The Campus History Series

LaSalle University

The Campus History Series

LaSalle University

Jeffrey LaMonica

ARCADIA
PUBLISHING

ISBN 978-0-7385-3922-5

Published by Arcadia Publishing
Charleston, South Carolina

Printed in the United States of America

Library of Congress Catalog Card Number: 2005931163

For all general information contact Arcadia Publishing at:
Telephone 843-853-2070
Fax 843-853-0044
E-mail sales@arcadiapublishing.com
For customer service and orders:
Toll-Free 1-888-313-2665

Visit us on the Internet at www.arcadiapublishing.com

*I dedicate this work to my family
and to the hundreds of LaSalle students that I have
had the privilege to teach over the years.*

Contents

ACKNOWLEDGMENTS

This book was made possible through the efforts and support of several individuals who personify Lasallian values. This compilation of photographs would not have been achievable without the tenacity of my research assistant Michael Gallen and the cooperation and guidance of LaSalle's archivist Brother Joseph Grabenstein. The technological genius of Timothy Smalarz provided solutions to challenges far beyond my level of computer literacy. Special recognition is owed to Brother Charles Gresh for endorsing this project from its inception. Thomas J. Donaghy's 1966 book *Conceived in Crisis: A History of LaSalle College*, Tonya Ellis's 2001 documentary *Finding a Place . . . Making a Name . . . The History of LaSalle University*, and Nicholas Smalarz's 2005 documentary *Together We Remember: The Legacy of LaSalle* were valuable sources of information for many of my captions.

INTRODUCTION

John Baptist de LaSalle was born to an upper-middle class family in Reims, France, in 1651. He earned a Ph.D. in theology from the University of Reims in 1680. After attending seminary, De LaSalle passed up an opportunity to enter the upper clergy and opened a school and orphanage for poor children in Reims with lay teacher Arien Nigel. His first school was a success, but more teachers were needed in order to expand. De LaSalle developed a brotherhood of educators who took vows but not Holy Orders. These consecrated teachers became the Institute of the Brothers of the Christian Schools, or the Christian Brothers. De LaSalle spent the rest of his life using his inheritance and soliciting charity to establish schools across France and train more Christian Brothers. He endured lawsuits and resistance from French aristocrats who believed that education should be reserved for the upper classes and was shunned by his own family. John Baptist de LaSalle died in 1719, but the Christian Brothers went on to gain the recognition of the Catholic Church under Pope Benedict XIII in 1725. The Christian Brothers were nearly persecuted out of existence during the French Revolution, but were reestablished under Napoleon Bonaparte. John Baptist de LaSalle was canonized in 1900 and named the Patron Saint of Teachers in 1950. The Christian Brothers founded schools in 80 countries around the world. They arrived in the United States in 1845 and focused upon offering education to Catholic immigrants. The Christian Brothers eventually established seven colleges in the United States, including LaSalle College in Philadelphia, which was chartered by the Commonwealth of Pennsylvania in 1863.

One

Buildings and Locations

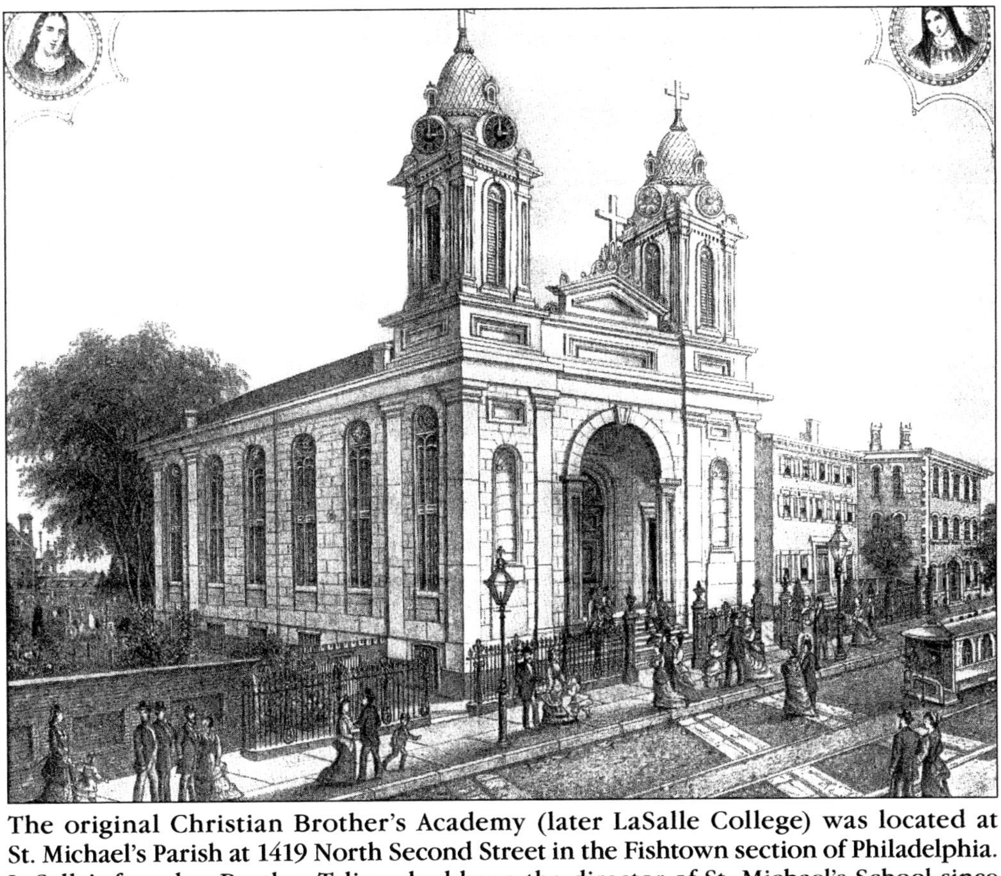

The original Christian Brother's Academy (later LaSalle College) was located at St. Michael's Parish at 1419 North Second Street in the Fishtown section of Philadelphia. LaSalle's founder, Brother Teliow, had been the director of St. Michael's School since 1858. Philadelphia's fifth bishop, James F. Wood, recognized the need for Catholic higher education in the city since its other Catholic colleges had closed due to the Civil War. The academy held its classes in the basement of St. Michael's.

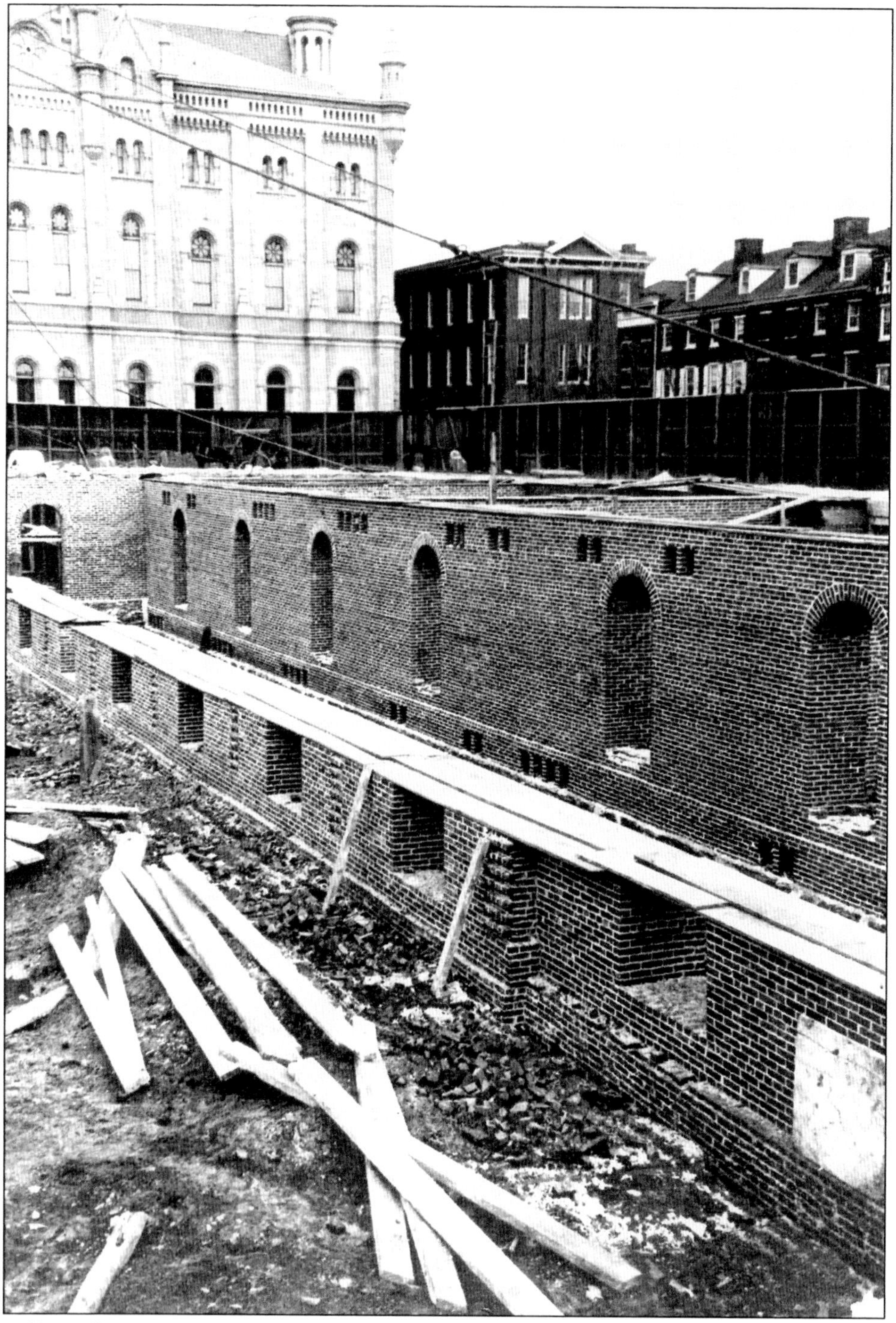

LaSalle College occupied a site in Center City, Philadelphia between Filbert and Juniper streets from 1867 until 1886. The property was purchased for $30,000, and under President Brother Oliver, enrollment grew to nearly 200 students. Yearly tuition was $80. Future Bishop of Philadelphia Philip McDevitt was one of LaSalle's first graduates at this location.

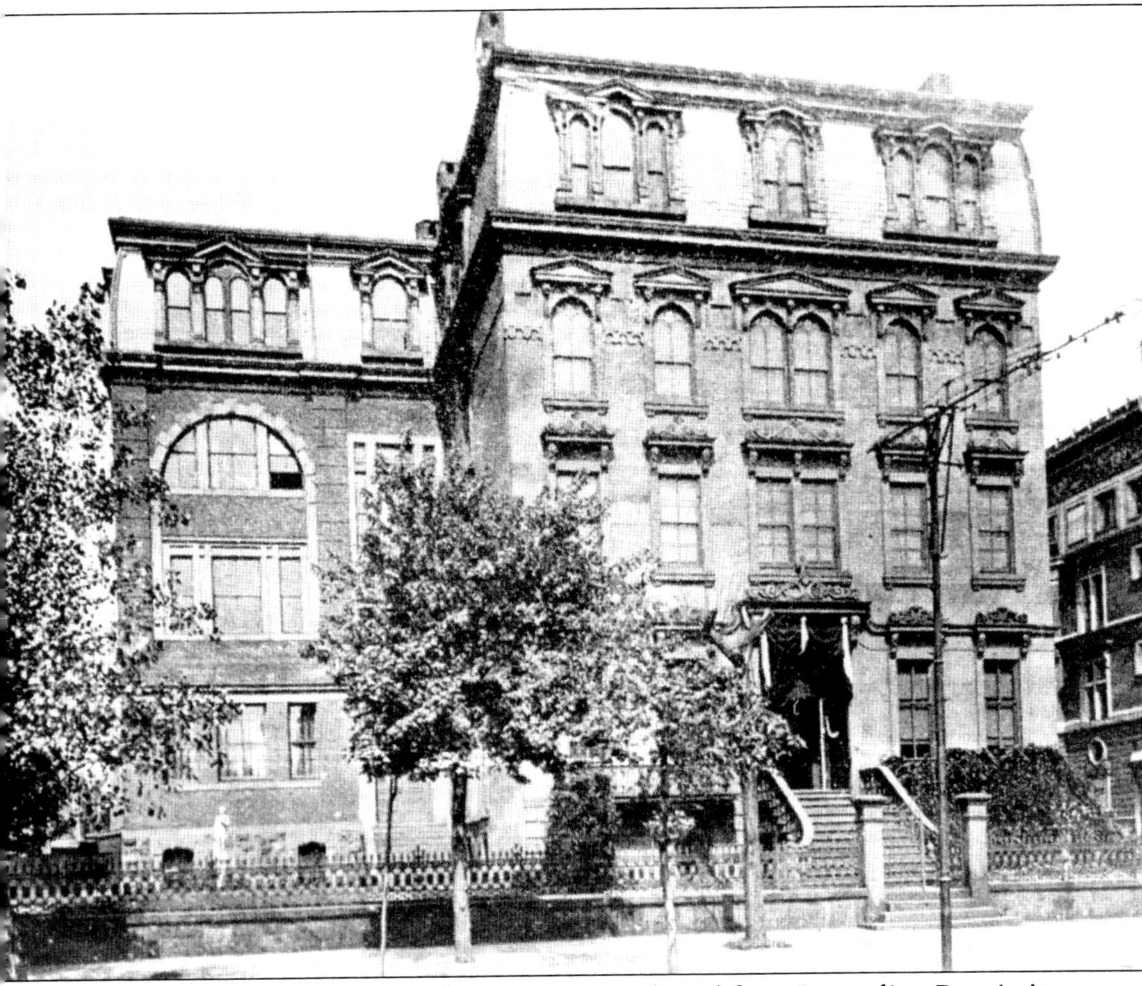

A mansion at 1240 North Broad Street was purchased from Jacqueline Bouvier's great-great-grandfather Michel Bouvier and served as LaSalle's home from 1886 until 1930. President Brother Noah was able to obtain the building for $67,500 with financial assistance from the Francis Drexel Estate.

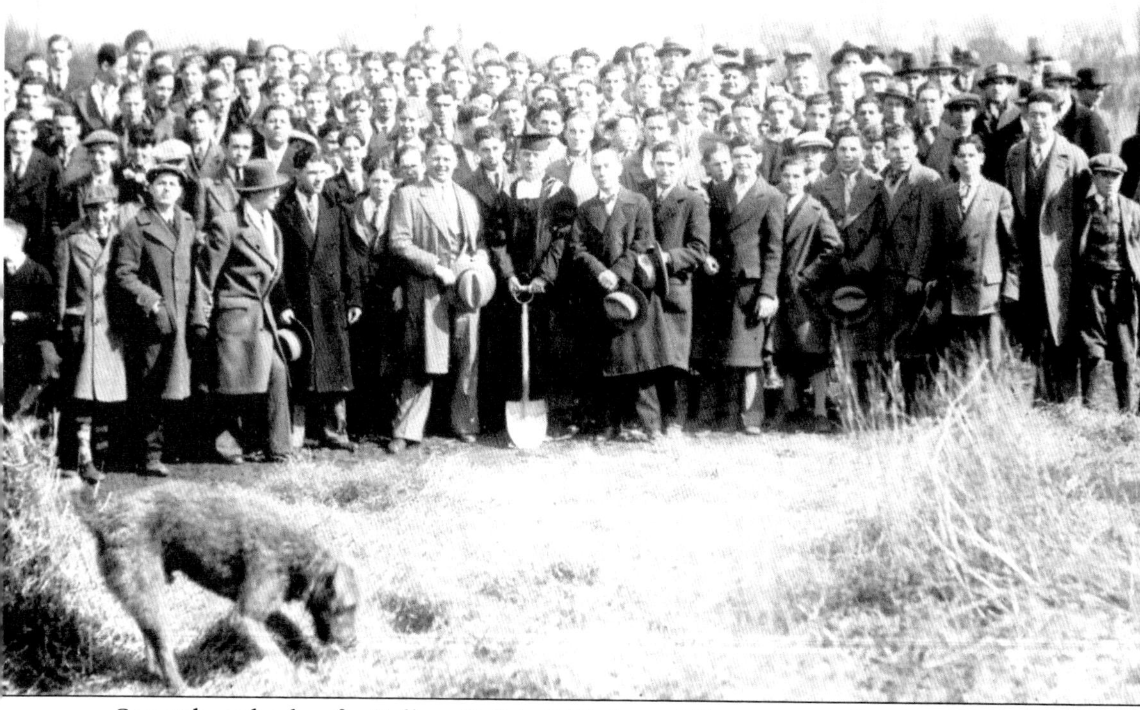

Ground was broken for College Hall in 1928. It would become LaSalle's signature building on the corner of Twentieth Street and Olney Avenue. The land was obtained from the heir of the Belfield and Fox estates James Starr for a total of $241,844. Famous American artist, scientist, and inventor Charles Willson Peale resided there from 1810 until the property was purchased by the Wister Family in 1826. Renowned builder and LaSalle alumnus John McShain built College Hall for $470,000. Seven hundred LaSalle students utilized automobiles and the subway to help transport the college's books, desks, and supplies up Broad Street when the project was completed in 1930.

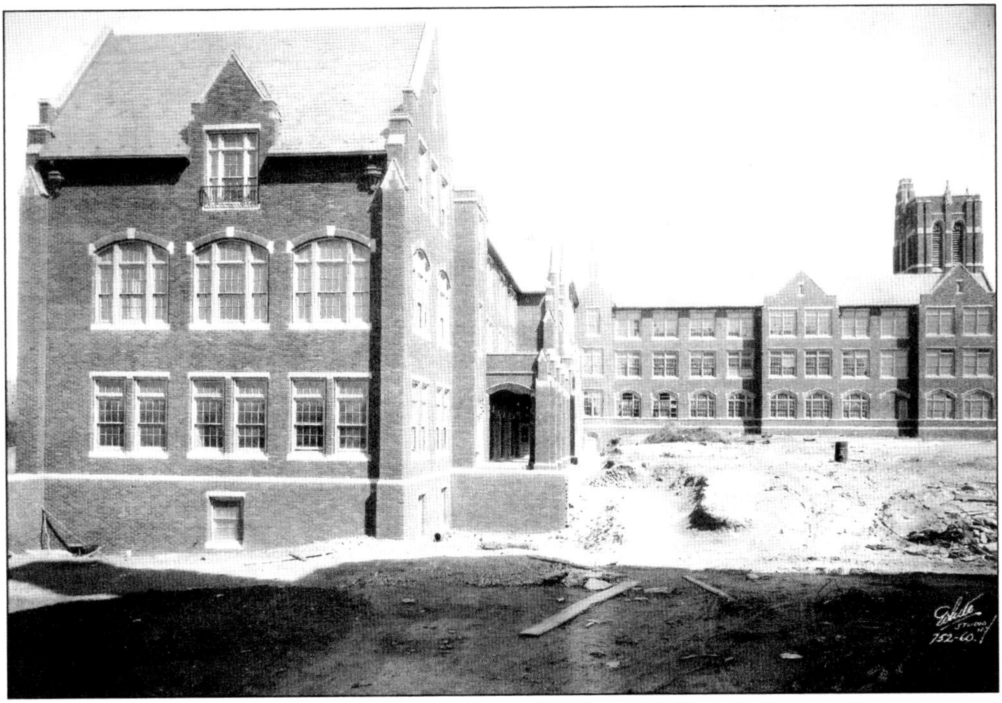
The Christian Brother's residence portion of College Hall and the quadrangle were under construction in 1929.

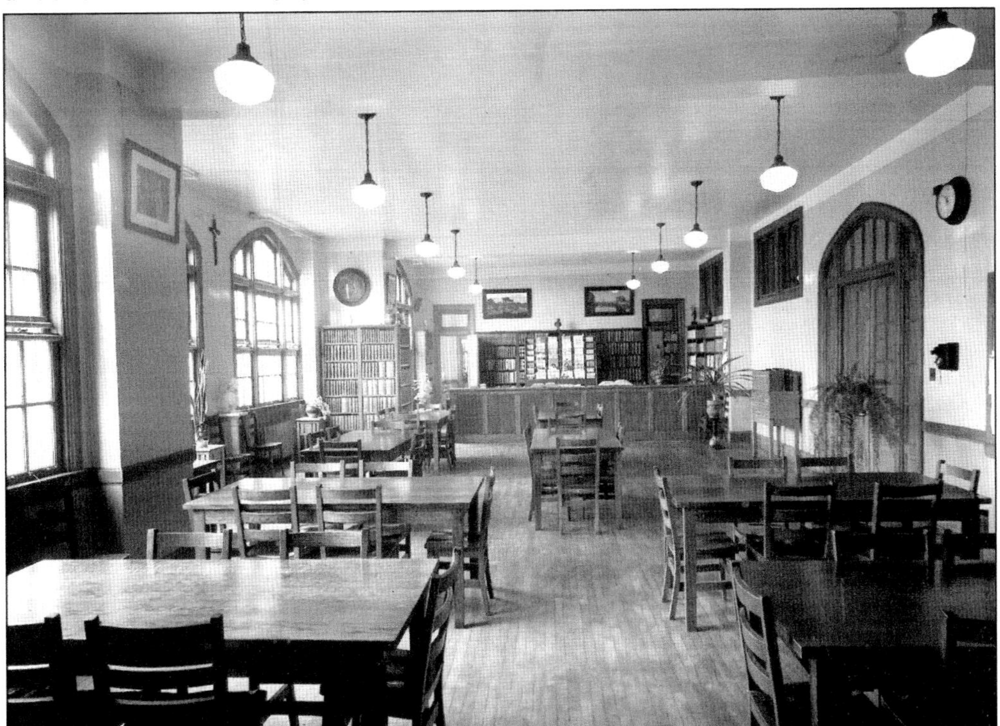
The first floor of College Hall housed LaSalle's library in the 1930s.

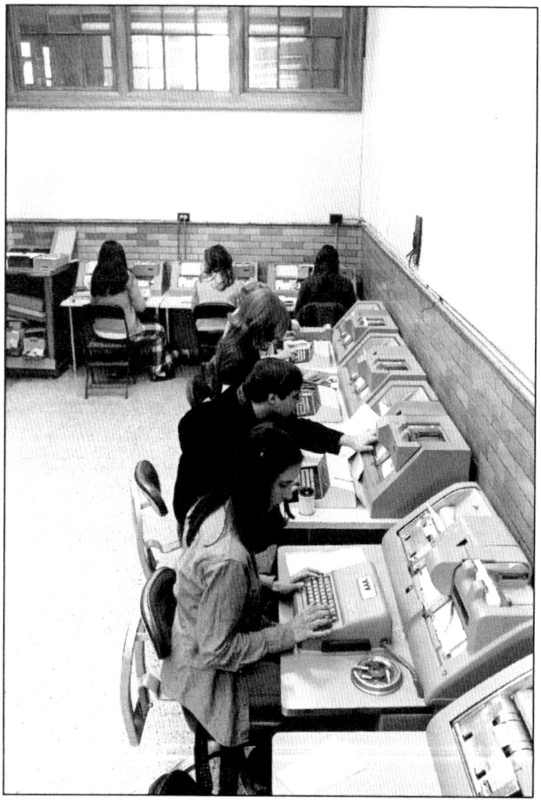

College Hall's information technology room featured state-of-the-art keypunch machines in the 1970s.

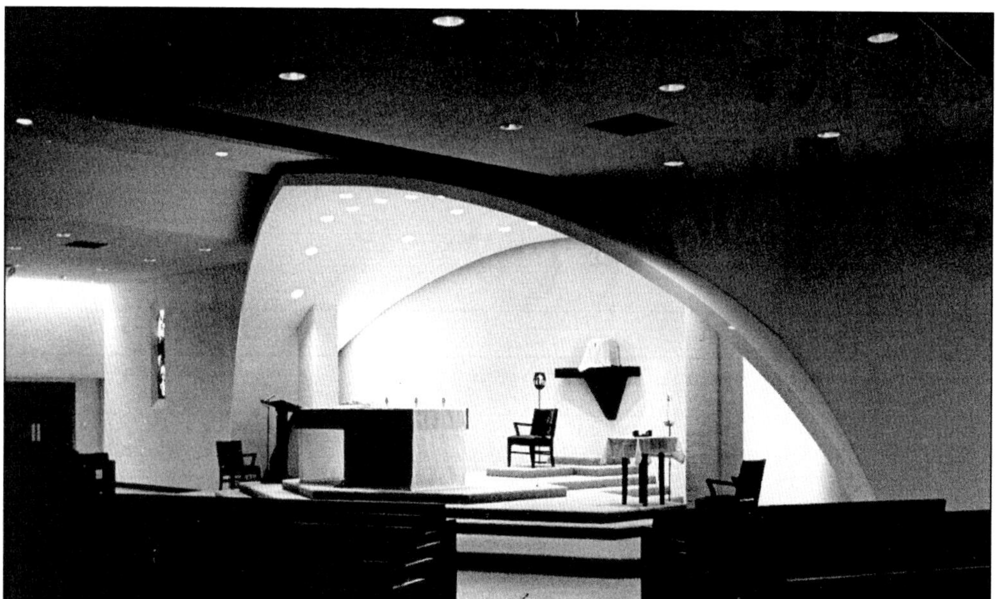

The De LaSalle Chapel opened in the basement of College Hall in 1965. It was originally an auditorium.

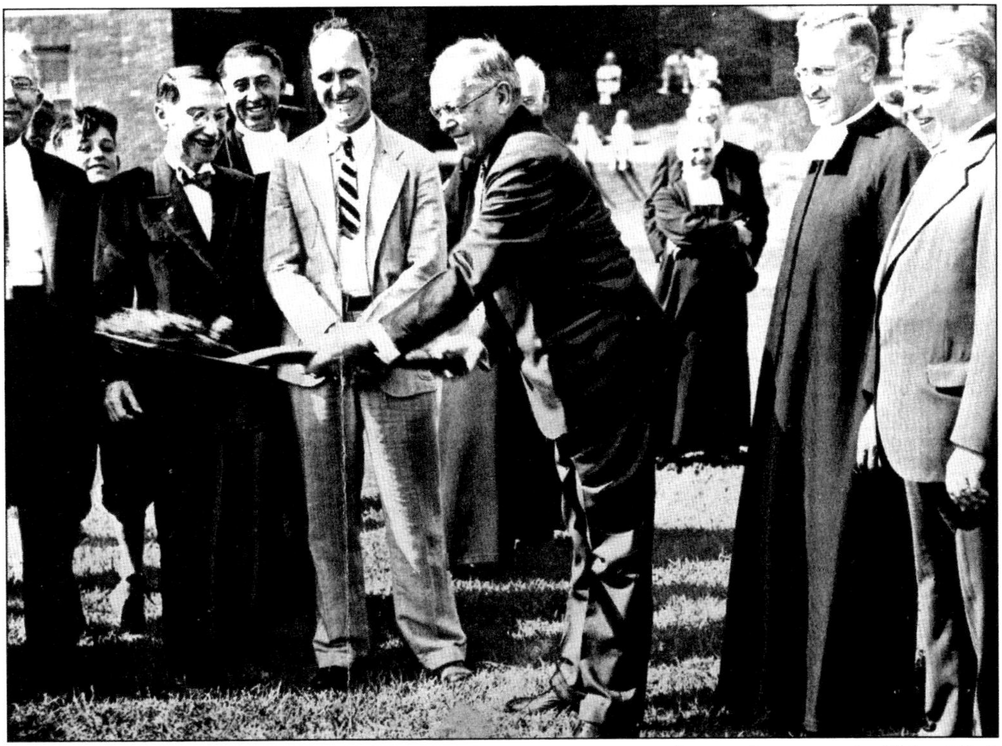

A ceremony celebrating the start of construction on McCarthy Stadium was held in 1936. Sir John A. McCarthy (holding the shovel) attended with J. Burrwood Daly, Brother Edward John, and President Brother Anselm. The college received a $10,000 gift from McCarthy to help offset the $38,126 cost of the project. President Brother Anselm hoped that a football program would boost enrollment during the Great Depression. LaSalle defeated St. Mary's of Minnesota, which was also a Christian Brother's school, 47–12 on the stadium's opening day later that year.

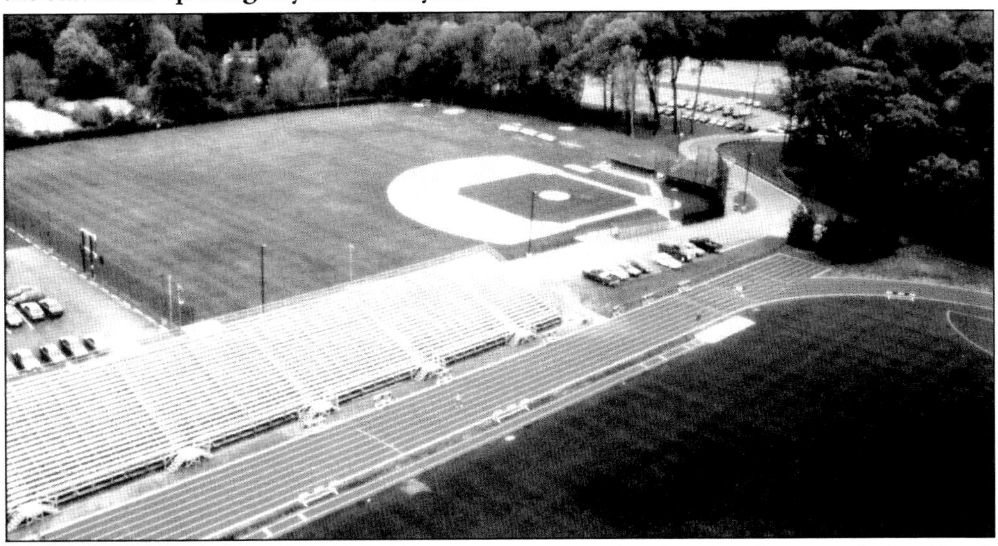

An aerial photograph was taken to survey McCarthy Stadium and the Hank DeVincent Field.

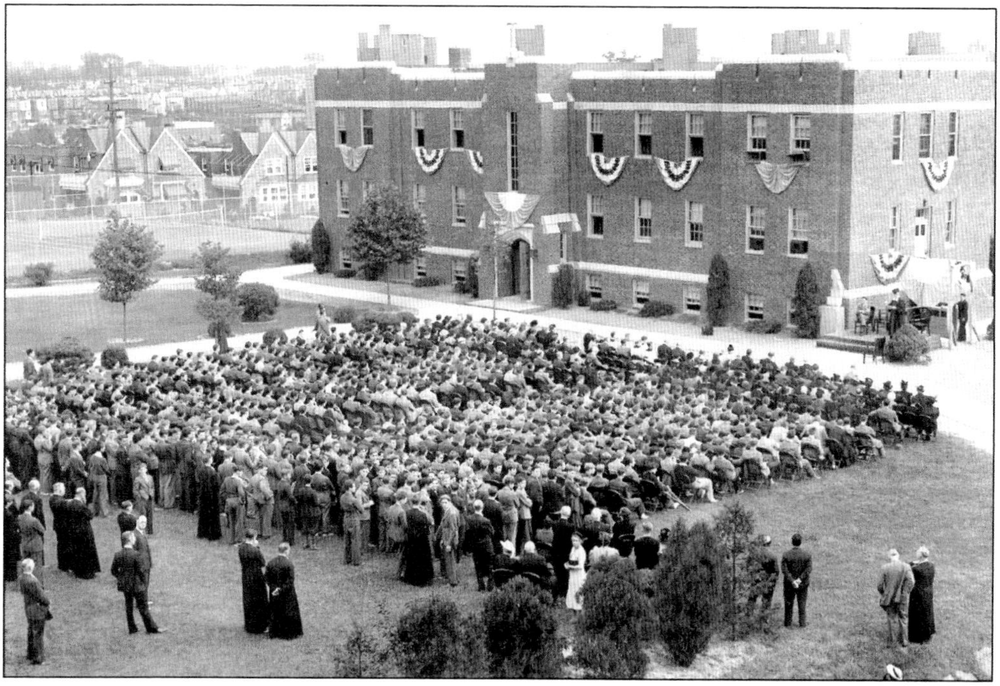

McShain Hall was dedicated in honor of builder John McShain in 1940. The basement served as a student lounge and recreation area, the first floor comprised of four classrooms and two offices, and the top floor was a residence hall. The building was converted into administrative and faculty offices in the 1960s.

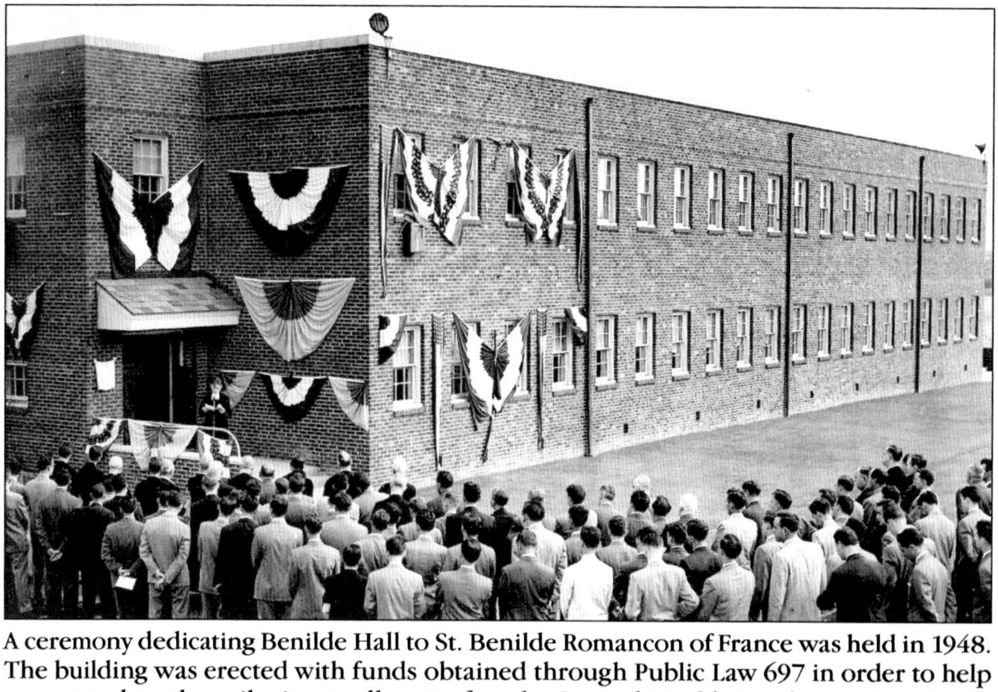

A ceremony dedicating Benilde Hall to St. Benilde Romancon of France was held in 1948. The building was erected with funds obtained through Public Law 697 in order to help accommodate the spike in enrollment after the Second World War due to the GI Bill. LaSalle was in need of classroom space for its 1,385 students.

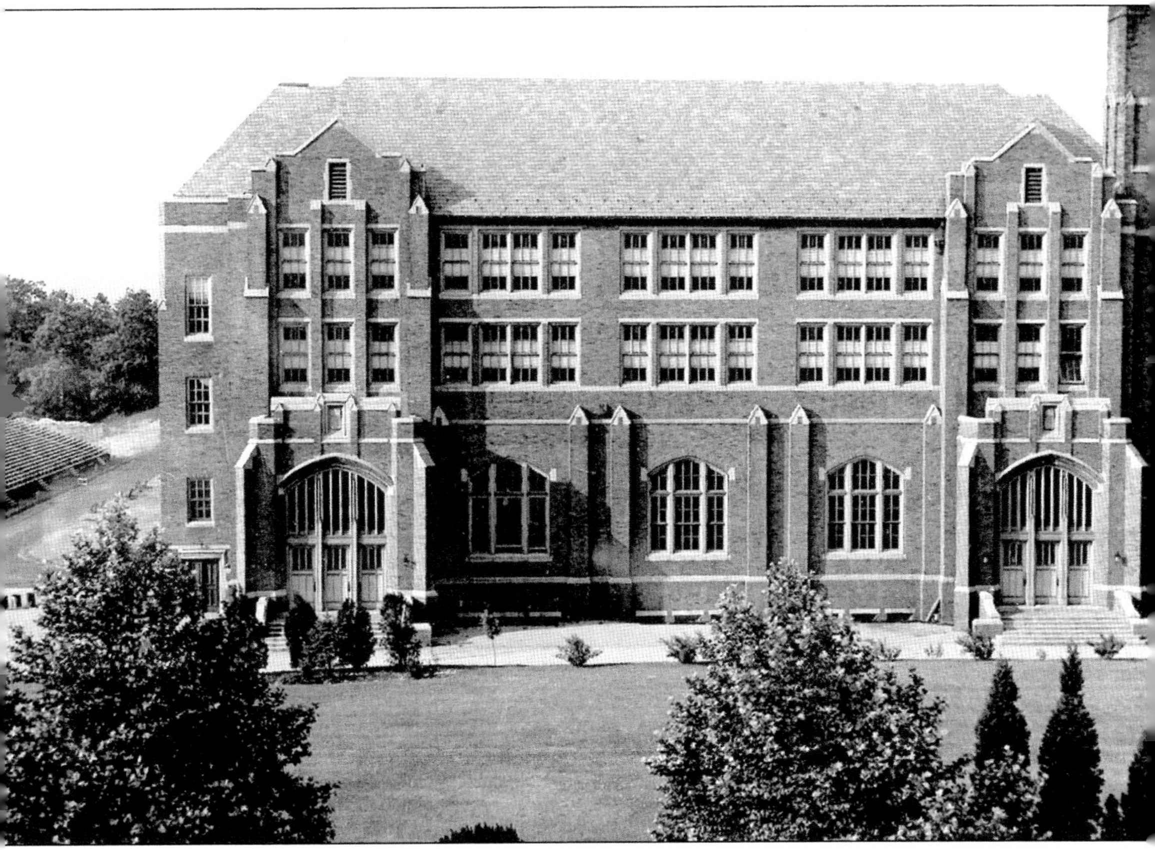

The Wister Building was named after the family who owned the Belfield Estate for nearly a century. The building became LaSalle College High School when its construction was completed in 1930. The high school was relocated to Springfield Township, Pennsylvania, in 1960, and Wister Hall was used by the college as classrooms, faculty offices, and a gymnasium.

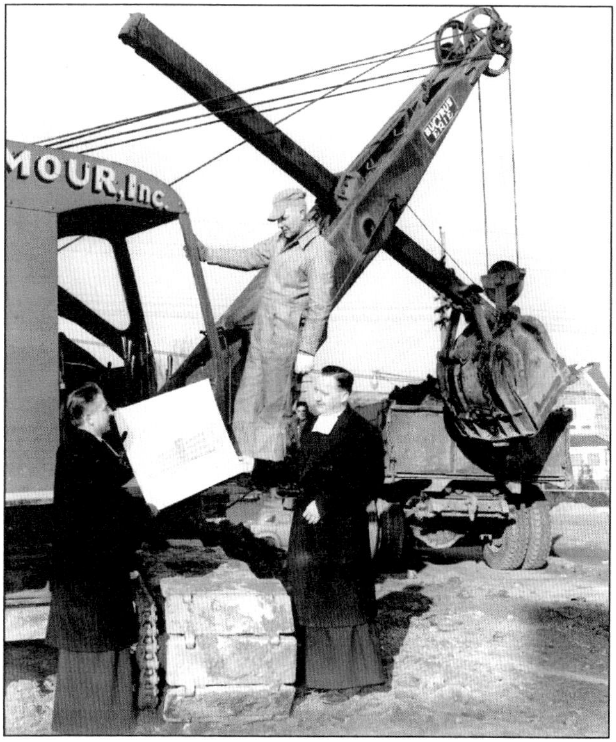

Philip Knutzen (center), Pres. Brother Gregorian Paul (left), and Brother E. Joseph participated in the groundbreaking for the LaSalle College Library in 1950. Brother Joseph became the first director of the library when it was opened in 1952. The building later became the Administration Center.

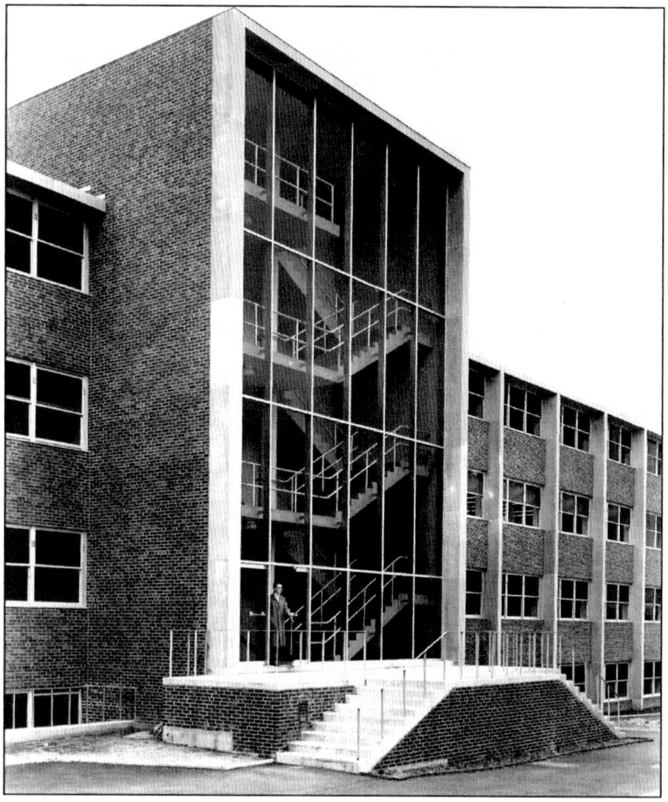

The LaSalle College library was named in honor of Pennsylvania Governor David Leo Lawrence in 1969. It was capable of holding 150,000 volumes.

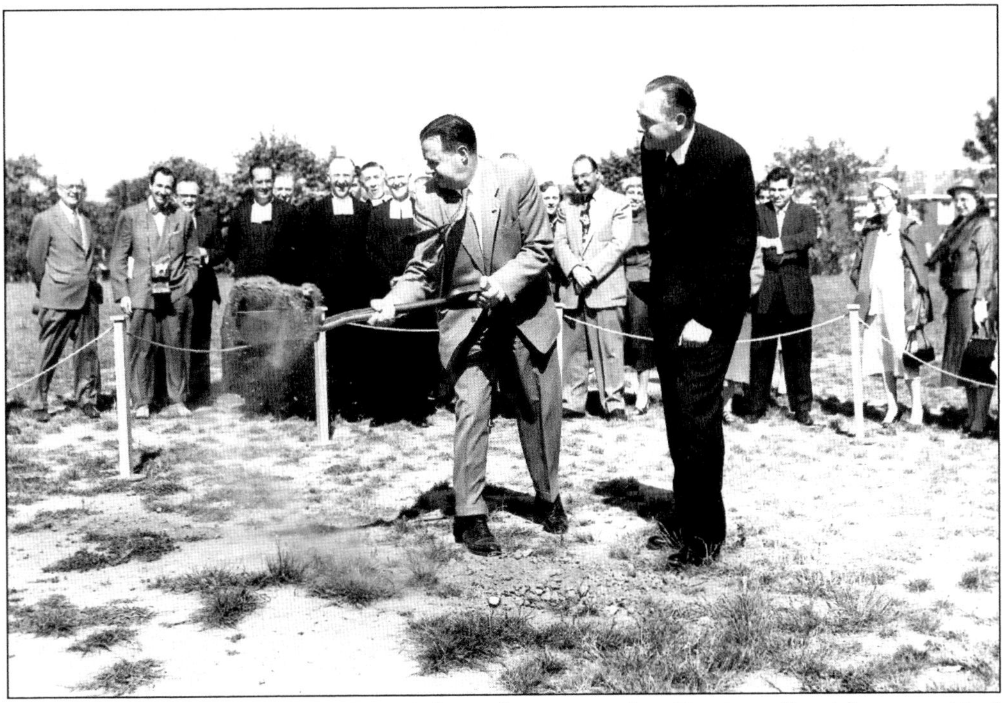

Congressman Hugh F. Scott (front left) and Pres. Brother Erminus Stanislaus presided over the groundbreaking for the LaSalle Student Union in 1956. Brother Stanislaus obtained a $1 million loan from the Federal Government for the project.

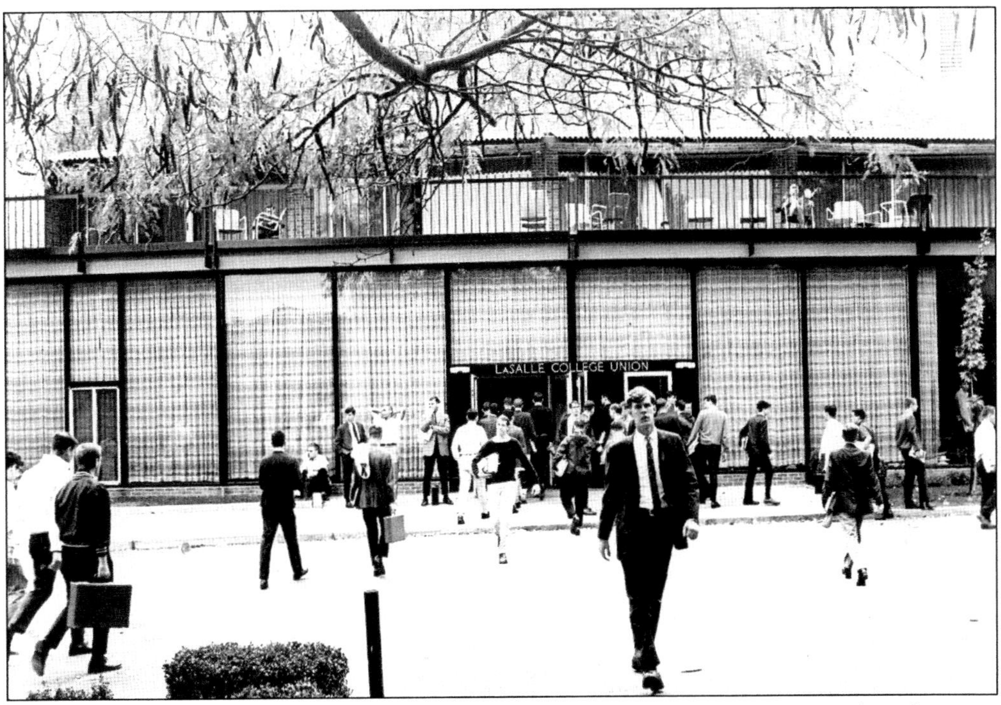

The LaSalle Student Union opened in 1959 and housed a cafeteria, student lounge, and theatre.

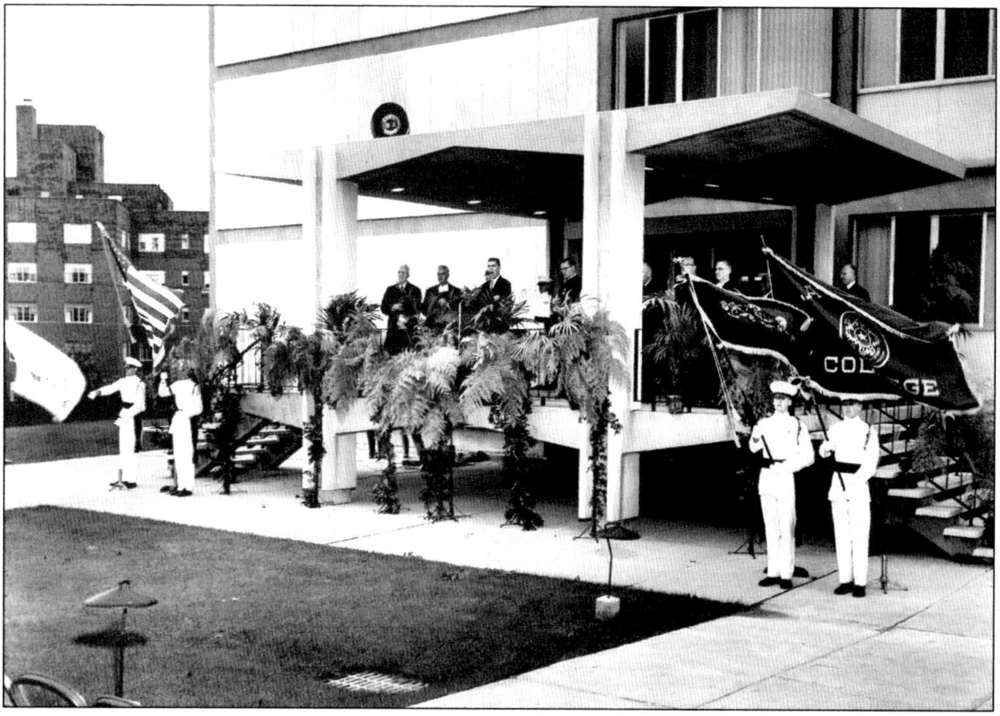

The opening of the Science Center in 1960 featured LaSalle's ROTC color guard. The $1.8 million facility contained an animal research room and a green house.

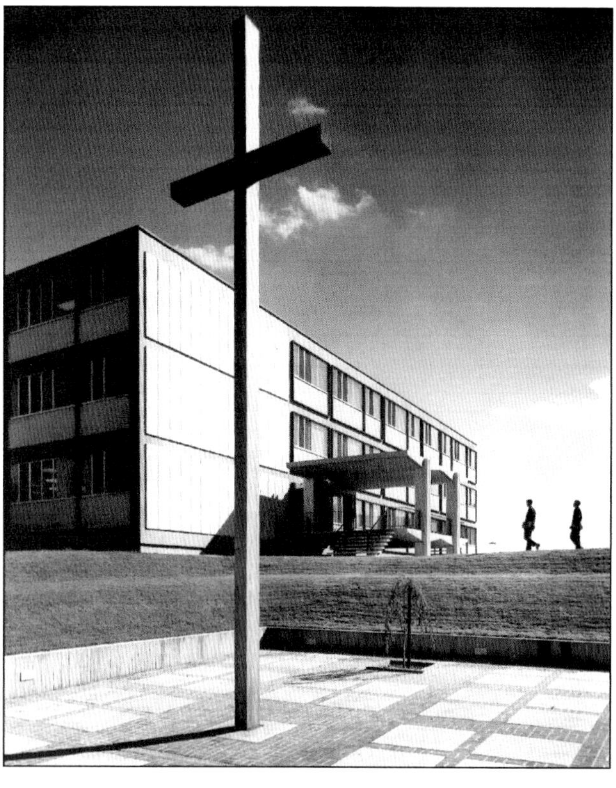

The Science Center was named in honor of Dr. Roland Holroyd in 1970. He was one of LaSalle's first recipients of the Lindback Foundation Award for Excellent Teaching.

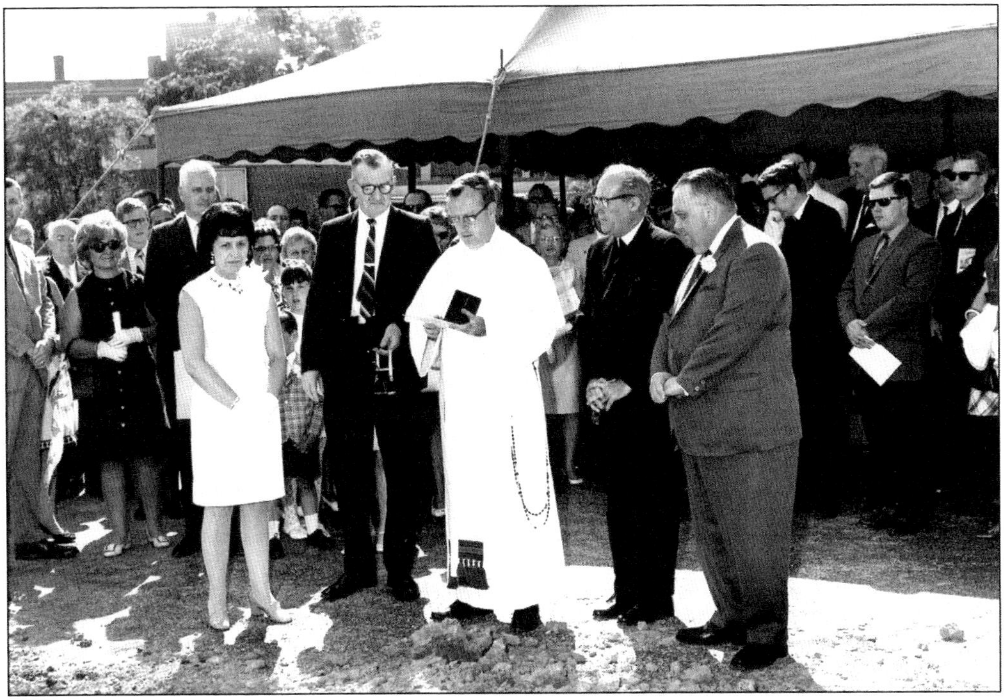

In the front shown from left to right are Emelia Hayman, Dr. Robert J. Courtney, Reverend Raymond Halligan, Pres. Brother Daniel Bernian, and LaSalle College alumnus Dr. H. Blake Hayman who participated in the groundbreaking celebration for Hayman Hall in 1969.

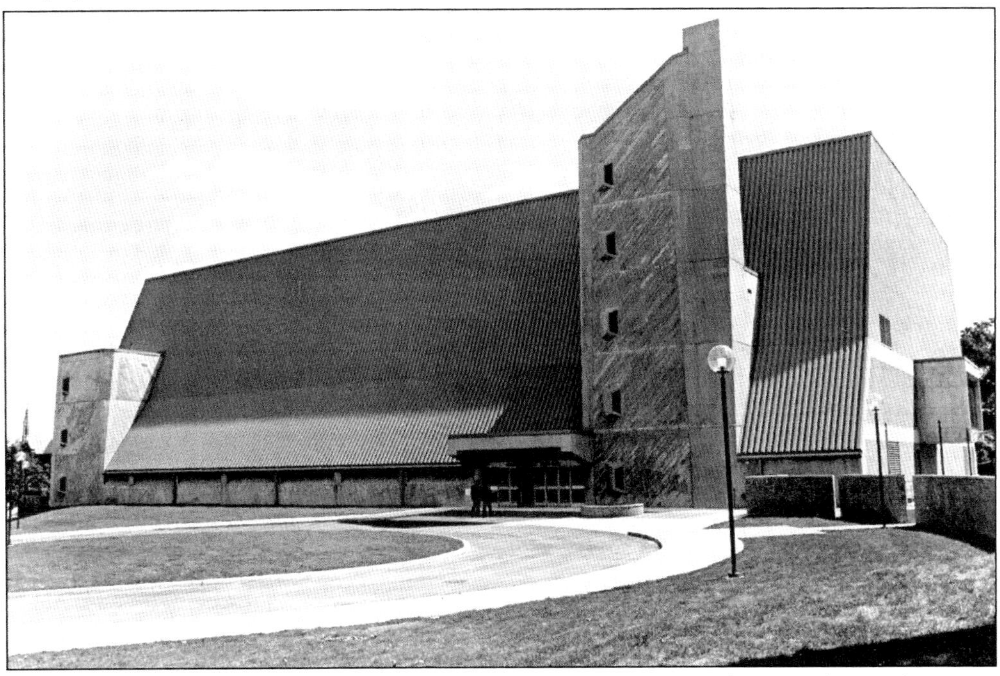

Hayman Hall opened in 1972. It contained a basketball court, indoor track, weight room, and swimming pool.

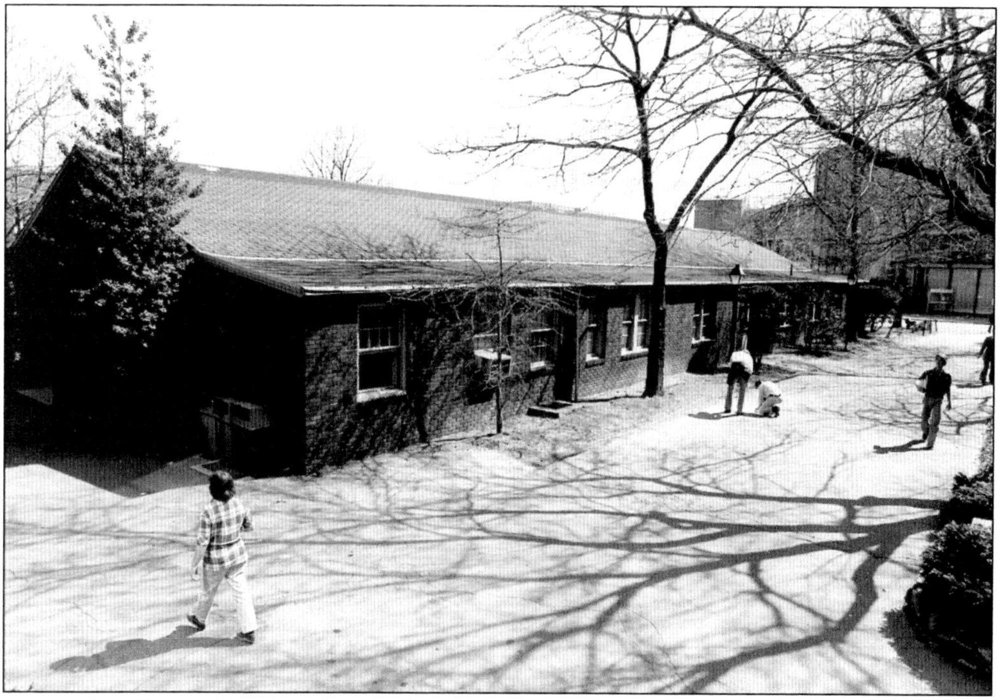

Leonard Hall was built in 1947 as a student center with funds from Public Law 697. It was demolished in 1977 and converted into a quadrangle.

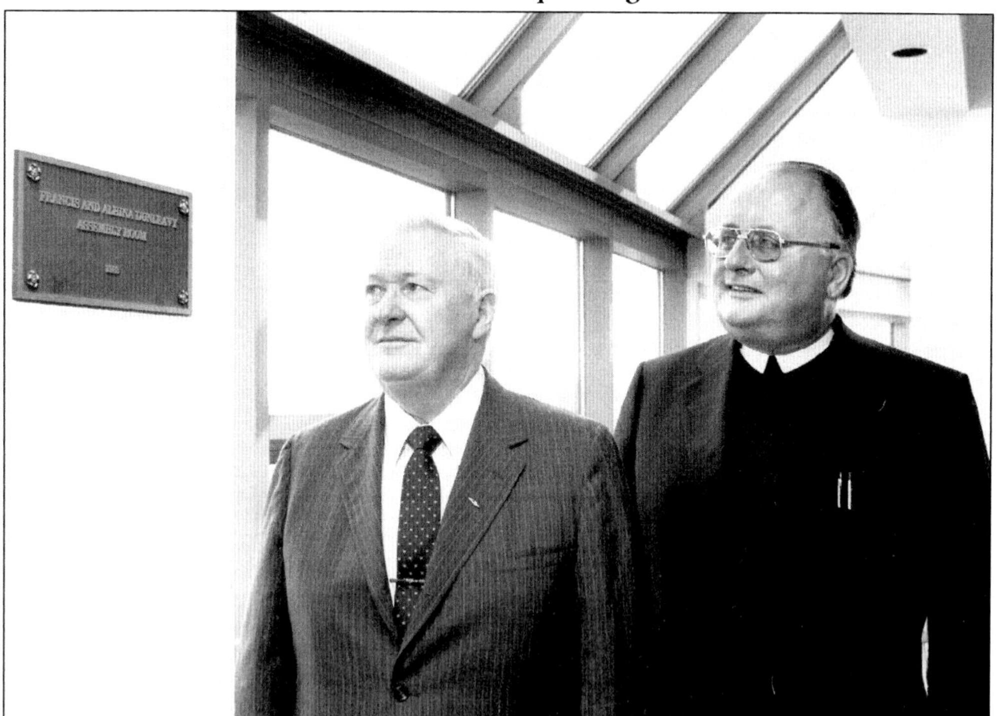

Francis J. Dunleavy (left) and Pres. Brother Patrick Ellis attended the dedication of the Dunleavy multipurpose room in the LaSalle Student Union in 1983.

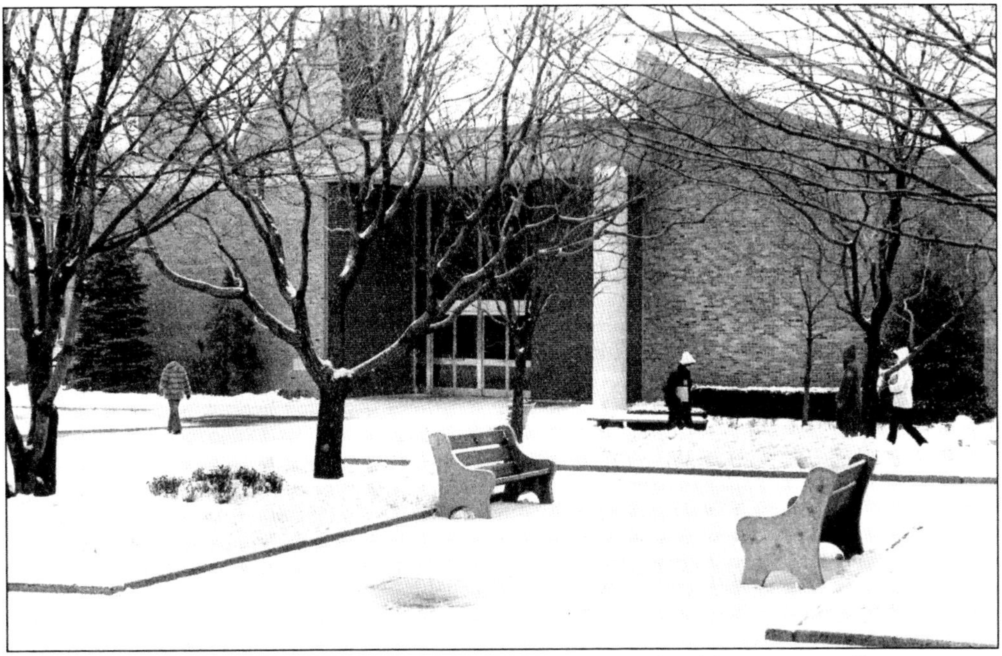

Olney Hall was opened in 1971 and became the largest building on LaSalle's campus. It contained classrooms, faculty offices, and a planetarium. Tuition was about $2,300 during the 1970s.

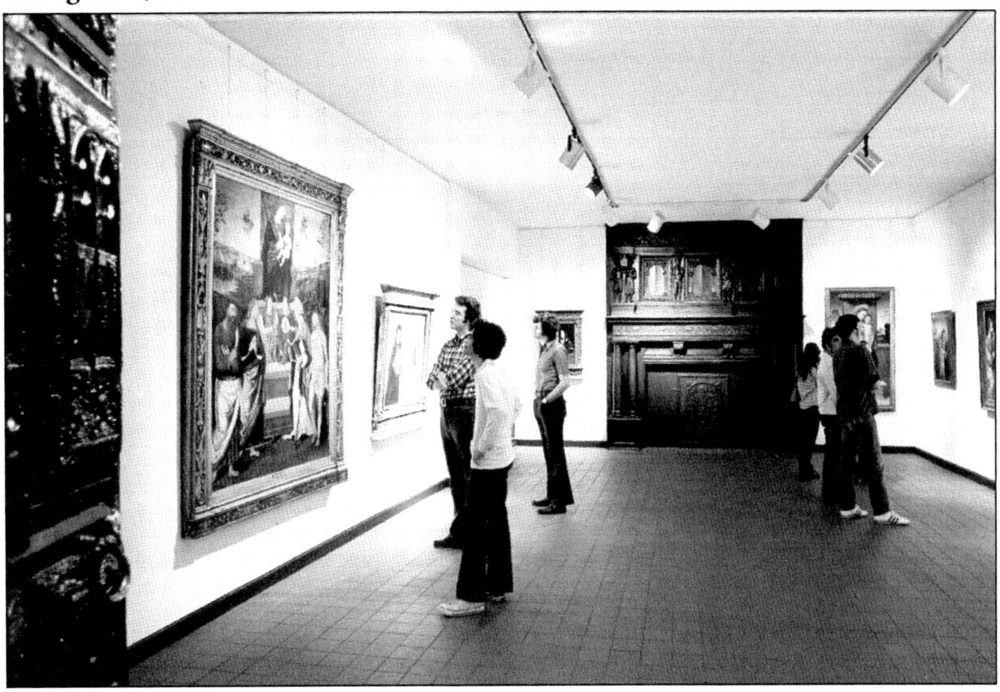

Brother Daniel Burke had been acquiring works of art since 1965 in anticipation of starting a museum at the college. The LaSalle Art Museum opened in the basement of Olney Hall in 1975, he became its director in 1976. The collection grew to over 200 paintings representing six periods of Western art.

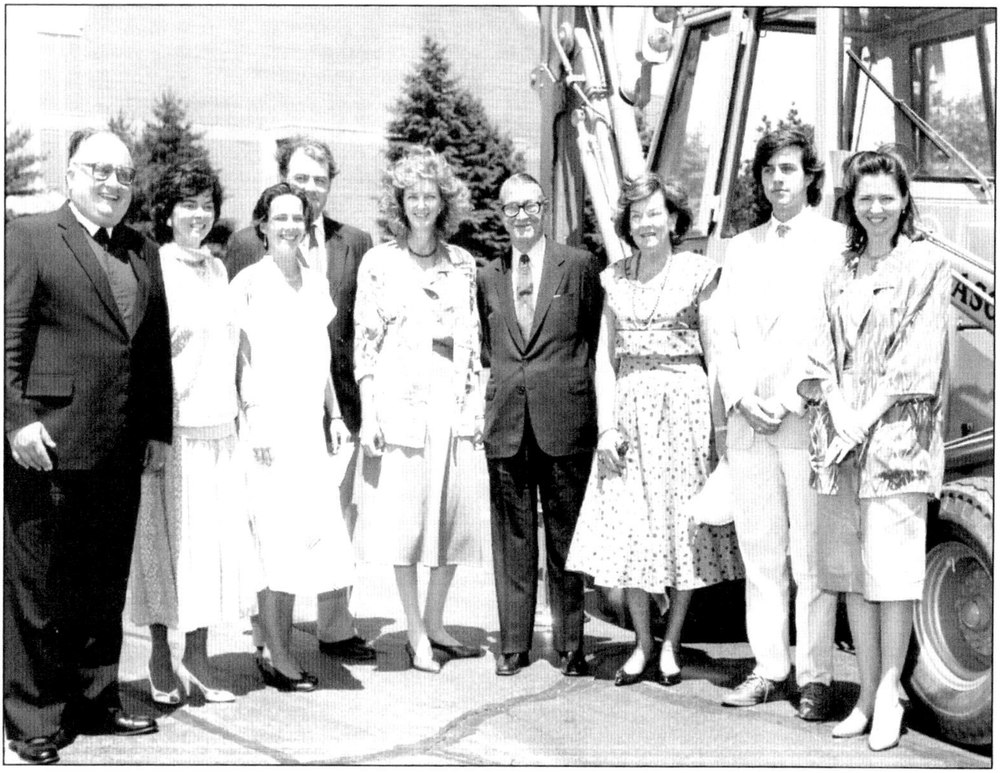

Pres. Brother Patrick Ellis (left) and the Connelly family celebrated the groundbreaking for the Connelly Library in 1986. The project was made possible by an $11 million contribution from the Connelly Foundation.

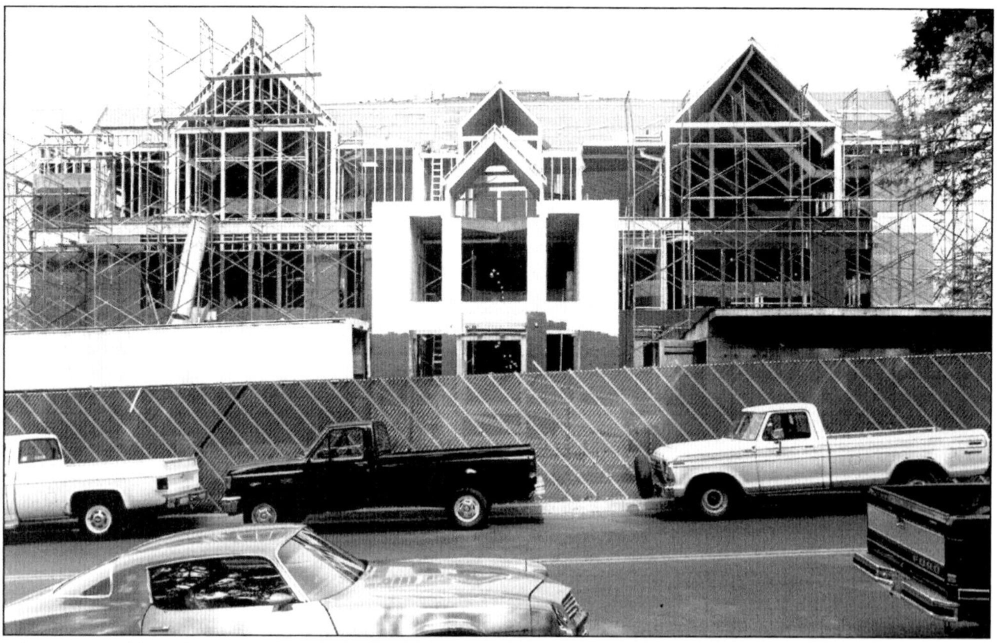

The Connelly Library was under construction in 1987.

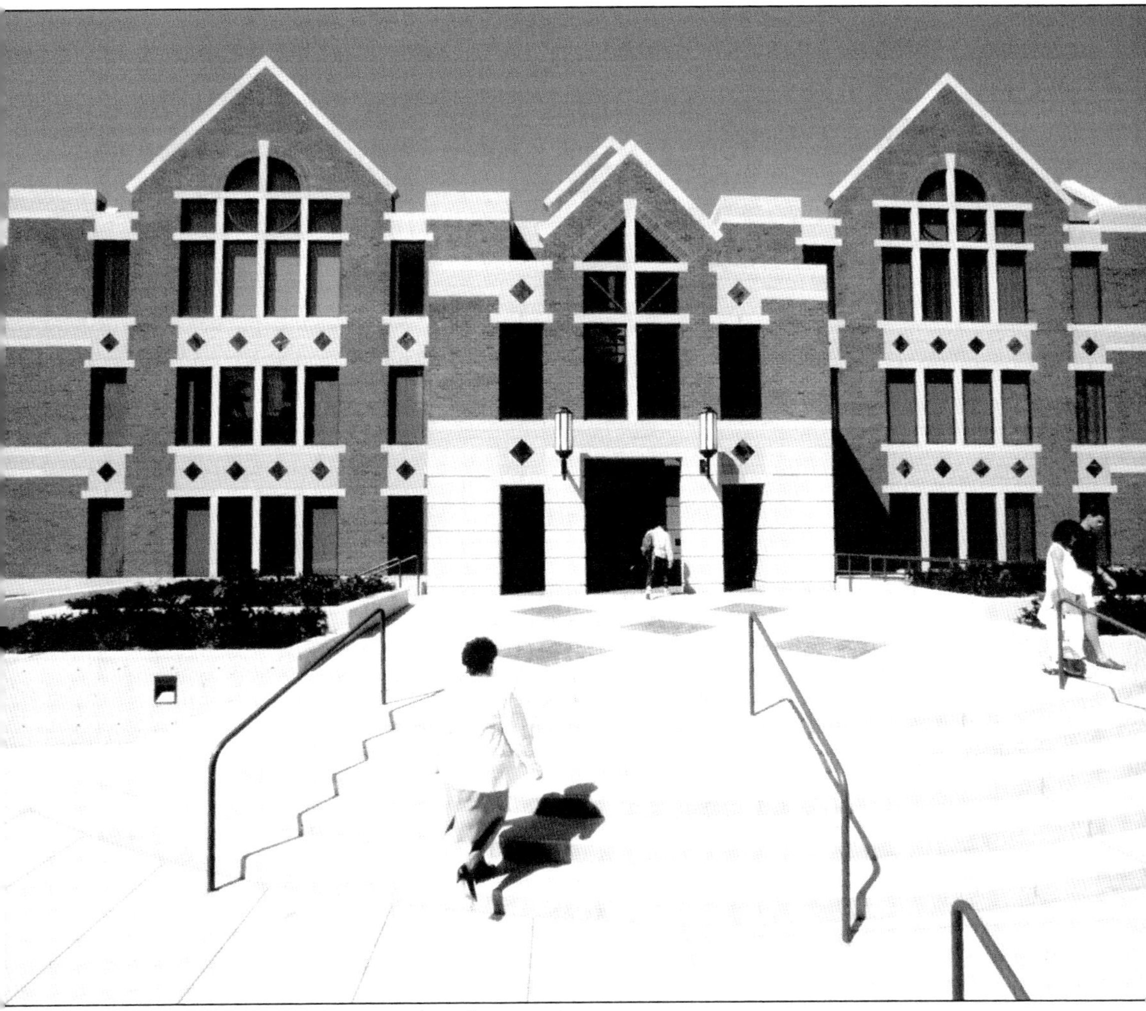

The Connelly Library was completed in 1988.

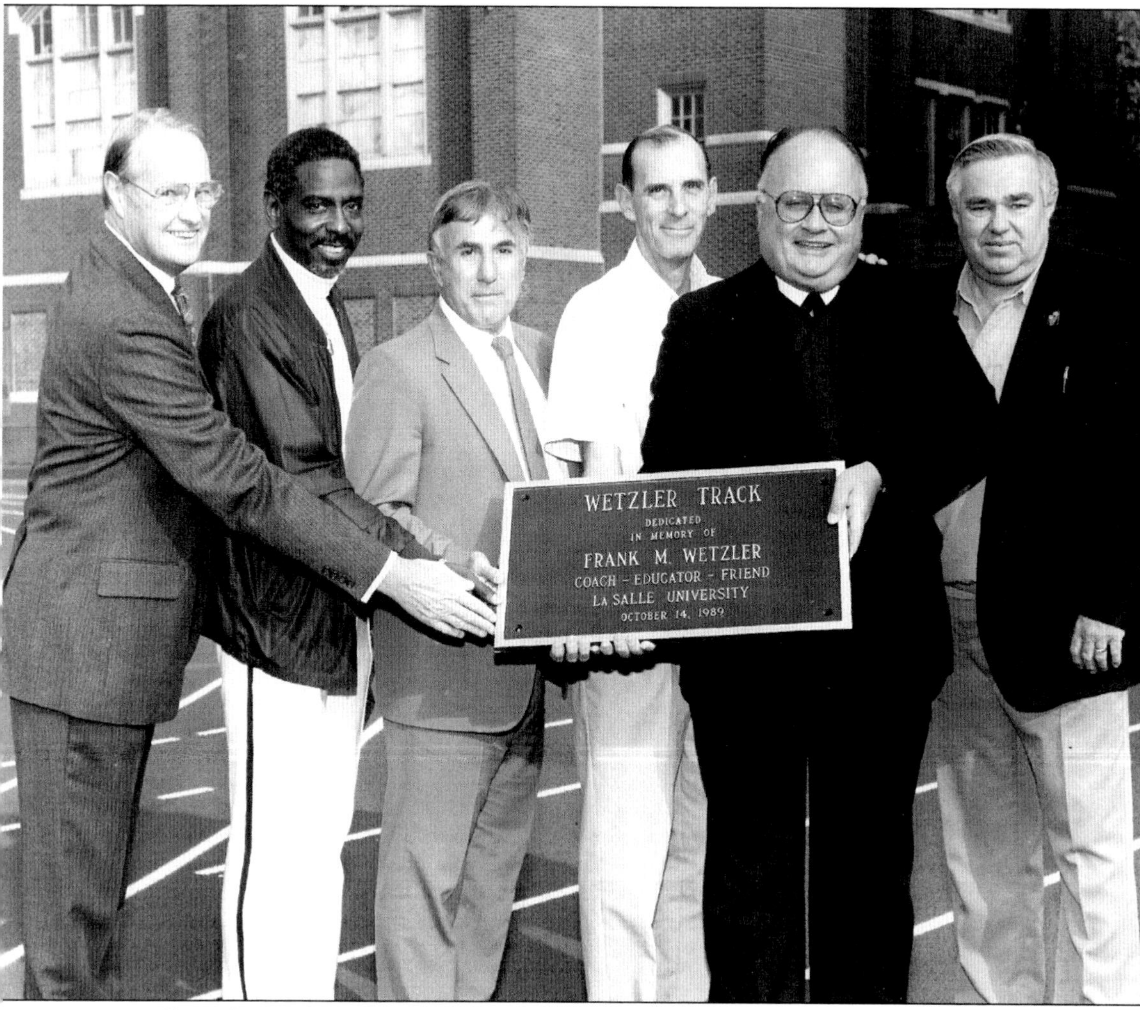

LaSalle's all-weather track was named in honor of track coach Frank M. Wetzler in 1989. Attending the ceremony (from left to right) were former LaSalle track stars Jim Tuppeny, Ira Davis, and Al Cantello along with William M. Wetzler, Pres. Brother Patrick Ellis, and athletic director Bob Mullen.

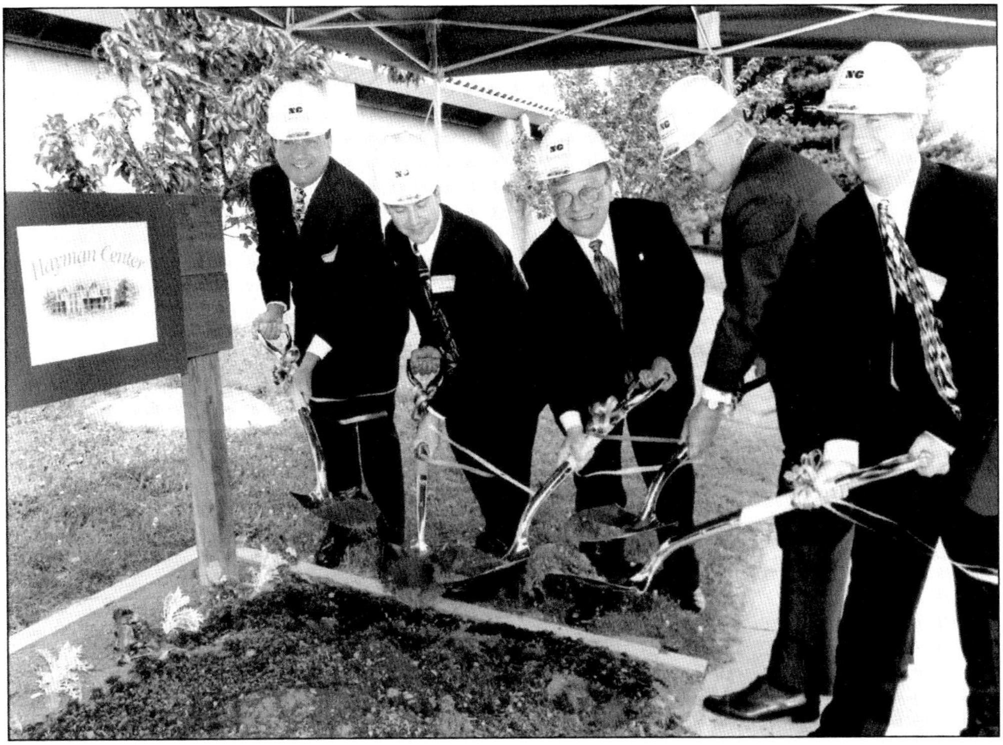

Pictured from left to right, LaSalle University's women's basketball coach John Miller, H. Blake Hayman Jr., Pres. Brother Joseph Burke, men's basketball coach Speedy Morris, and Trey Ulrich took part in the groundbreaking for renovations to Hayman Hall in 1997.

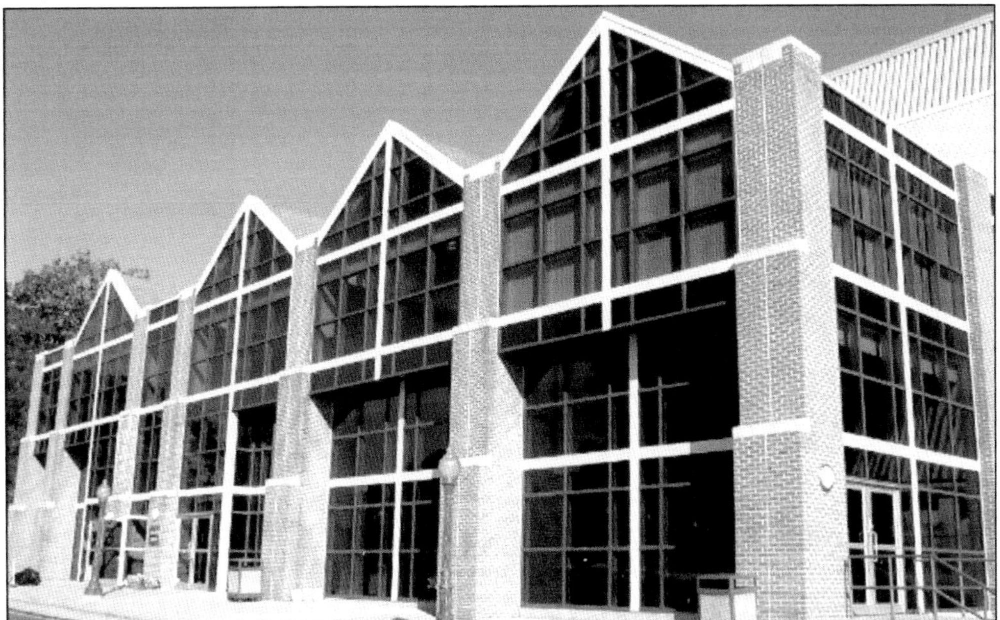

Hayman Hall was renamed the Hayman Athletic Center upon its reopening. Its new basketball arena was named in honor of Tom Gola. (Photograph courtesy of Timothy Smalarz.)

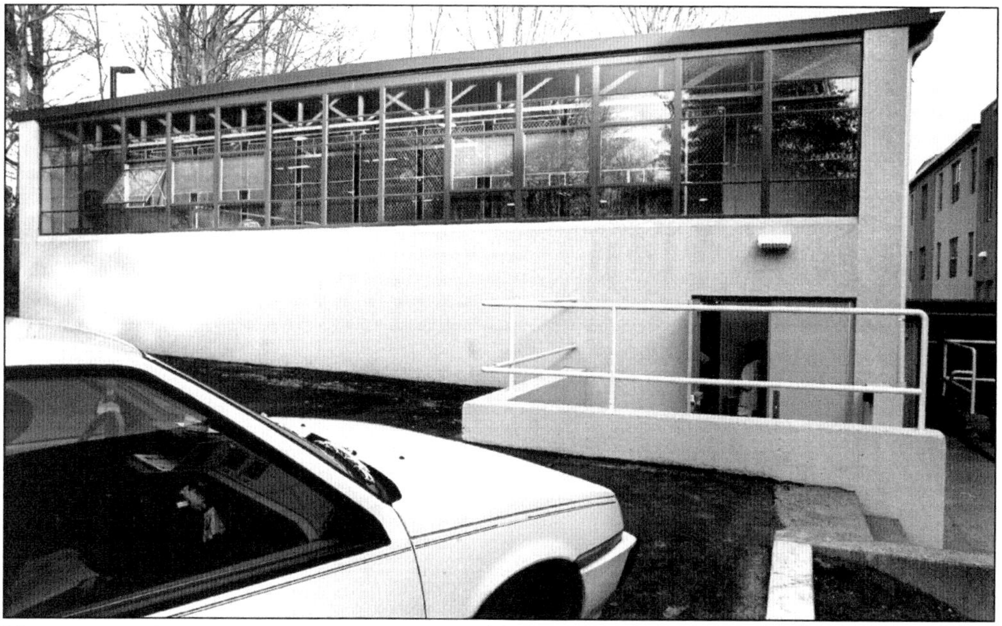

The James J. Binns Fitness Center was established in the early 1990s on LaSalle's south campus. It was later renamed the Independence Blue Cross Fitness Center.

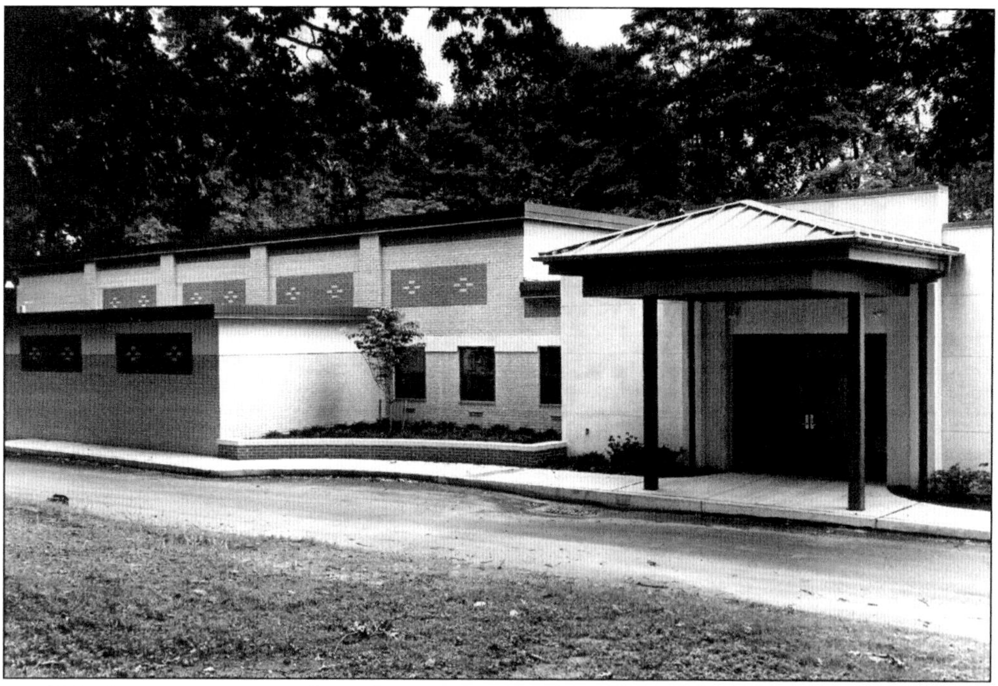

In 1989, the university purchased 19 acres of land from the Sisters of St. Basil the Great, a Ukrainian Byzantine order which had resided there since 1954. It became LaSalle's south campus. The Communication Center was opened there in 1994.

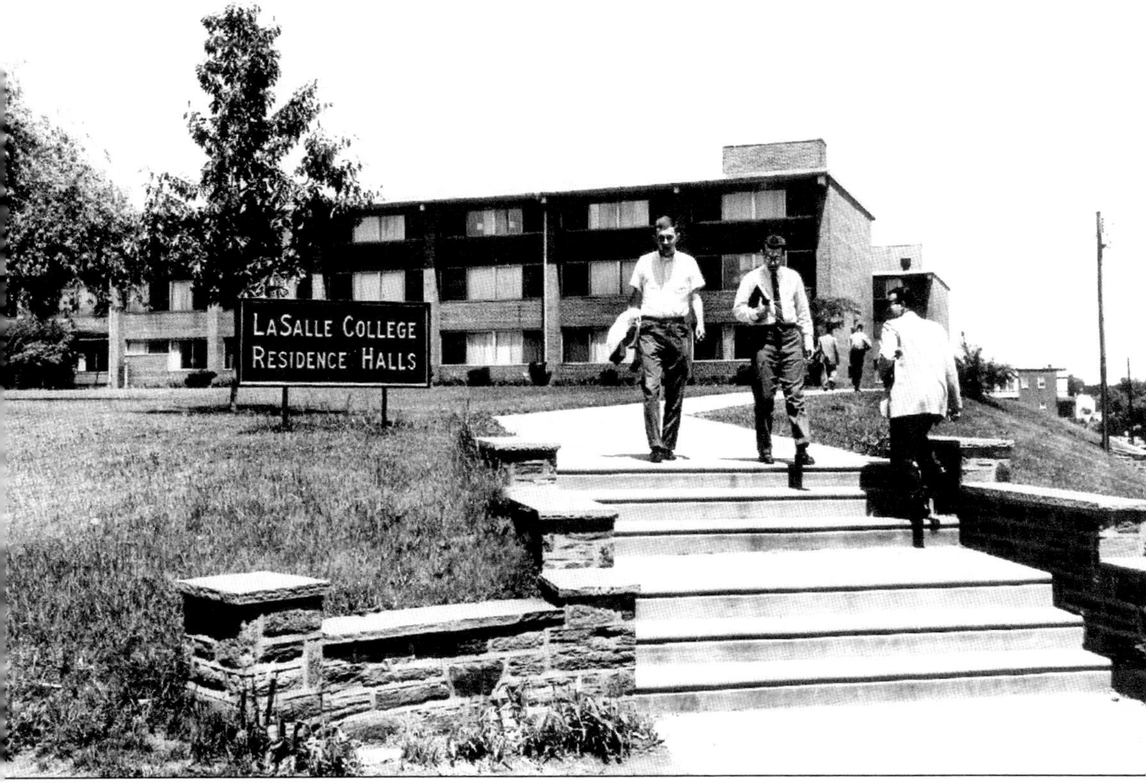

Resident students lived in College Hall and McShain Hall prior to the opening of St. Albert's Residence Hall in 1953 and St. Cassian's Residence Hall in 1956.

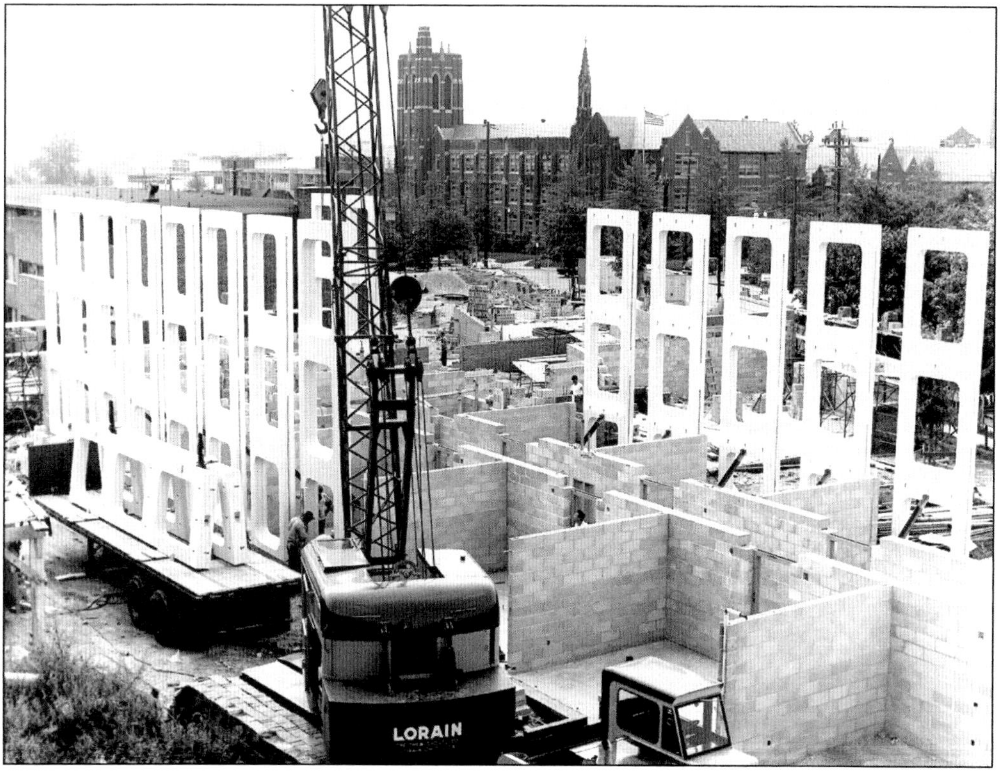

The construction of St. George's Residence Hall was underway in the mid-1960s.

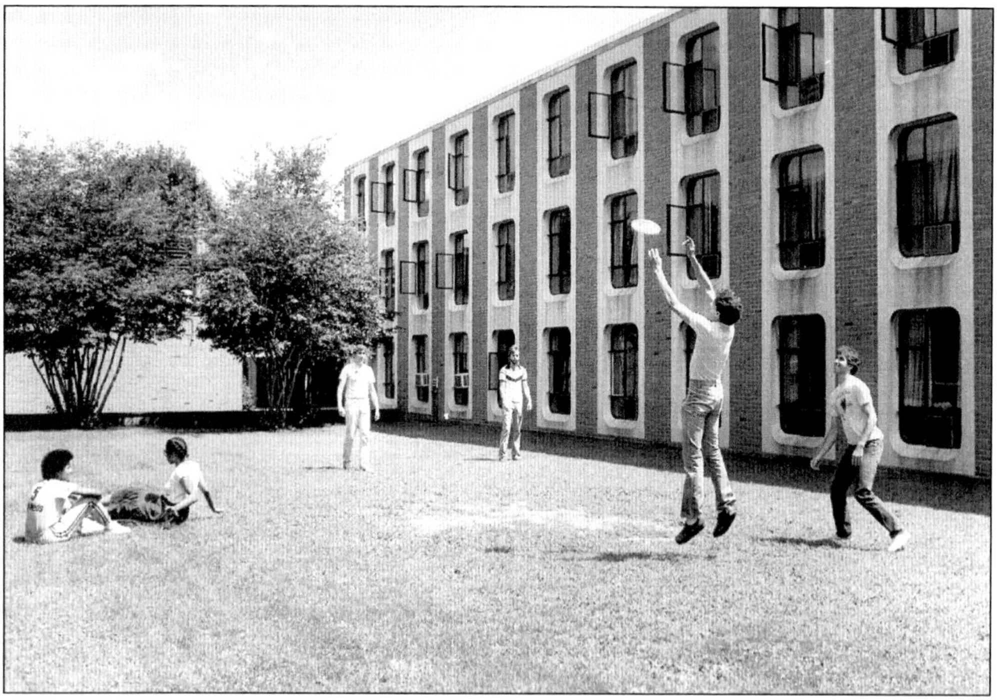

St. George's Residence Hall was completed in 1966.

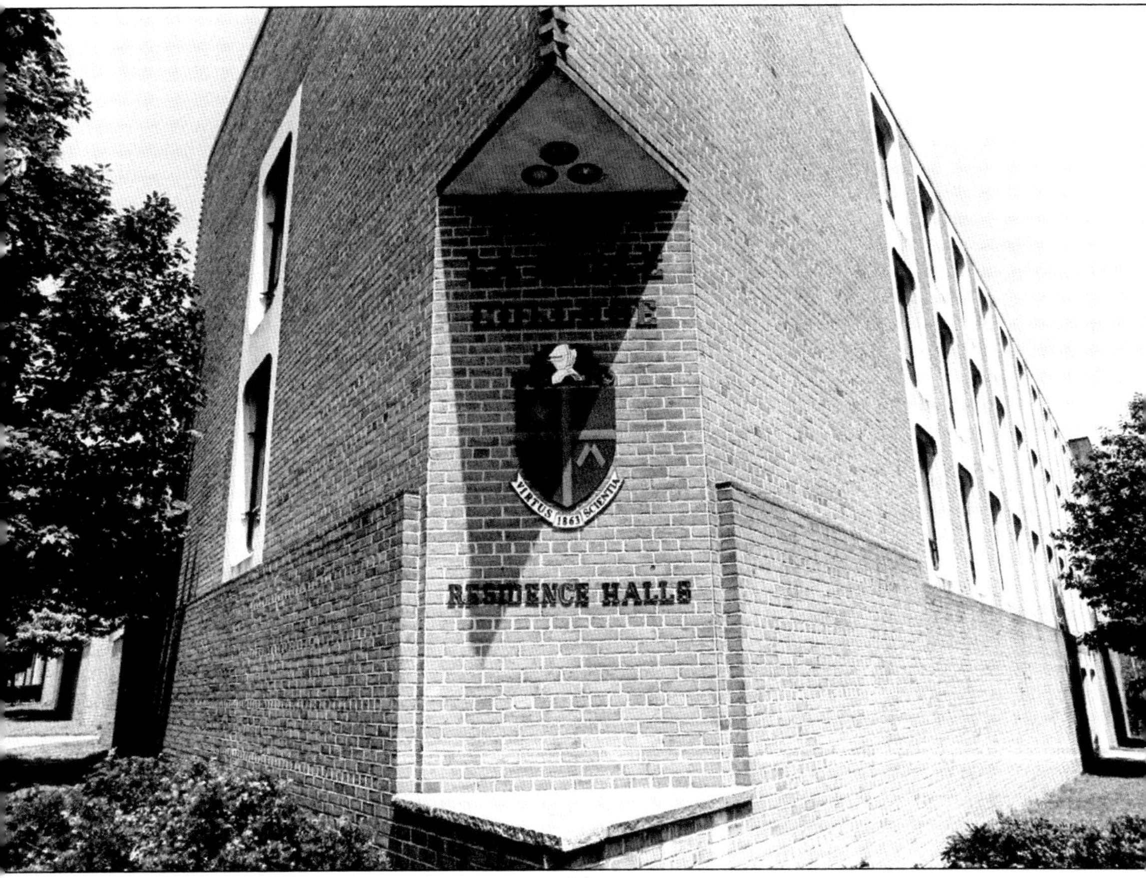

St. Hilary's Residence Hall was erected in 1966.

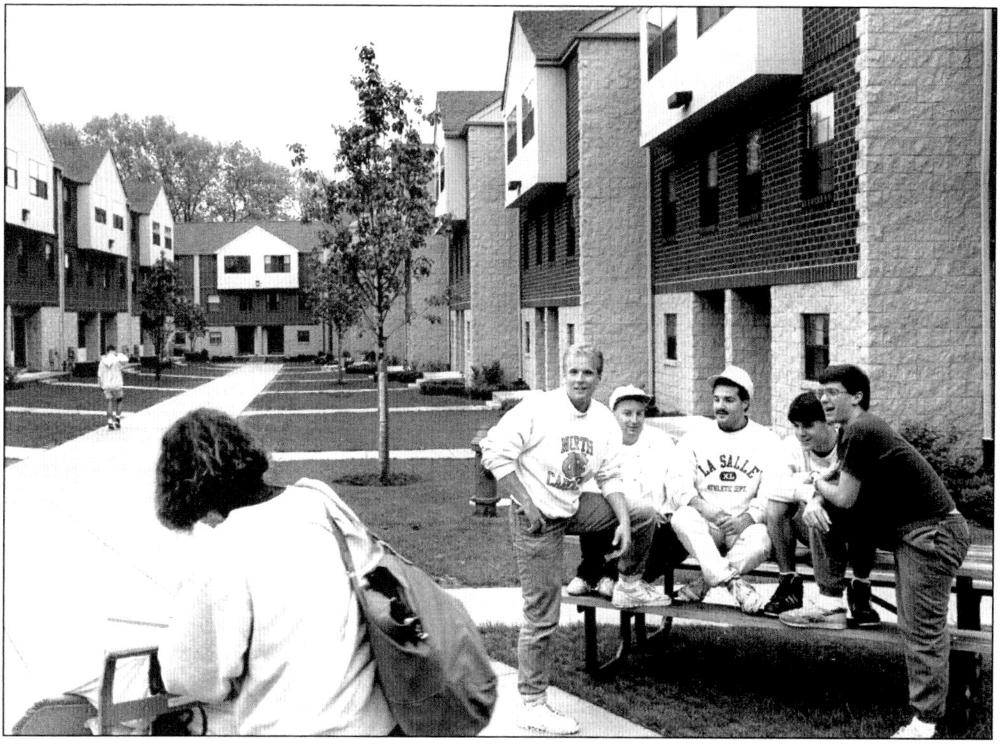

The St. Miguel Court Townhouses were named in honor of St. Miguel Febres Cordero of Ecuador and opened in 1989.

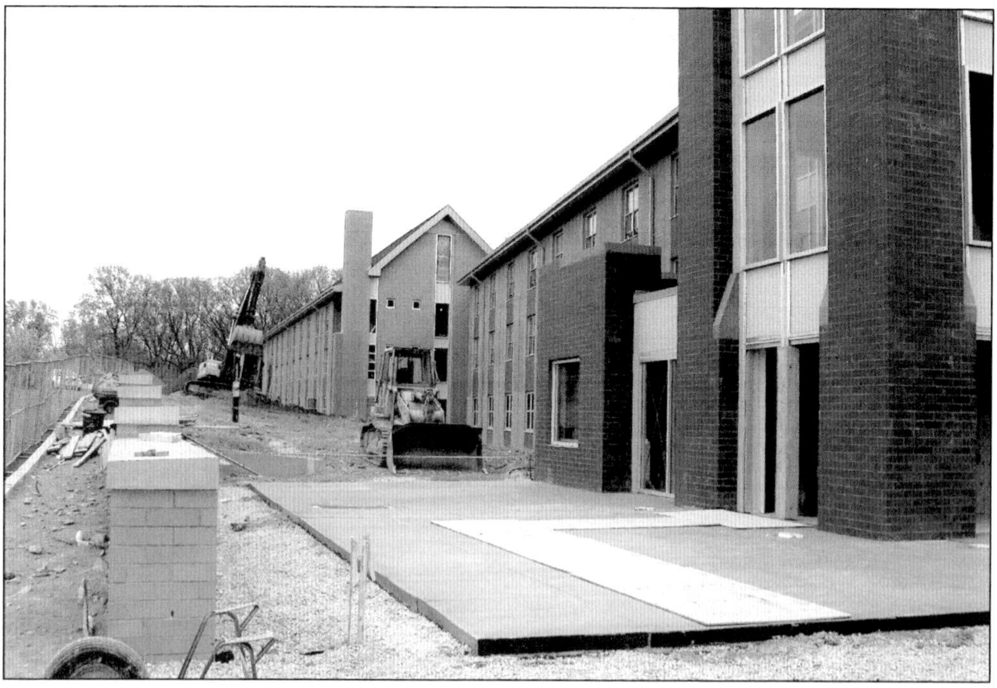

Construction began on the St. Basil's Court dormitory and dining hall in 2004. (Photograph courtesy of Michael Gallen.)

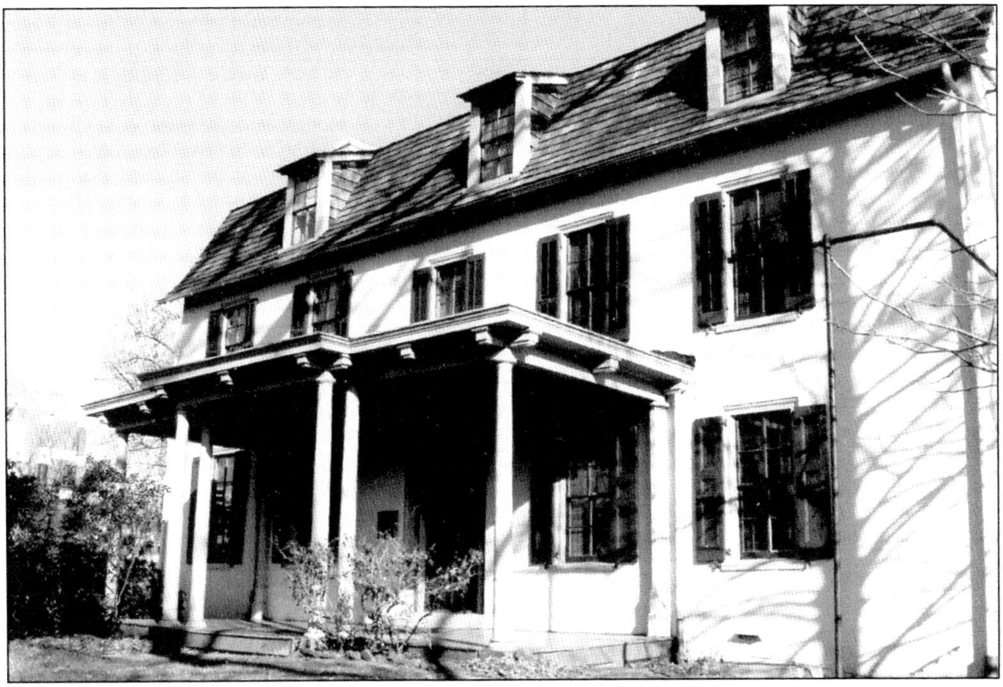

The original home of Charles Willson Peale sat upon 100 acres, which he named the Belfield Estate. He paid $9,500 for the property in 1810. Peale painted his famous portrait of George Washington prior to living in the house.

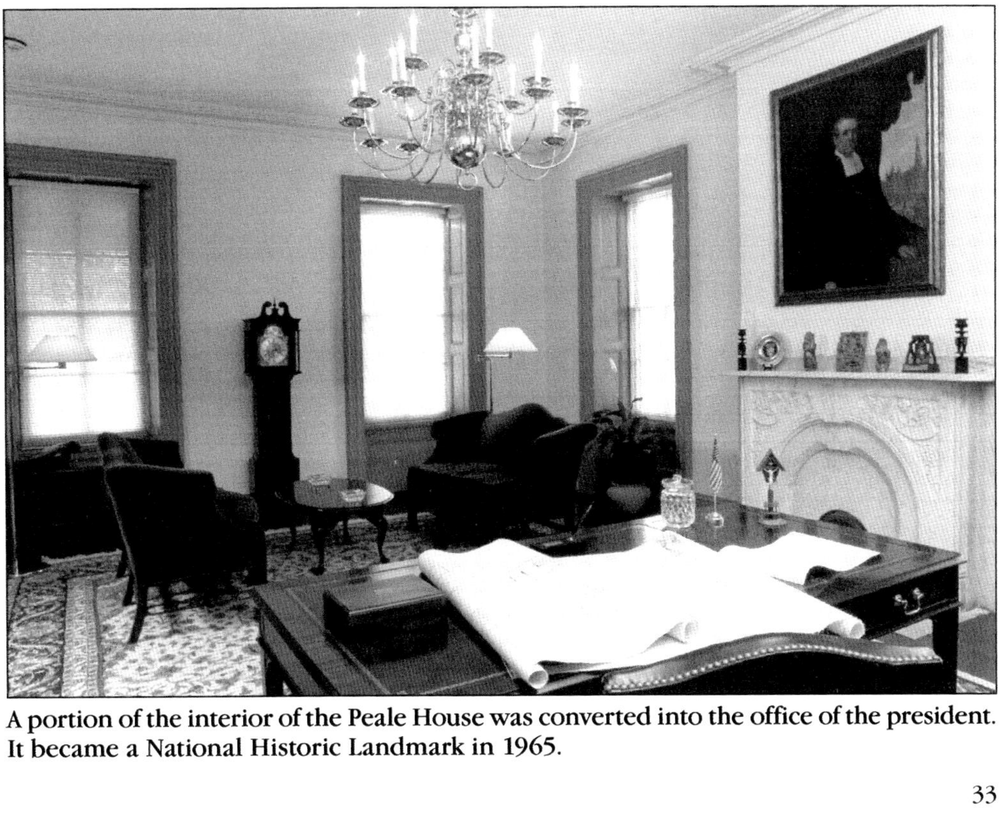

A portion of the interior of the Peale House was converted into the office of the president. It became a National Historic Landmark in 1965.

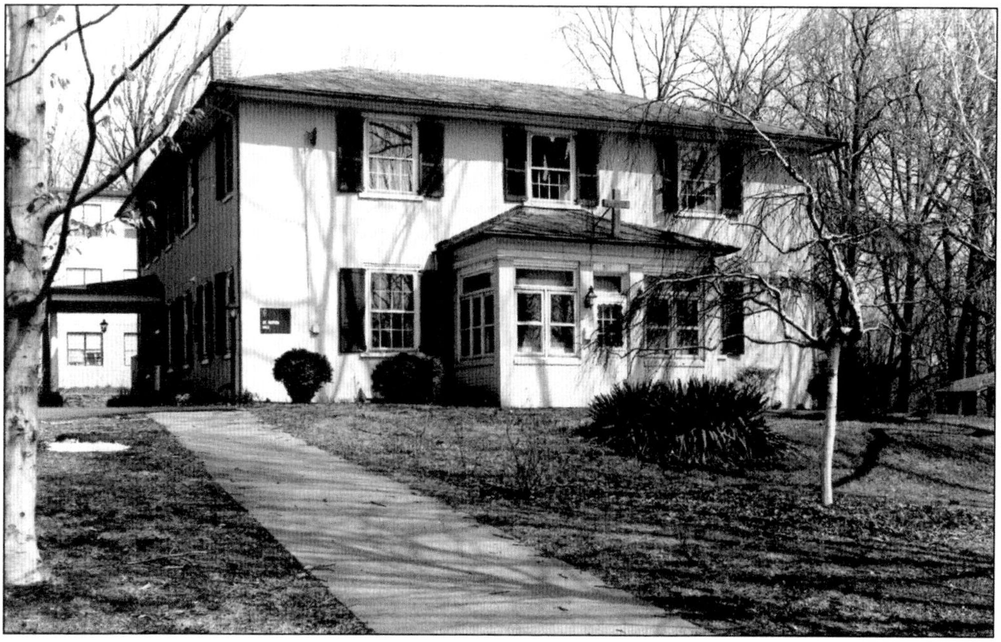

St. Mutien's Hall, named in honor of St. Mutien Marie Wianx of Belgium, was purchased in 1989 along with the south campus property and utilized as a Christian Brothers residence. It stood as a farmhouse during the Civil War and was used as a nursery school and convent by the Sisters of St. Basil.

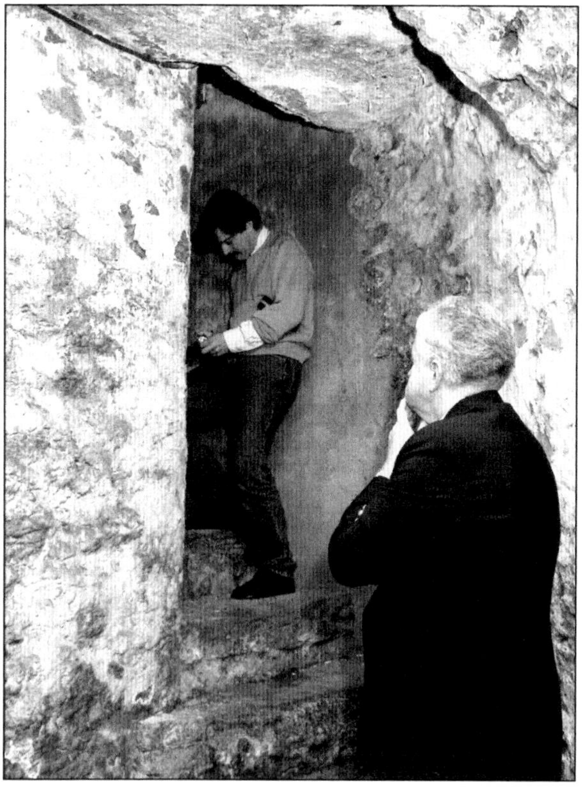

Brother Charles Gresh, director of St. Mutien's Hall, and architect John M. Bacon explore the subcellar of St. Mutien's, which served as the farmhouse's dairy vault.

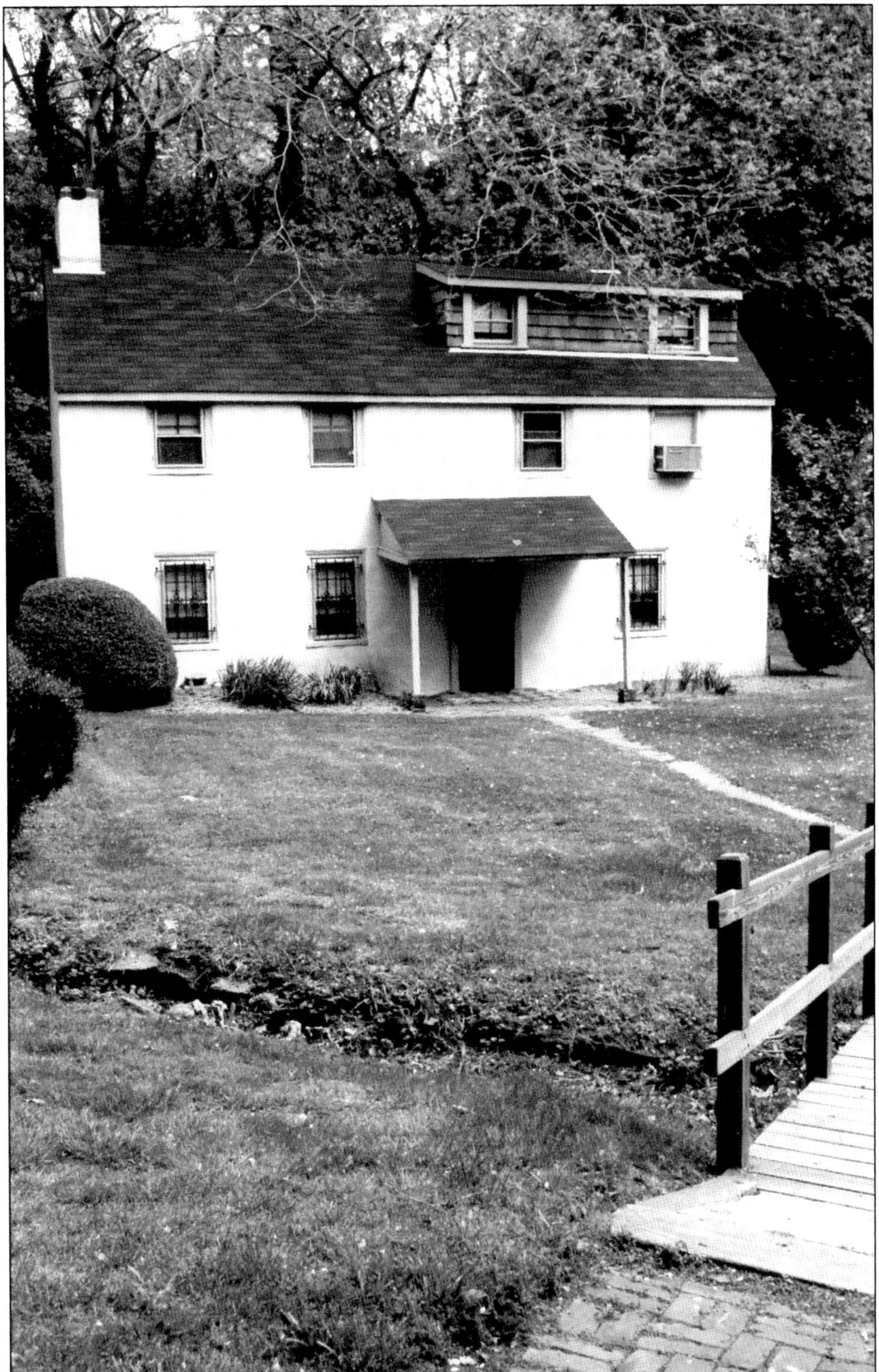

A tenant farmhouse located on the Belfield Estate became LaSalle University's Japanese Tea House, used for conducting authentic Japanese tea ceremonies.

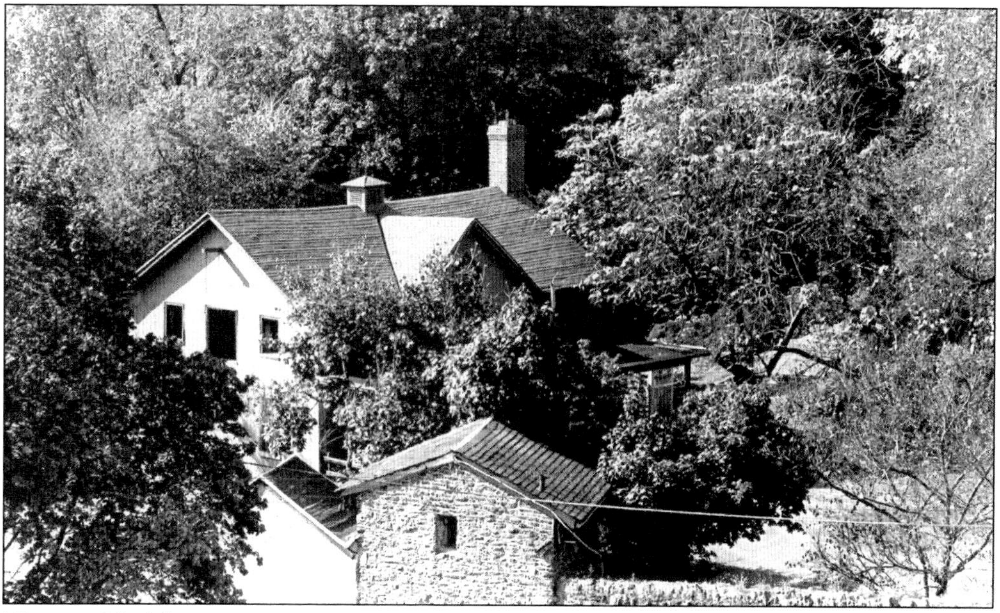

The Belfield Estate's barn and stable were converted into the LaSalle Security Headquarters.

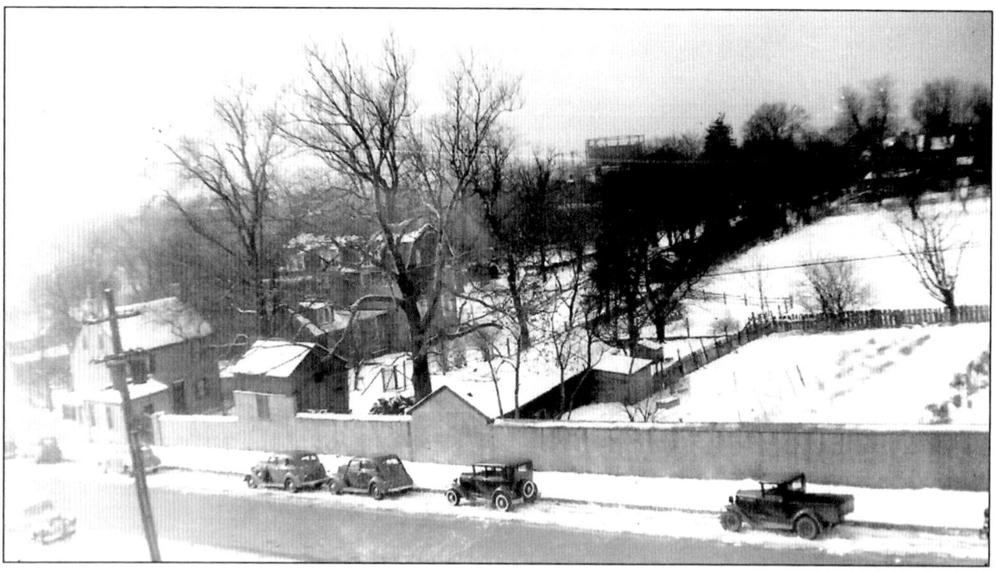

The Peale House, farmhouse, barn, and stable were all standing on the Belfield Estate when the Christian Brothers purchased the land in 1926.

Two

FOUNDERS AND FIRSTS

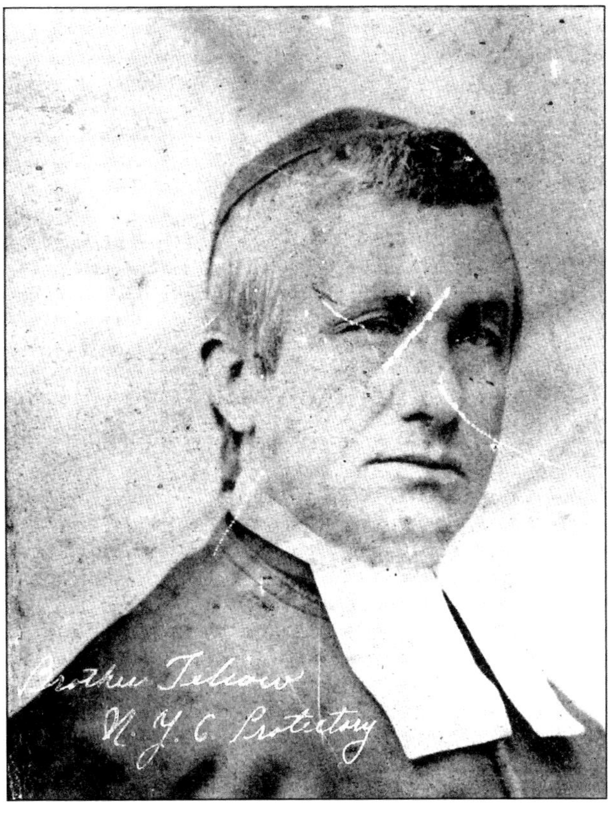

Brother Teliow was LaSalle's founding Christian Brother and first president, serving in 1863. He was a Prussian immigrant who spent time in Wisconsin, Iowa, and Michigan before coming to Philadelphia in 1854.

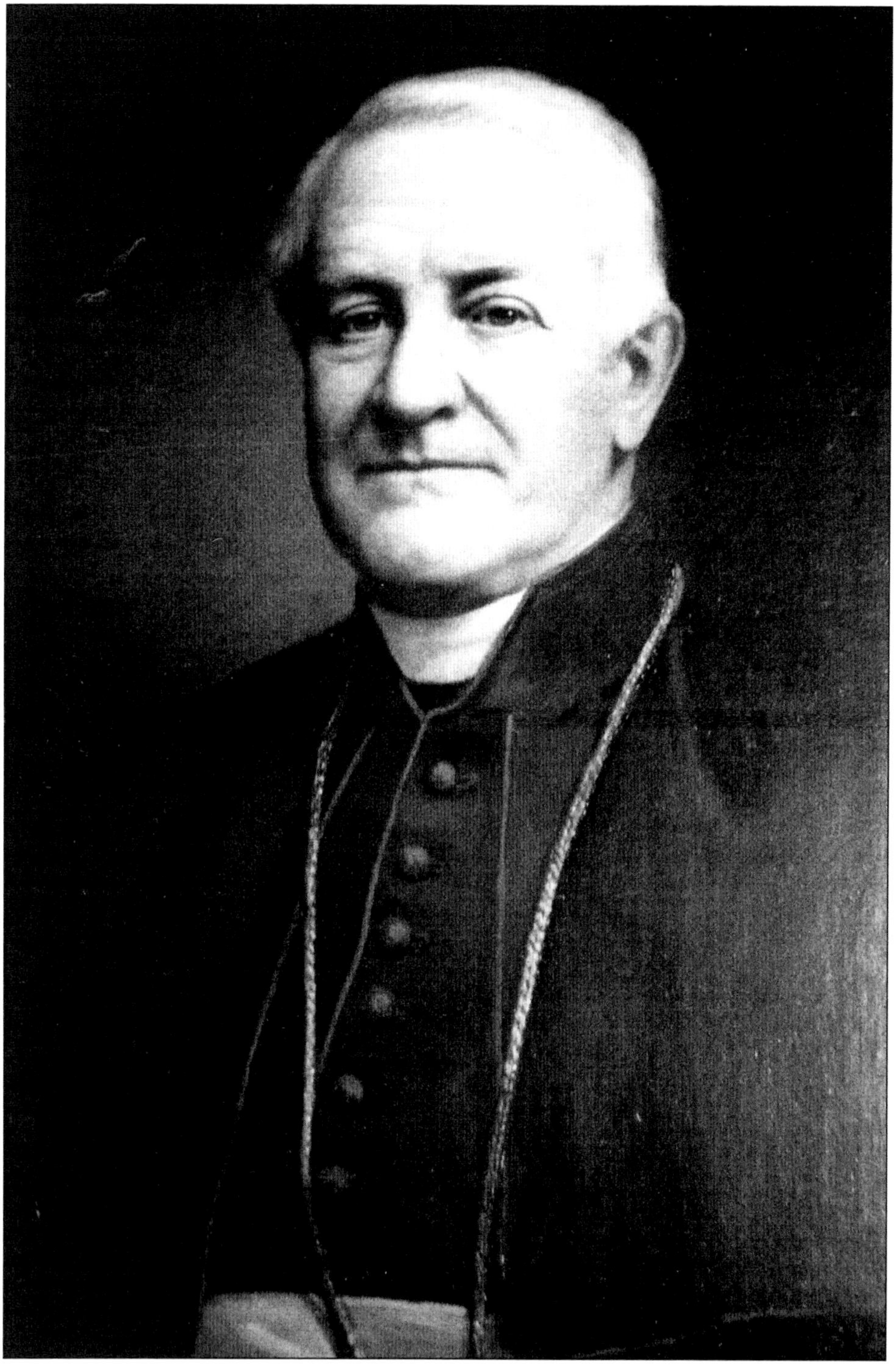

Bishop James F. Wood approached Brother Teliow in 1863 about establishing a Catholic institute of higher education in Philadelphia, as the city's other Catholic colleges had closed due to the Civil War. Brother Teliow, who was director of St. Michael's School at the time, organized the Christian Brother's Academy in the school's basement.

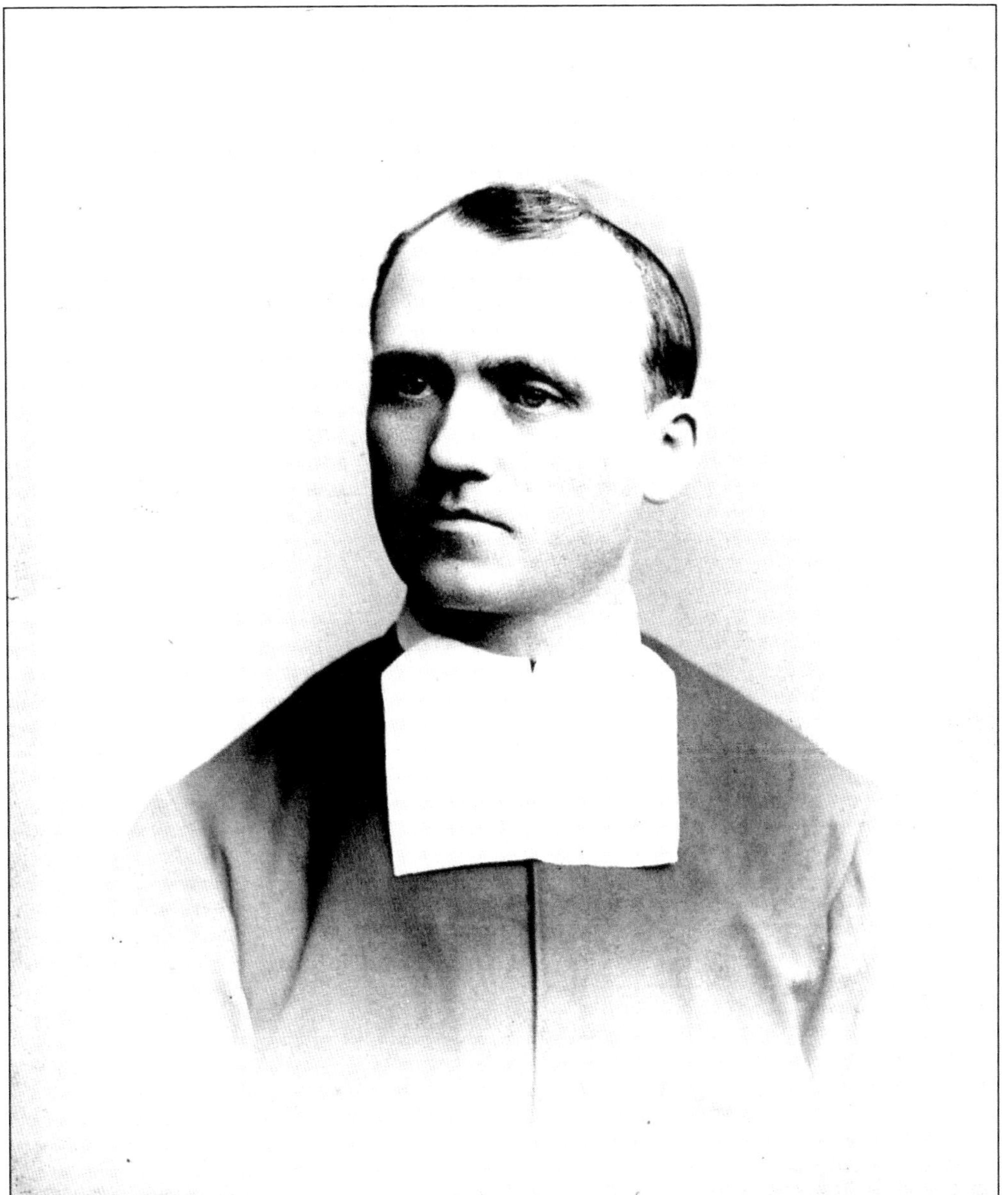

Brother Isidore John, an Irish immigrant, was president of LaSalle College for two terms, one from 1887 until 1889 and another from 1890 until 1900. He and other Christian Brothers assisted in repairing the roof of the Bouvier Mansion when renovations ran over budget in 1897.

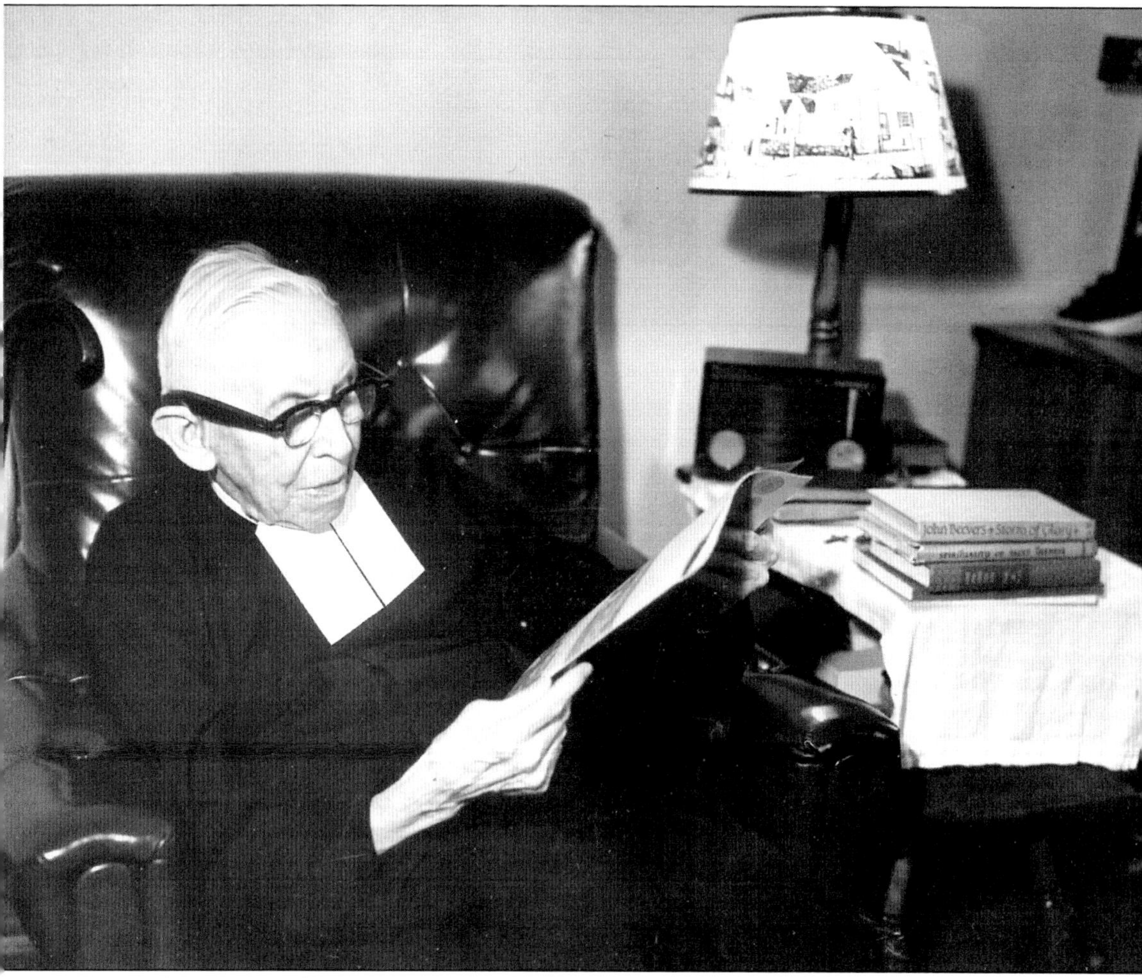

Brother Denis Edward earned a Ph.D. from Fordham University at the age of 57 and was president of LaSalle from 1911 until 1917. He enriched the college's curriculum with the introduction of physical science courses and raised admissions standards.

Brother Ennodius Richard was the first LaSalle alumnus to become president. He graduated in 1914 and was president from 1917 until 1922. Brother Richard was forced to close the college due to the lack of enrollment during the Great War but retained its charter by offering engineering courses to a handful of students.

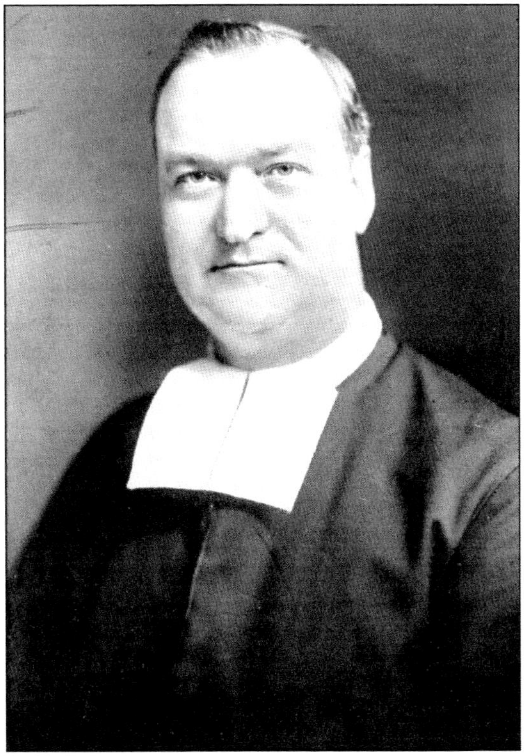

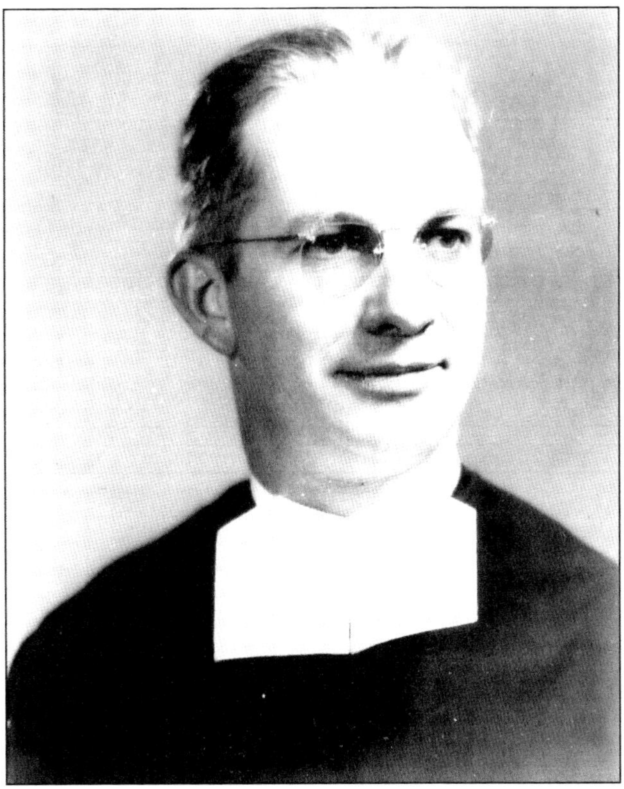

LaSalle College faced another enrollment crisis during Brother Emilian James's presidency from 1941 until 1945. LaSalle's student body dropped to 97 during the Second World War. Brother Emilian refused to allow the military to take over the school and offered courses during the summer in order to accelerate the degree program for students who faced the draft. He left LaSalle when he was promoted to provincial superior of the Baltimore Province in 1945.

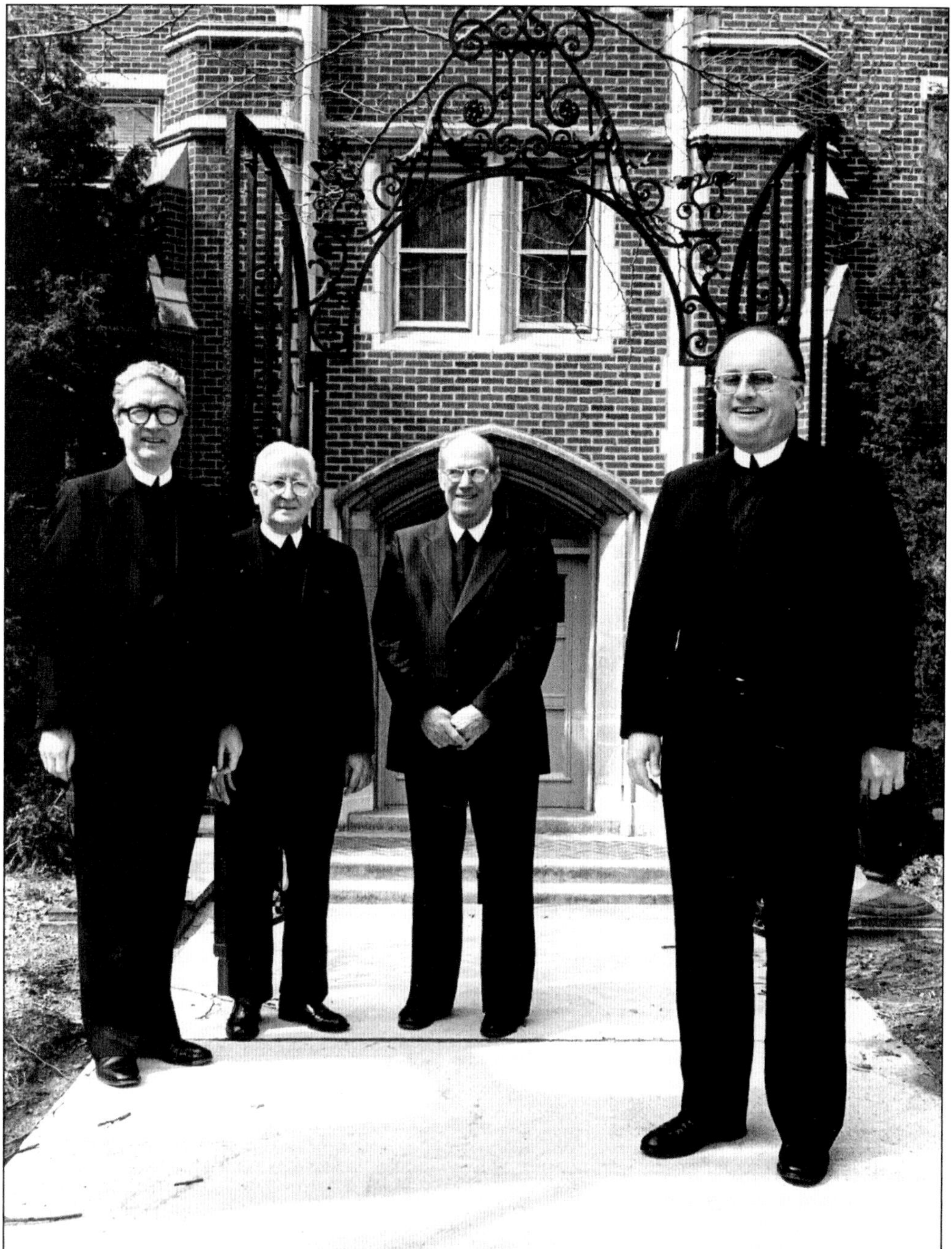

Four former LaSalle presidents, Brother Daniel Burke (1969 to 1976), Brother Gregorian Paul (1945 to 1952), Brother Daniel Bernian (1958 to 1969), and Brother Patrick Ellis (1977 to 1992) are seen here. Brother Paul taught chemistry in the 1930s and was dean in the early 1940s. Brother Bernian received a Ph.D. in French from Laval University in Canada, taught French, and was the first vice-president of student affairs in the early 1950s. Brother Patrick was the first director of LaSalle's Honors Program in the 1960s. LaSalle became a university during Brother Patrick's presidency in 1984.

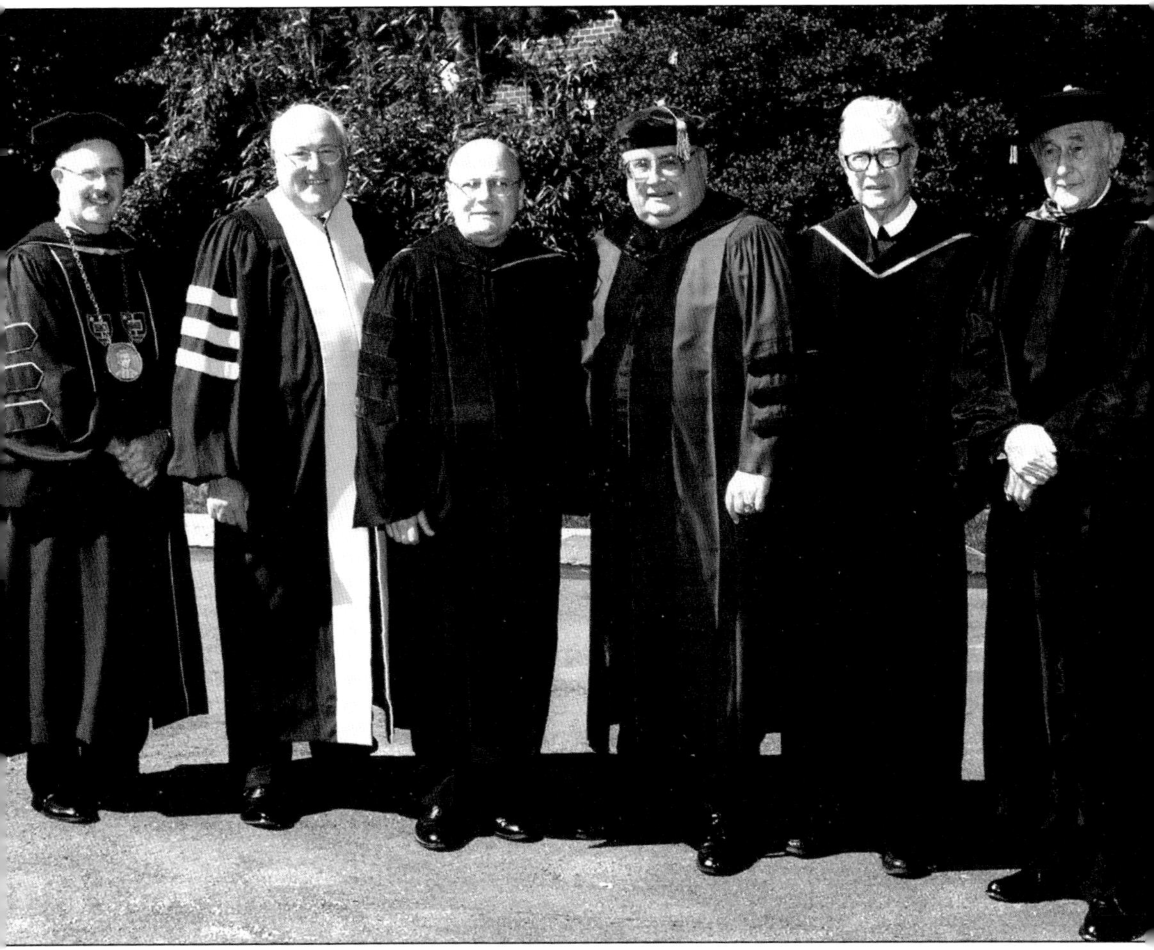

Brother Michael McGinniss's inauguration as president in 1999 was attended by (from left to right) former interim president Nicholas Giordano (1998 to 1999), former presidents Brother Joseph Burke (1992 to 1998), Brother Patrick Ellis (1977 to 1992), Brother Daniel Burke (1969 to 1976), and Brother Erminus Stanislaus (1952 to 1958).

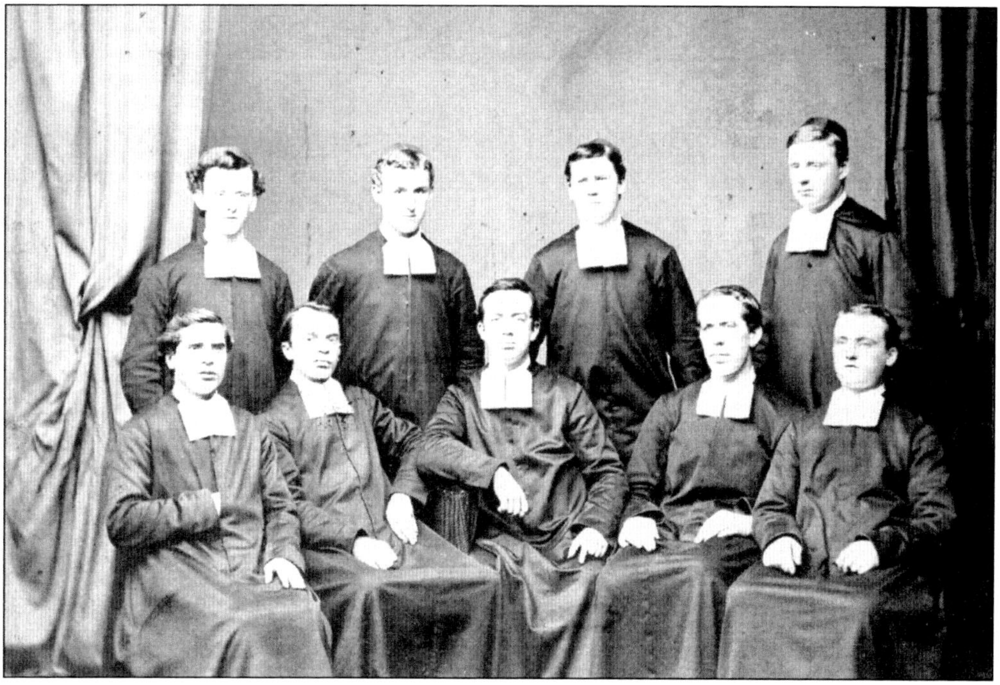

The faculty of LaSalle College pose for a Christmas photograph in 1873.

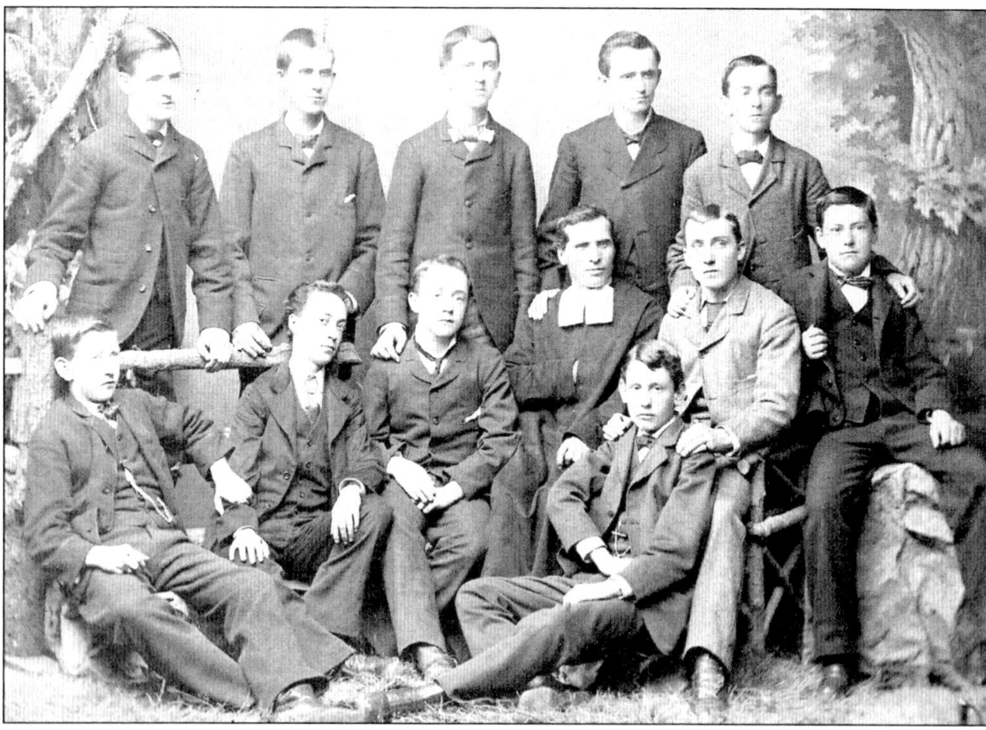

Brother Paphylinus is photographed with a group of LaSalle students in the 1880s. Brother Paphylinus was the college's treasurer and director of its drama club.

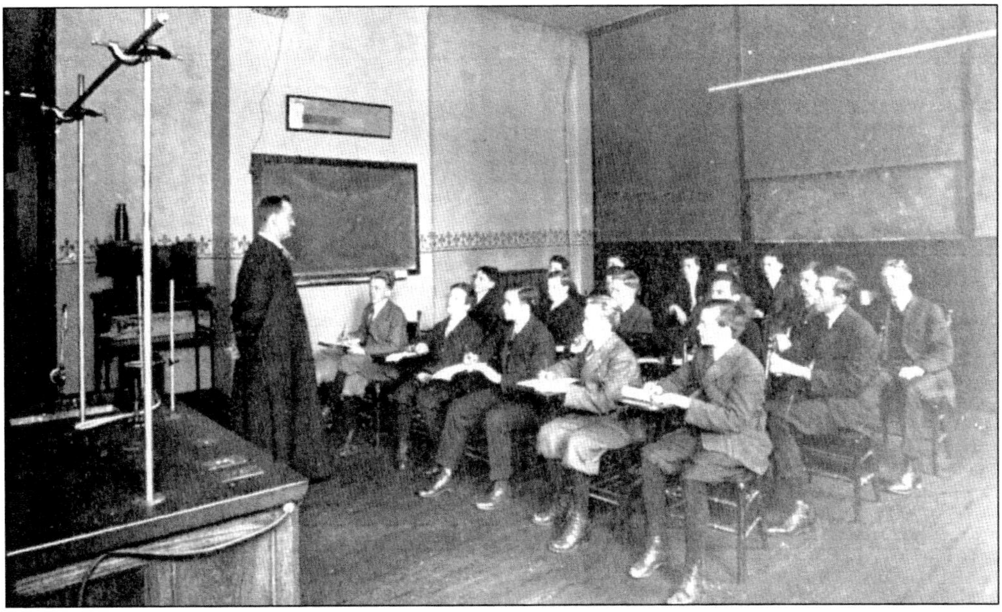

A promotional pamphlet from the early 1900s showcases various classes offered at LaSalle College.

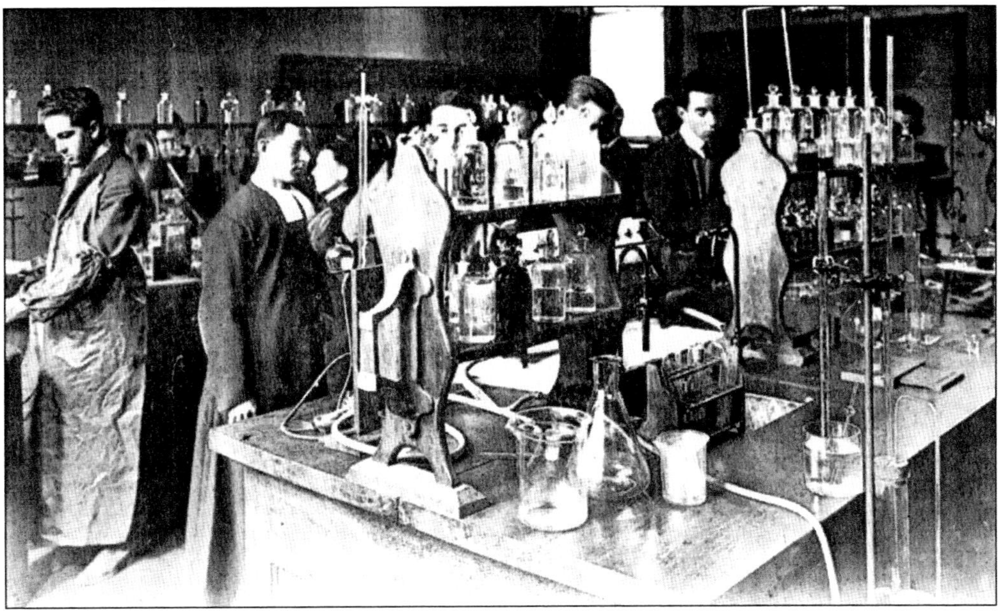

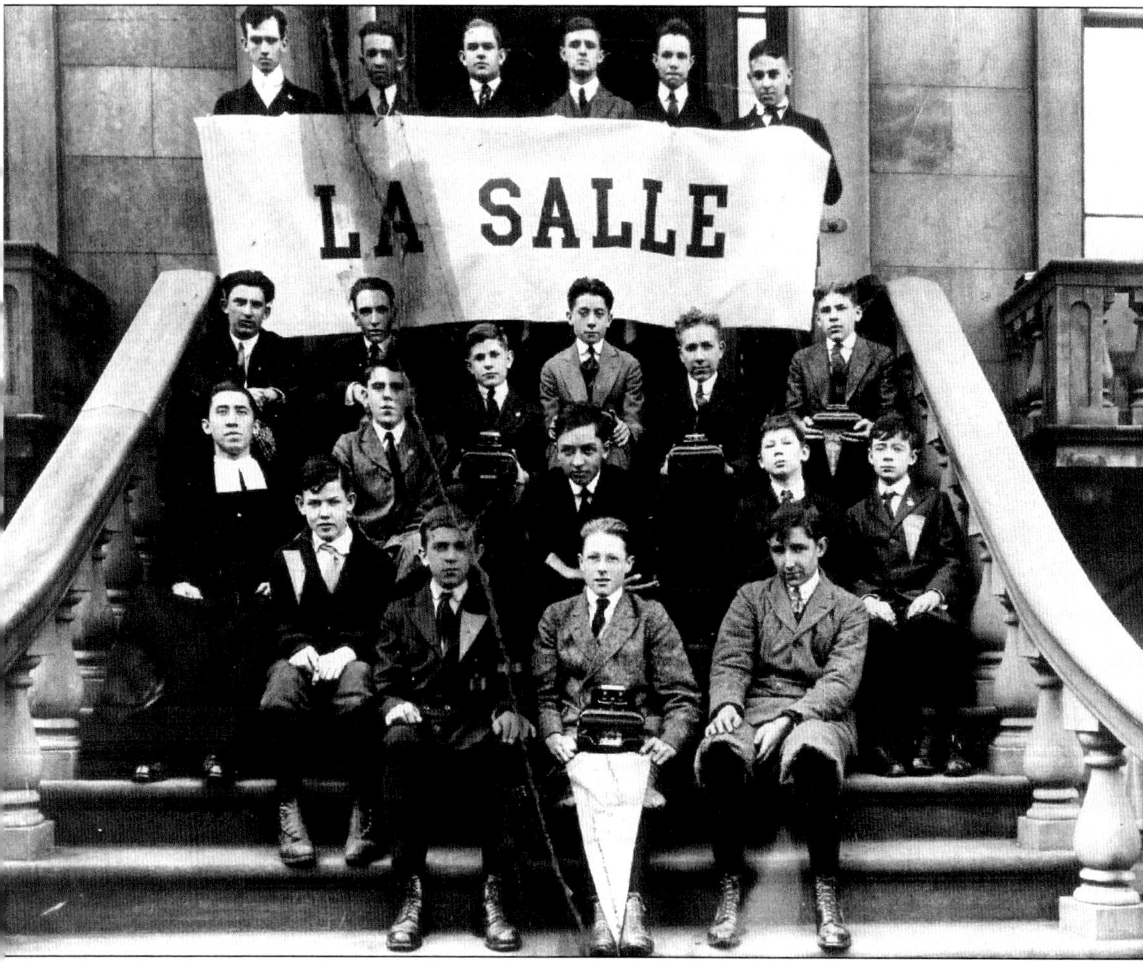

Brother Edward John and his students show the latest adding machines in 1919.

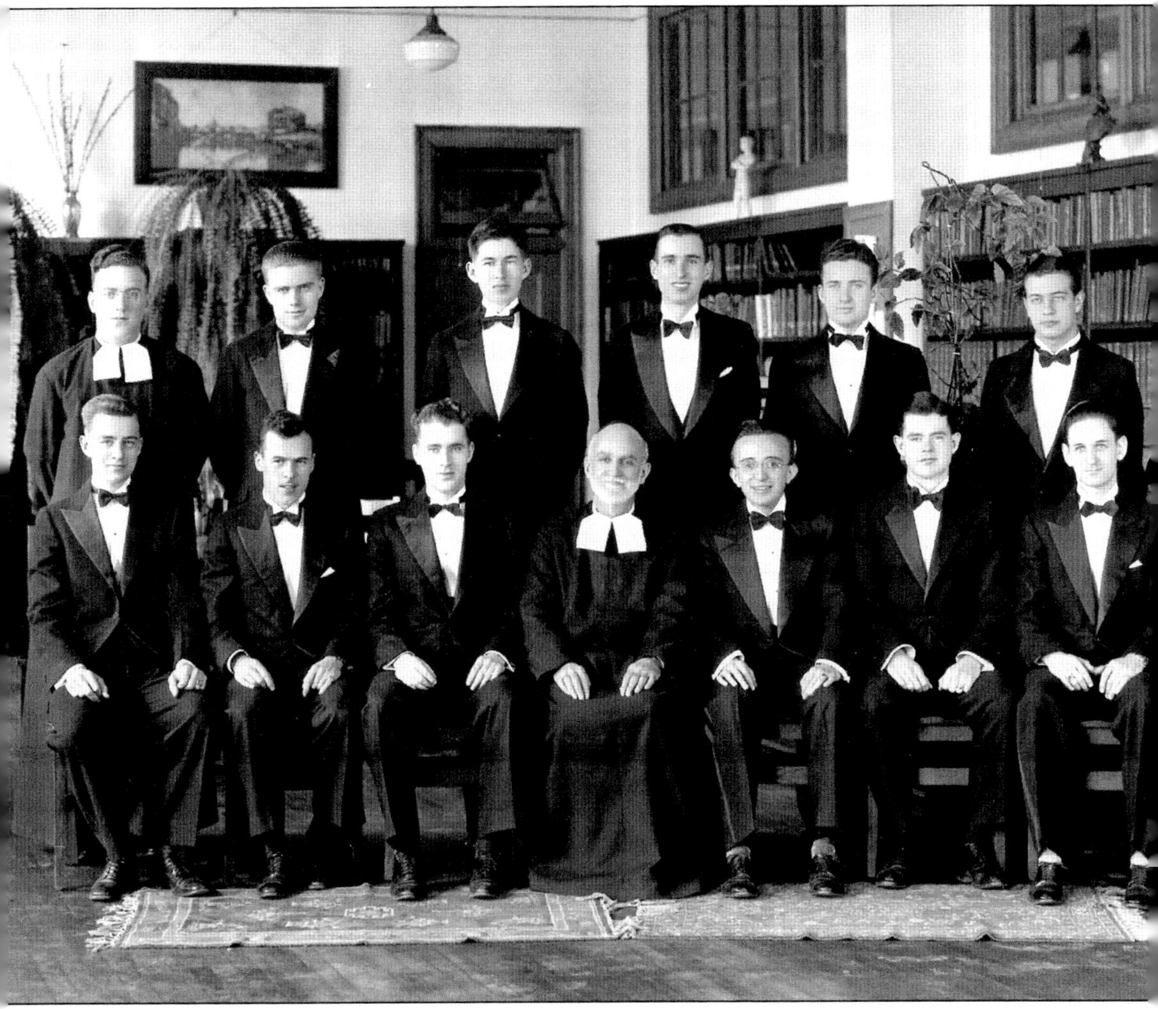

Brother Elzear Alfred (seated center) was faculty moderator of LaSalle's debate team, which included Joseph Flubacher (seated third from right), in the 1930s. Flubacher later taught economics at LaSalle and became one of the first recipients of the Lindback Foundation Award for Excellent Teaching. Brother Alfred was president from 1928 until 1932 and saw the college through the Great Depression. He refused to close the school in 1930, despite having only $1,805 left in the treasury. After serving as president, Brother Alfred organized the Sunday Labor Management School, which offered lectures on labor, management, and government throughout the city of Philadelphia.

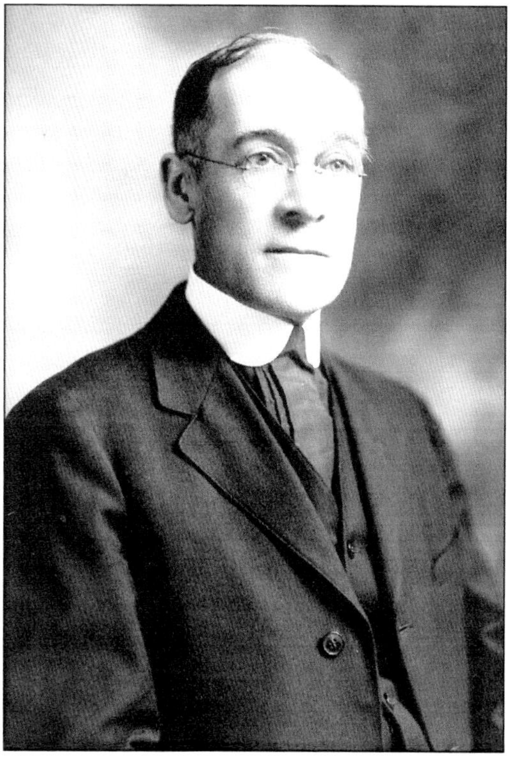

Brother Firmus Edward was the first dean of LaSalle College from 1925 until 1928.

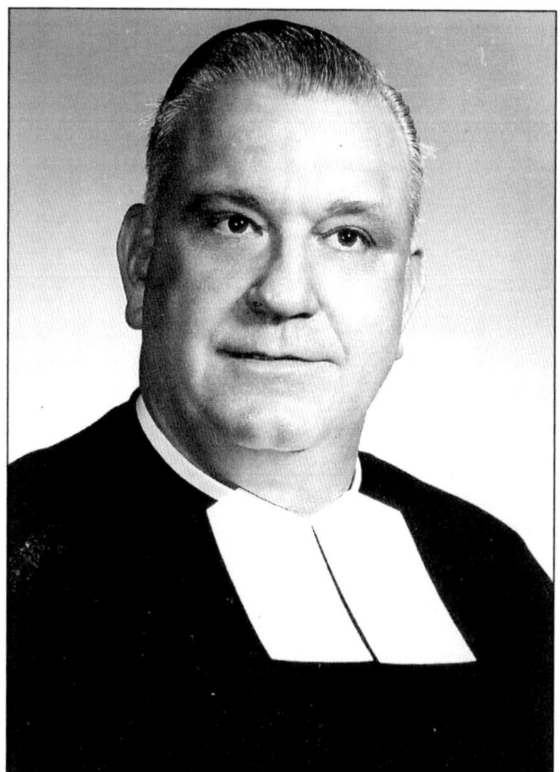

Brother Donatus Vincent Grimes was LaSalle's first dean of arts and sciences from 1955 until 1956.

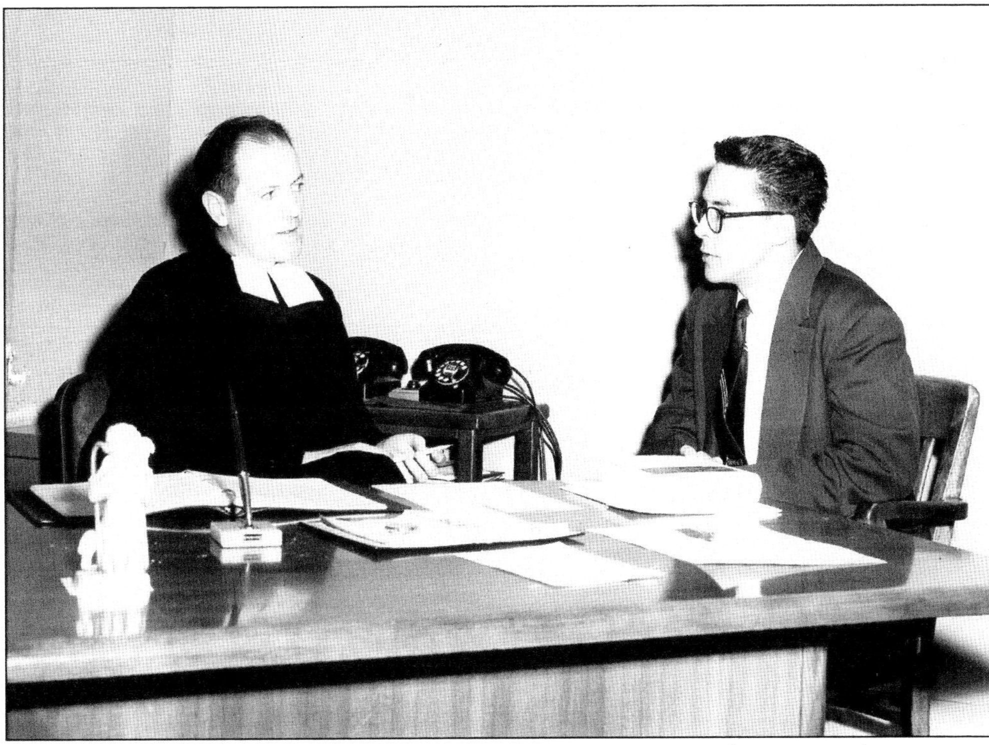

Brother David Cassian Pendergast was the first dean of the School of Business Administration from 1955 until 1969.

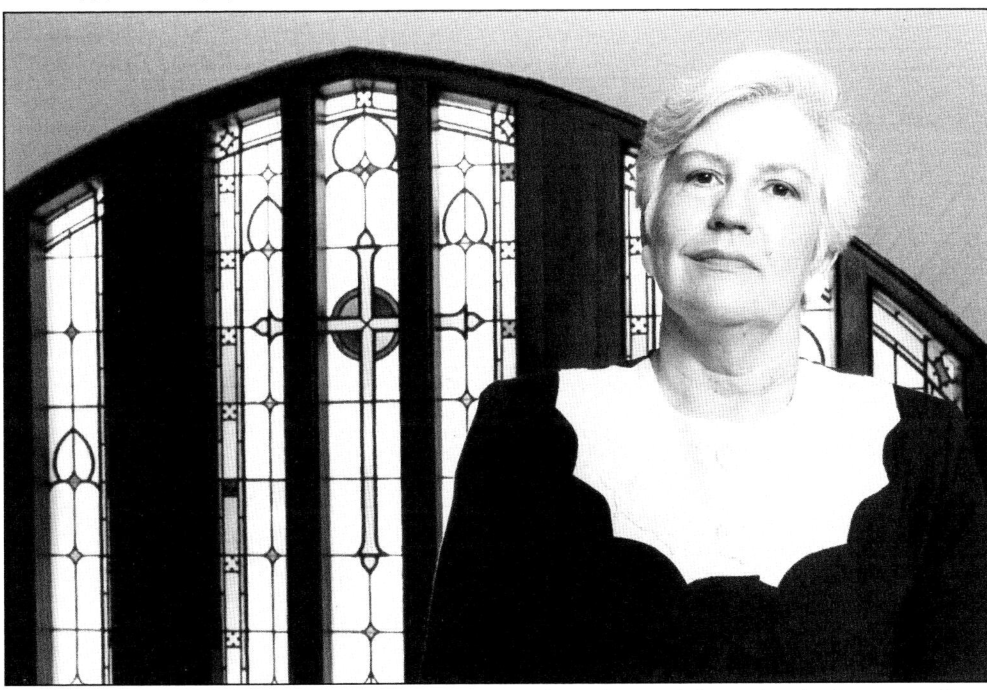

Dr. Gloria F. Donnelly was LaSalle University's first dean of the School of Nursing from 1992 until 1996.

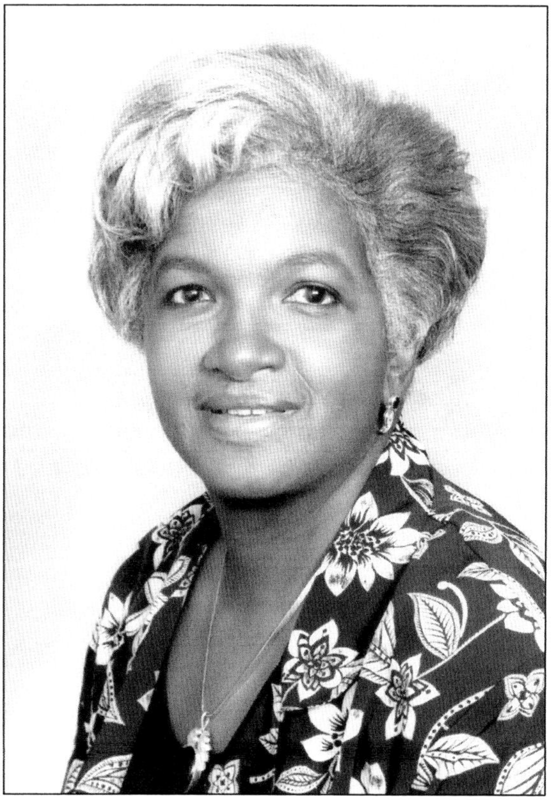

Dr. Cynthia Capers was LaSalle's first African American administrator. She was interim dean of the School of Nursing from 1996 until 1997.

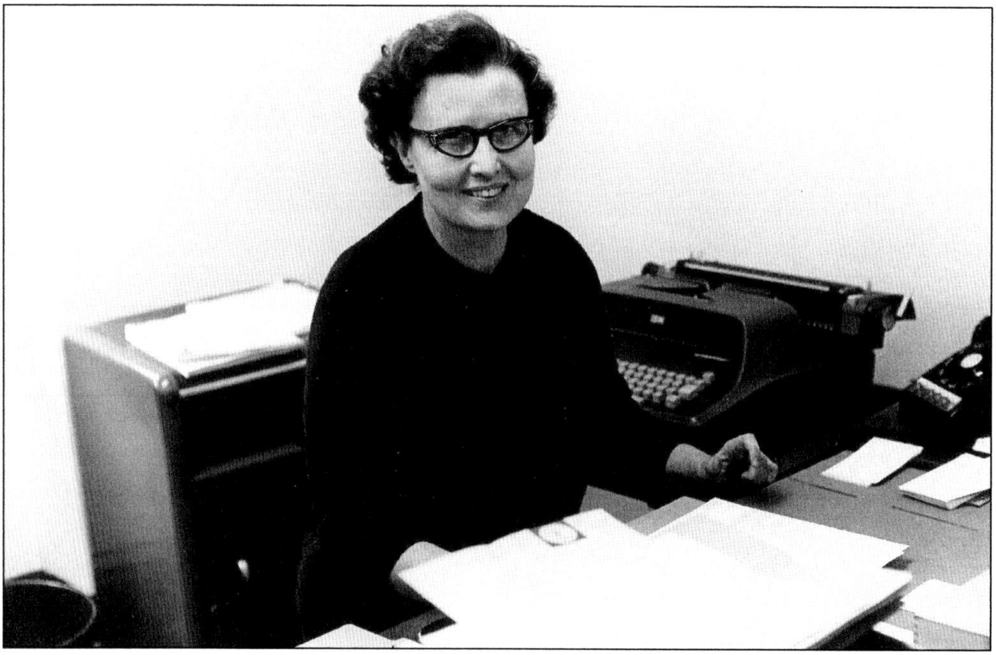

Margaret Keily Lennon was the college's first female staff member with administrative status. She started working in the Registrar's Office in the mid-1940s.

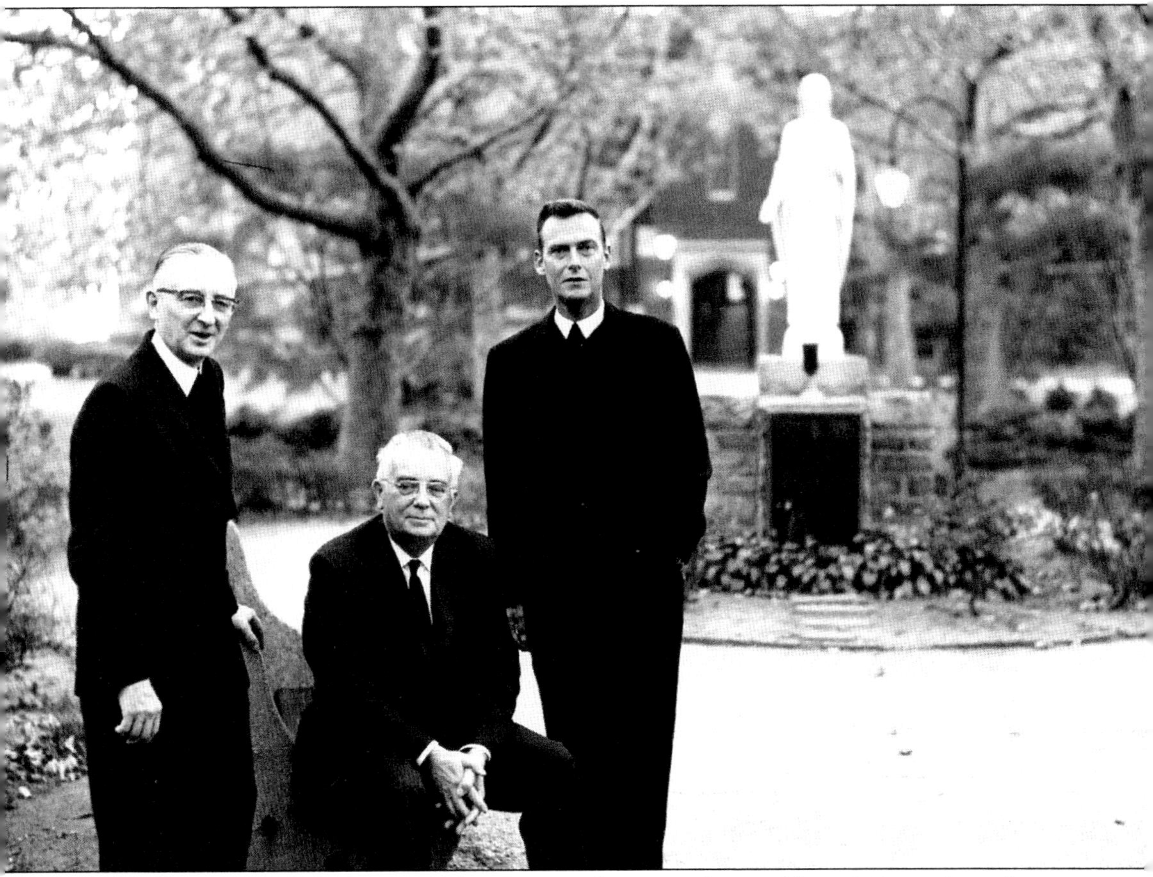

Brother Gregorian Paul (1953 to 1961), Dr. Joseph J. Sprissler (1946 to 1953), and Brother Emery Mollenhauer (1961 to 1969) were the first three directors/Deans of LaSalle's Evening Division. LaSalle College was one of the first institutes of higher education in Philadelphia to have a fully accredited evening program and was the first school in Pennsylvania to offer the opportunity to earn a bachelor's degree at night. The program began with 36 students in 1946.

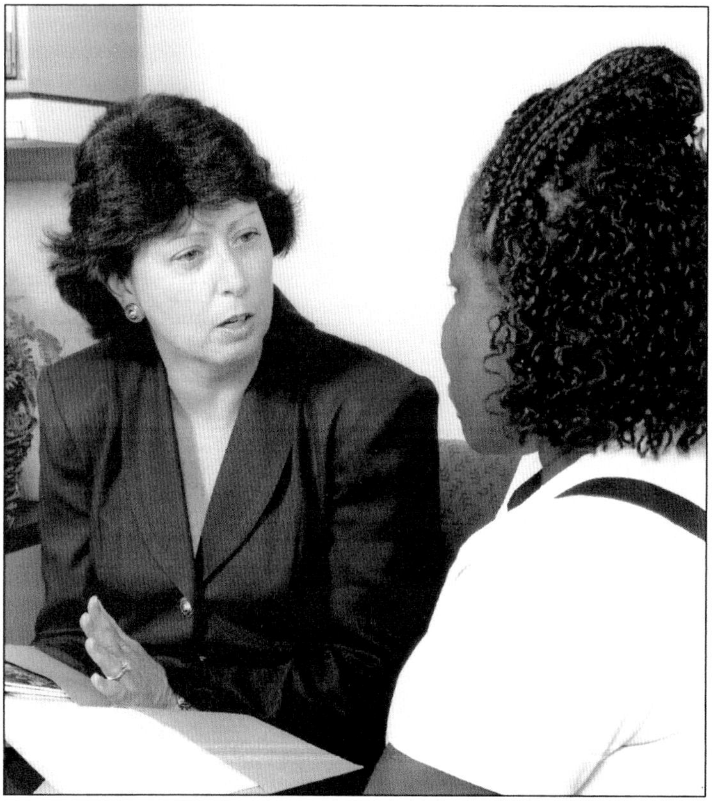

Elizabeth Heenan became the university's first director of the Office of Continuing Studies in 1996.

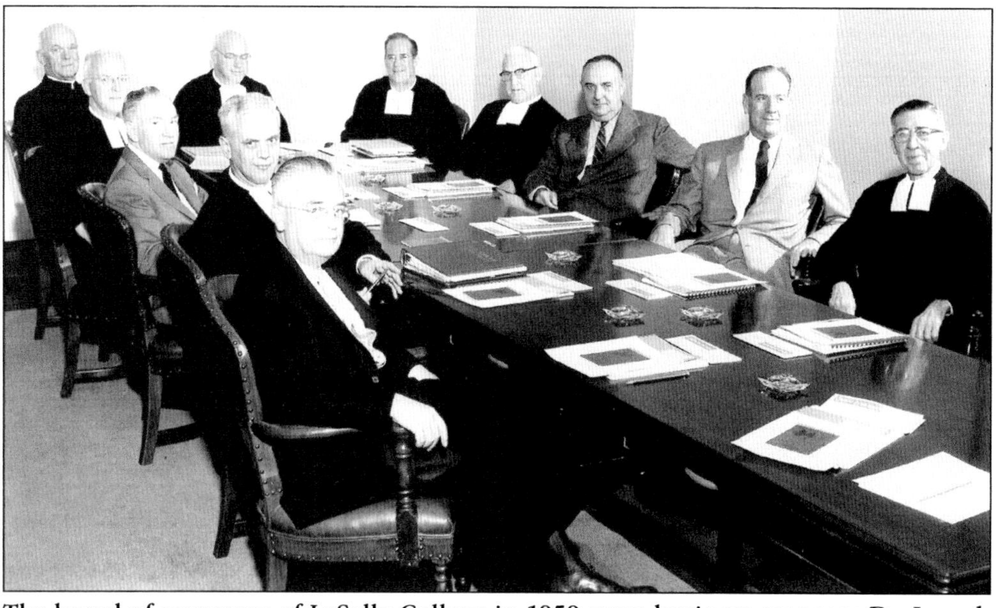

The board of managers of LaSalle College in 1959 were business manager Dr. Joseph J. Sprissler, vice-president and dean of the college Brother D. John, John McShain, Brother Felix Francis, Monsignor Thomas F. McNally, Brother E. James, Pres. Brother Daniel Bernian, Brother Edwin Anselm, Joseph Schmitz, William F. Kelly, and Bursar Brother E. John.

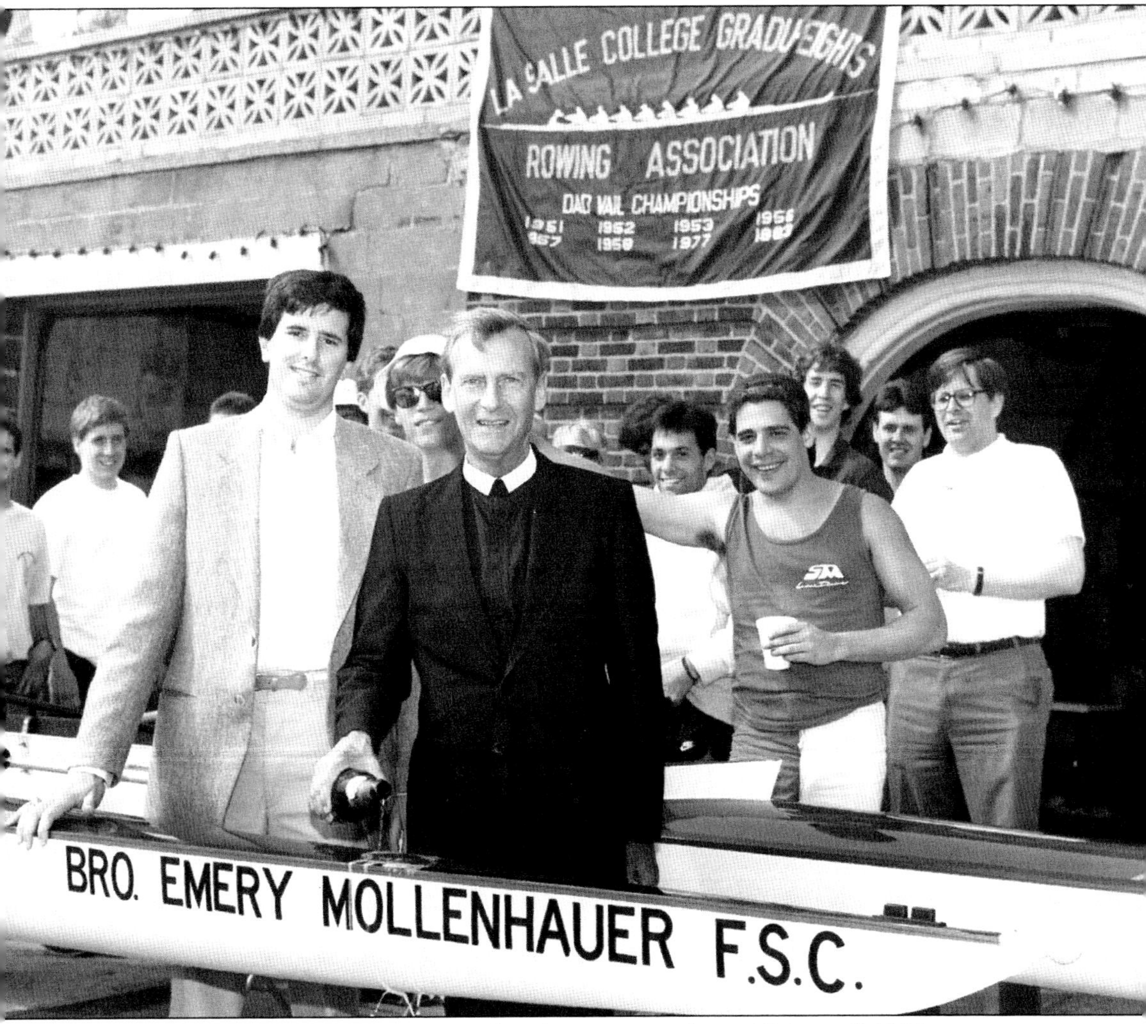

Brother Emery Mollenhauer was LaSalle's first provost from 1977 until 1990.

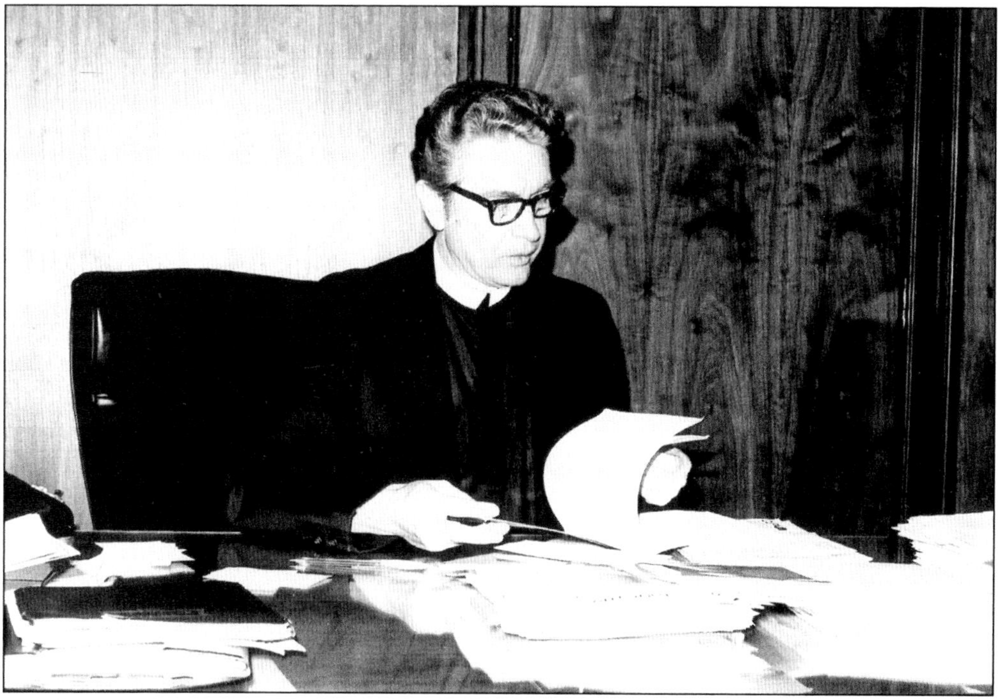

Brother Daniel Burke was the first vice-president for academic affairs from 1960 until 1969.

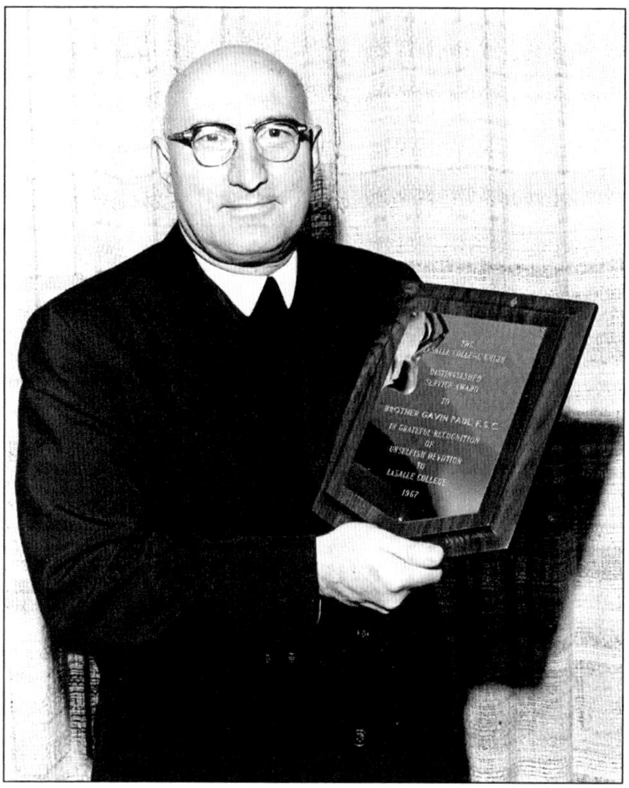

Brother Gavin Paul was LaSalle College's first vice-president for student affairs from 1960 until 1967.

Dr. Joseph J. Sprissler was the first vice-president for business affairs from 1960 until 1976. He had been the college's business manager since 1946.

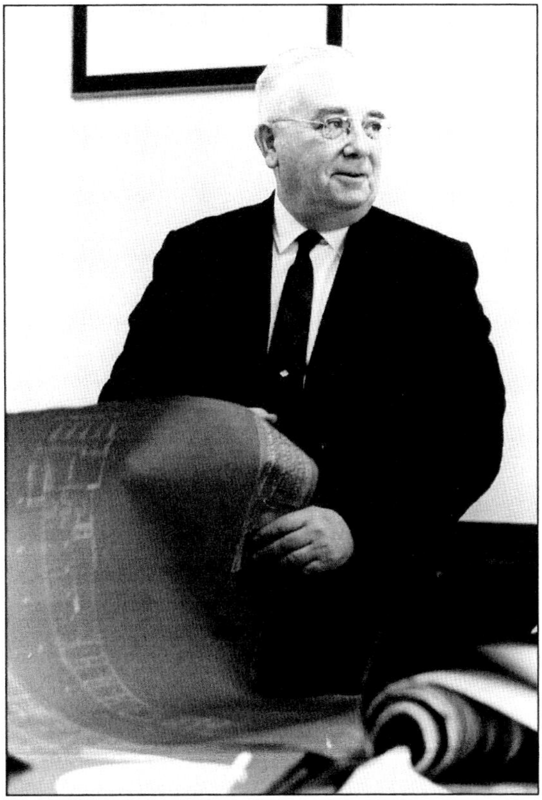

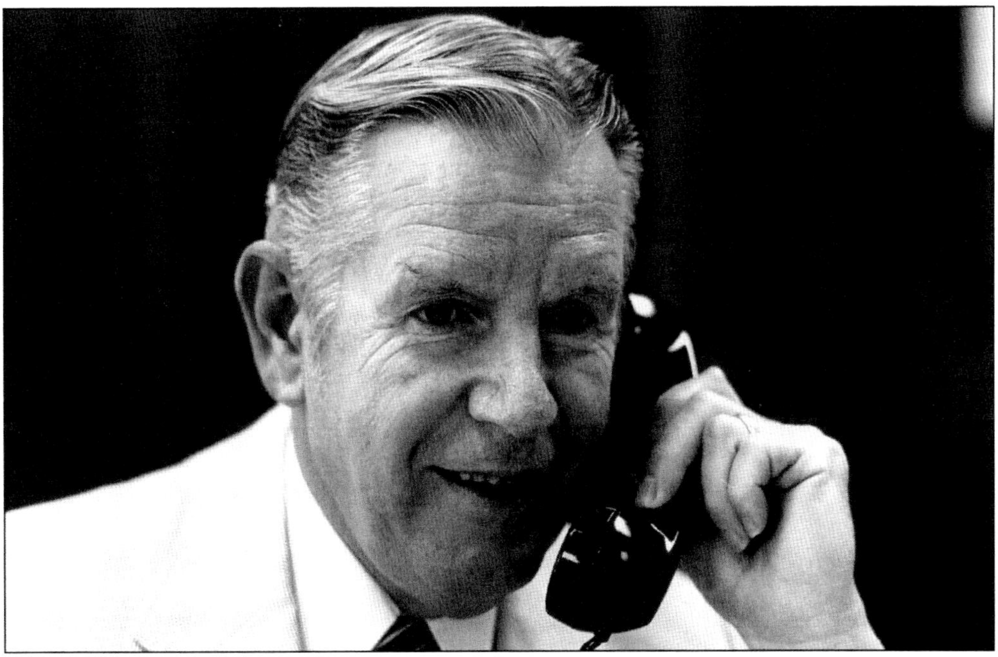

John L. McCloskey was LaSalle's first vice-president for public relations from 1960 until 1986. He graduated from LaSalle in 1948 and had worked as an assistant to the college's president.

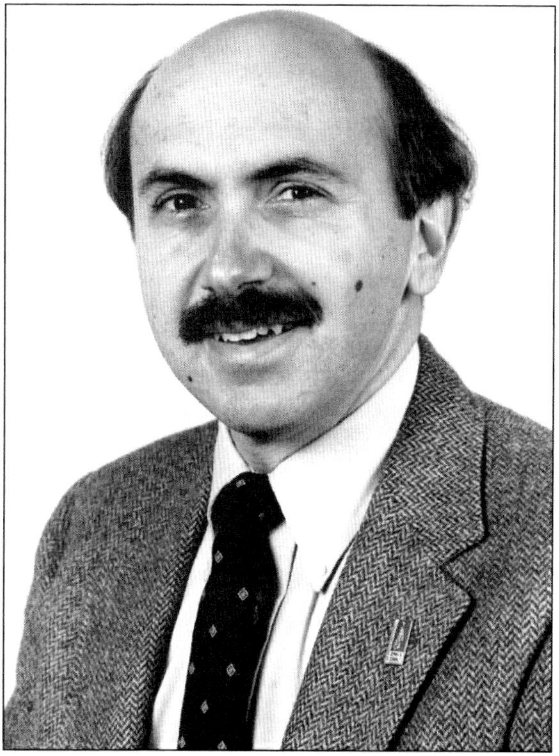

Raymond A. Ricci became the first vice-president for enrollment services in 1990. He graduated from LaSalle College in 1967.

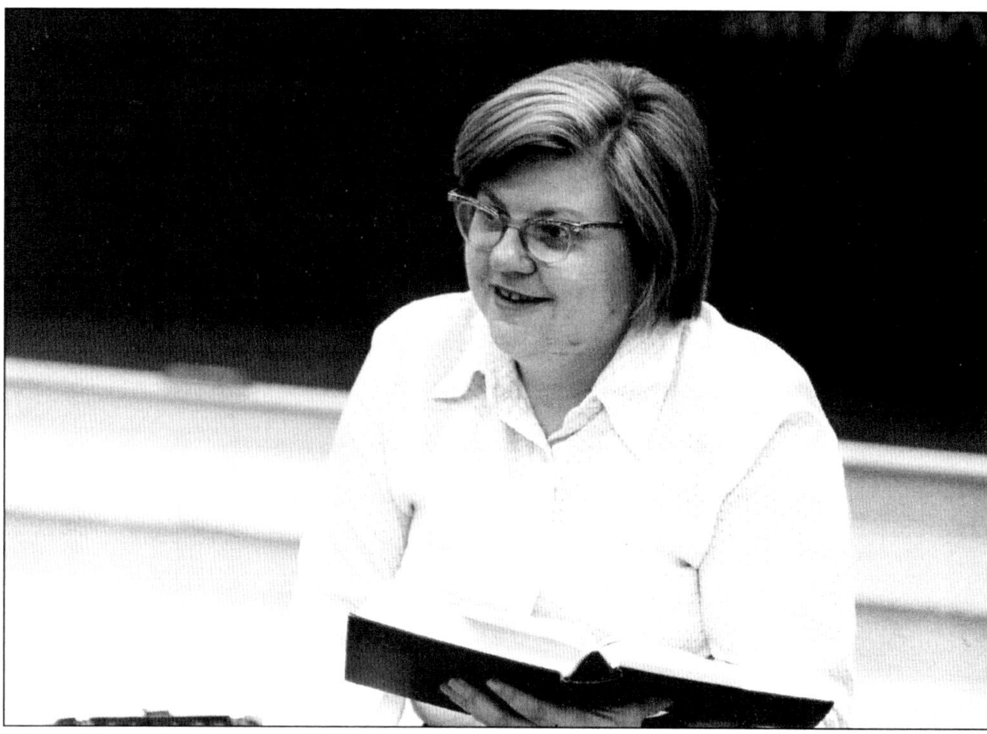

Shirley Ann Eriksson was the first female instructor in the evening division. She was hired to teach English in 1965.

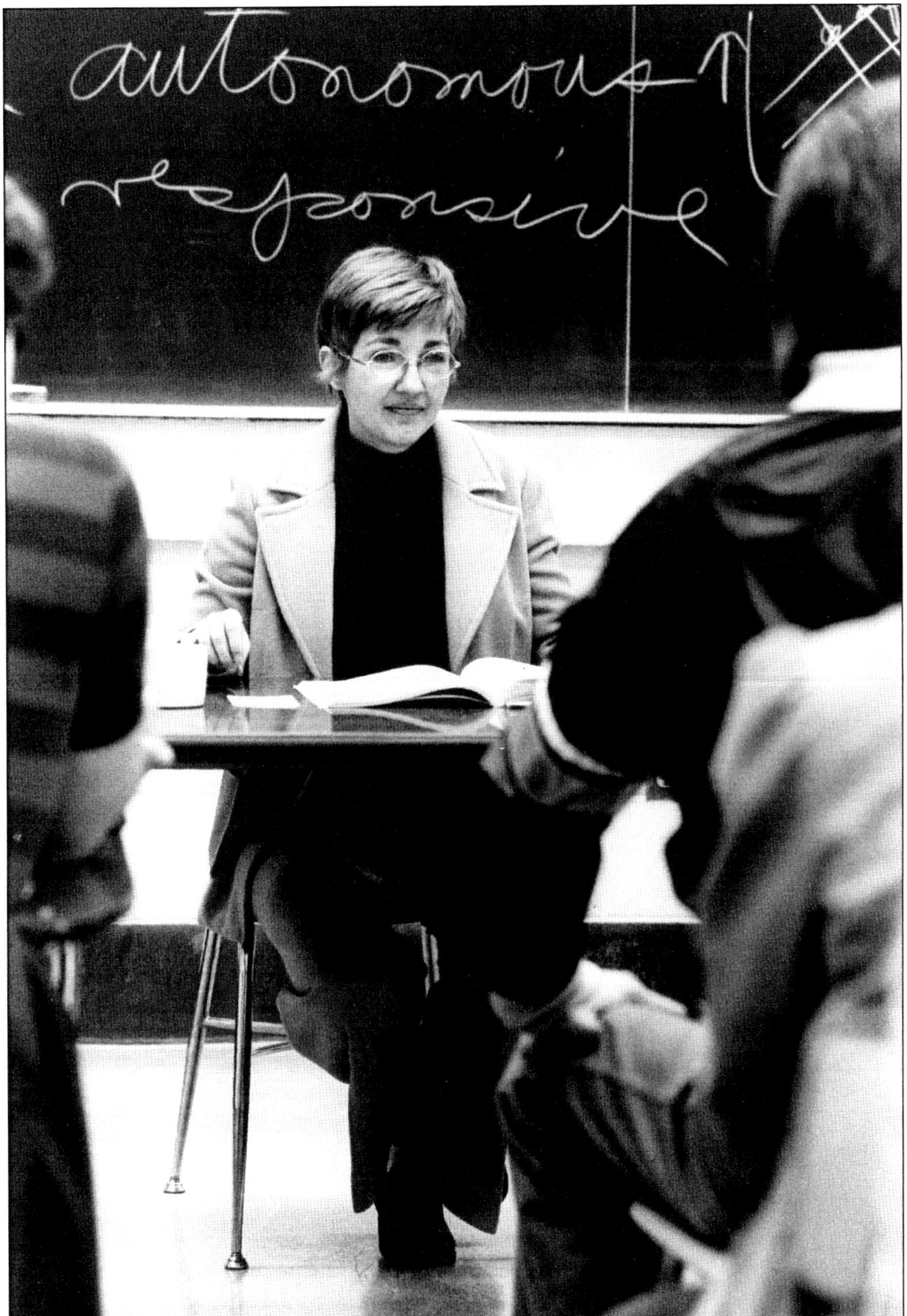

Dr. Diane Blumenthal was one of LaSalle's first two full-time female instructors hired in 1967. She taught foreign languages.

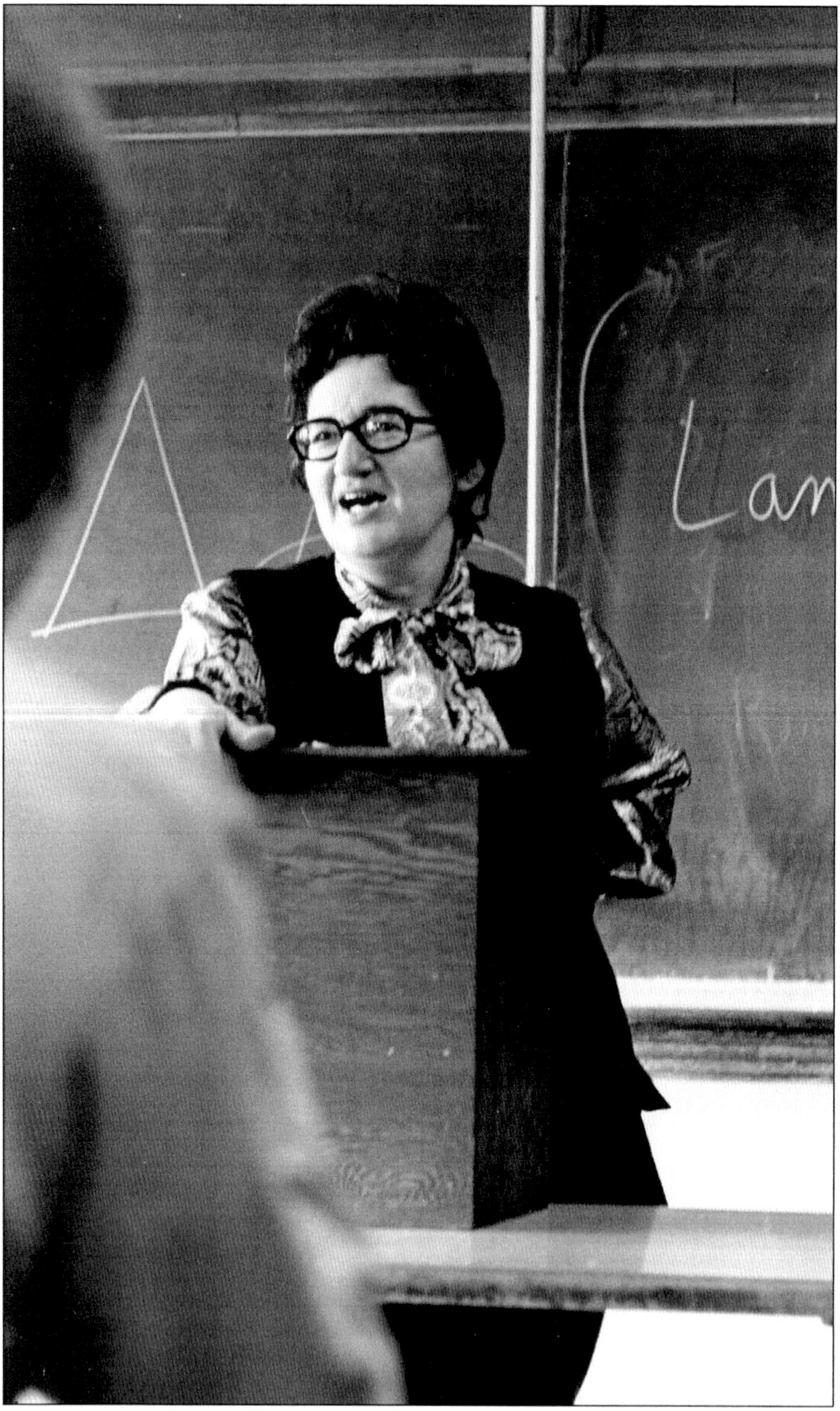

Dr. Minna Weinstein was the other female instructor hired in 1967. She taught history and was a recipient of the Lindback Foundation Award for Excellent Teaching in 1969.

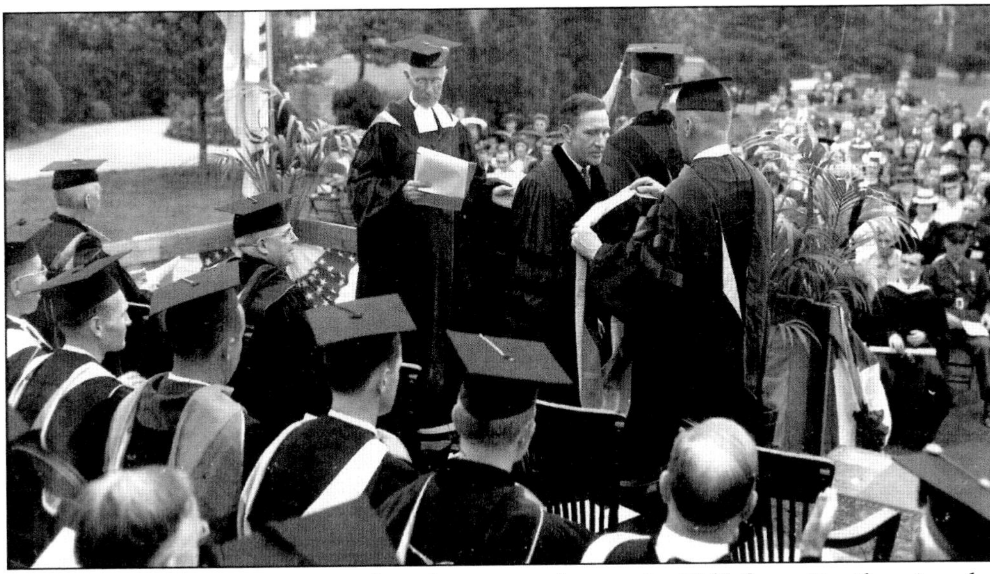

Builder John McShain received an honorary degree in 1943 from Brother Anselm in front of the building that bears his name. The Pentagon, the Jefferson Memorial, and St. Joseph's University are among the many structures built by McShain. Brother Anselm was president of LaSalle from 1932 until 1941. He found creative ways to keep the college open during the Great Depression, including accepting manual labor and groceries as tuition. He left LaSalle in 1941 to become principal of Philadelphia's West Catholic High School.

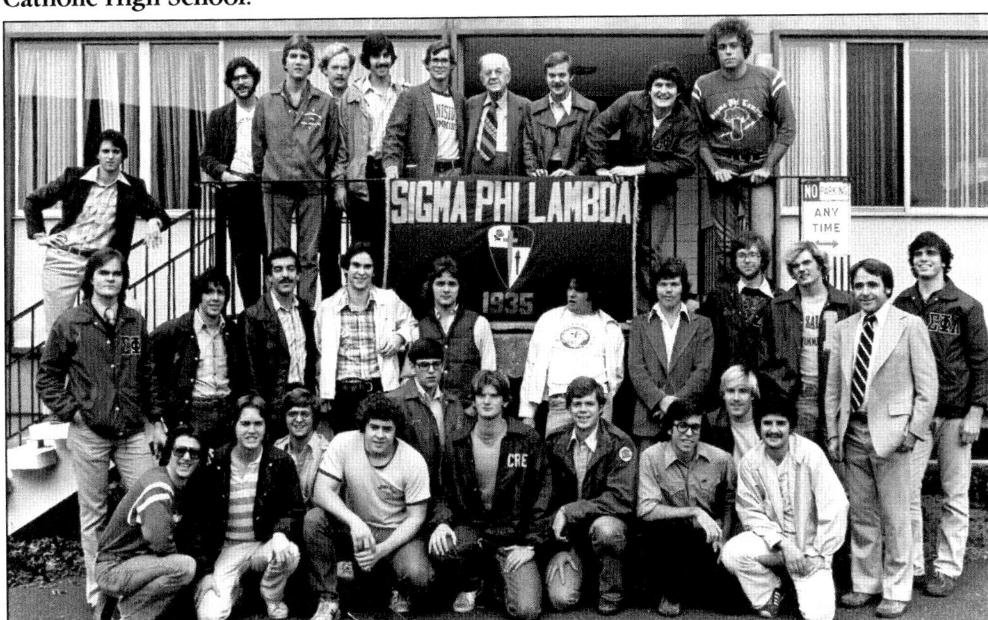

Brother Gerald Molyneaux (standing bottom second from right) became moderator of the Sigma Phi Lambda fraternity in 1976. Science professor Dr. Roland Holroyd (top center) was a member of the fraternity. Founded in 1935 by Brother Leonard, Sigma Phi Lambda was LaSalle's first fraternity. It dissolved with the drop in enrollment during the Second World War but reemerged in 1960 under the leadership of Dr. John Guischard.

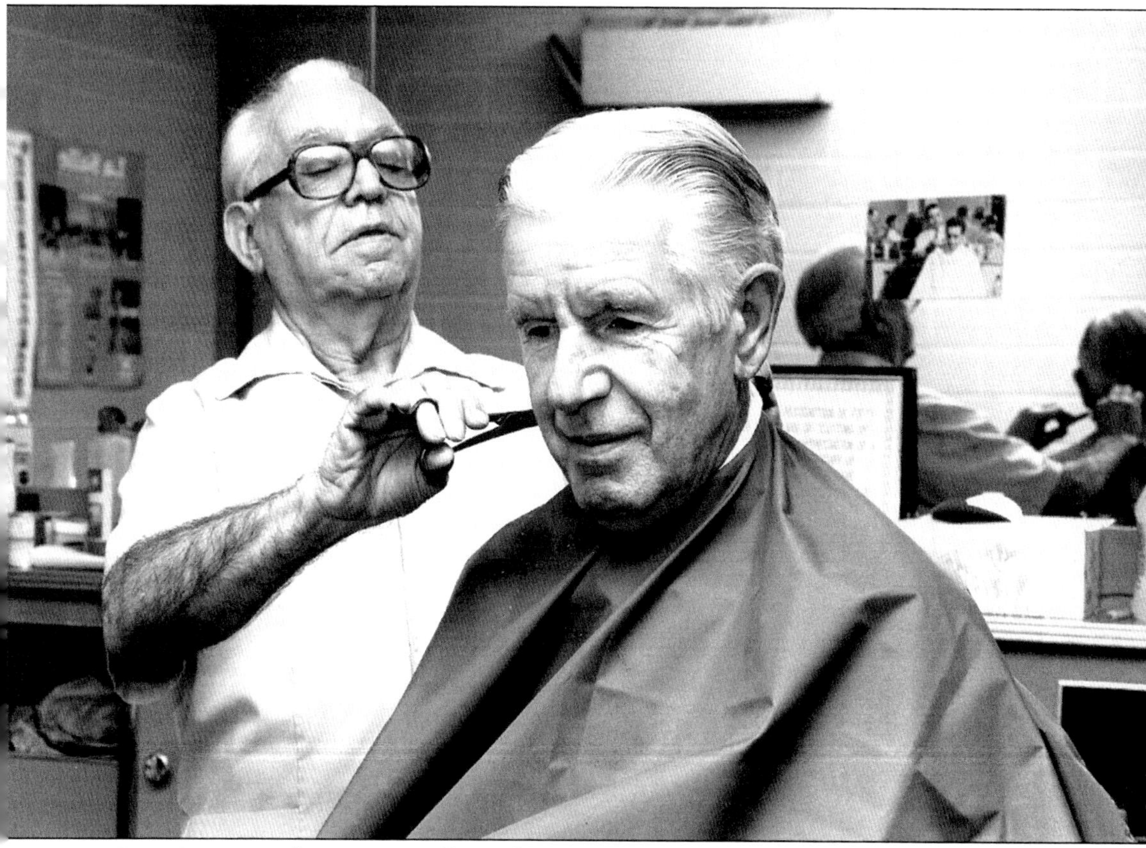

Pete Paranzino became LaSalle College's official barber in 1939.

Three

Athletics

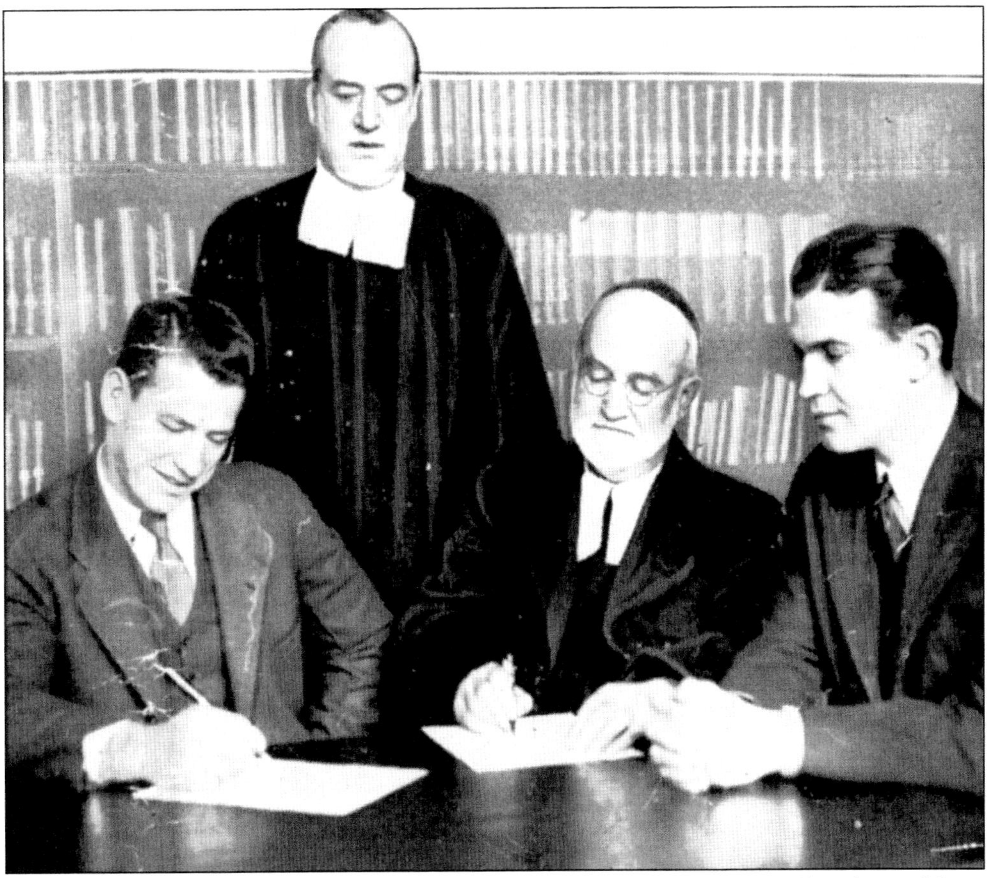

Brother Leonard and Brother Alfred hired Thomas A. Conley as LaSalle's first athletic director in 1931 upon the recommendation of Knute Rockne. Conley and Marty Brill became LaSalle's first football coaches in 1936.

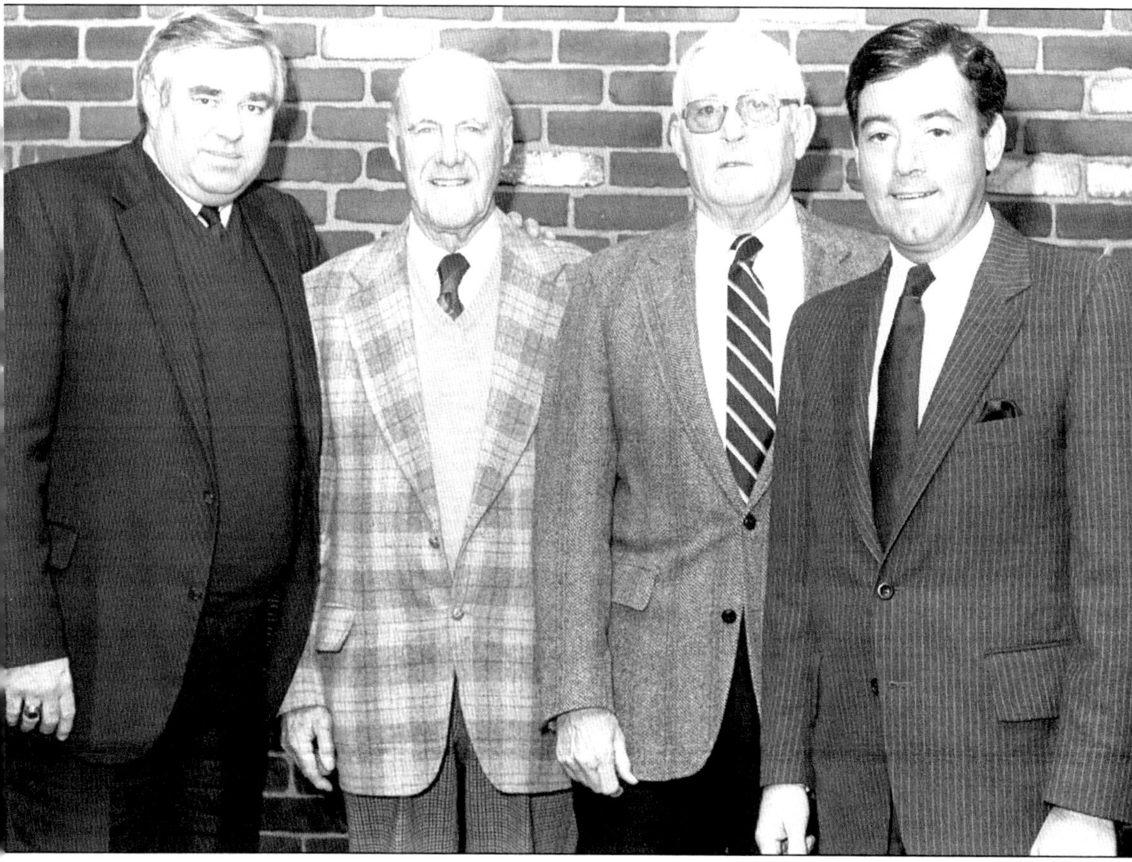

Pictured from left to right, Bob Mullen was LaSalle's athletic director from 1986 until 1997, Jim Henry (who also taught economics) served from 1935 until 1968, Jack Conboy was director from 1969 until 1977, and Bill Bradshaw held the position from 1978 until 1986.

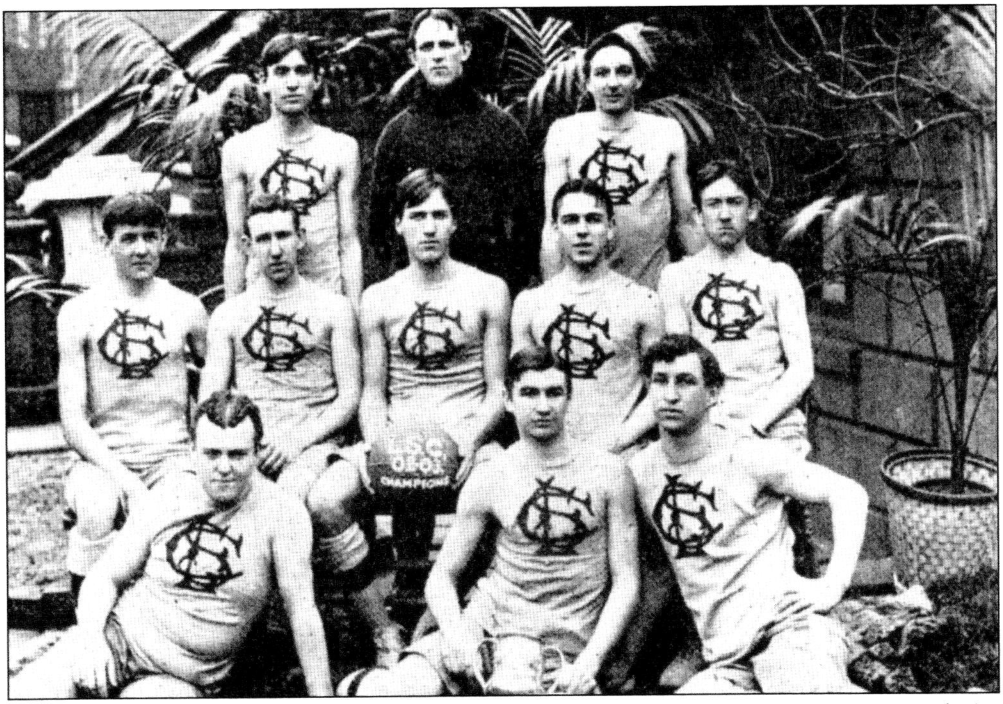

LaSalle's basketball team won a championship in 1903. After winning again in 1904, the basketball program was cut. It did not reemerge until the 1930s.

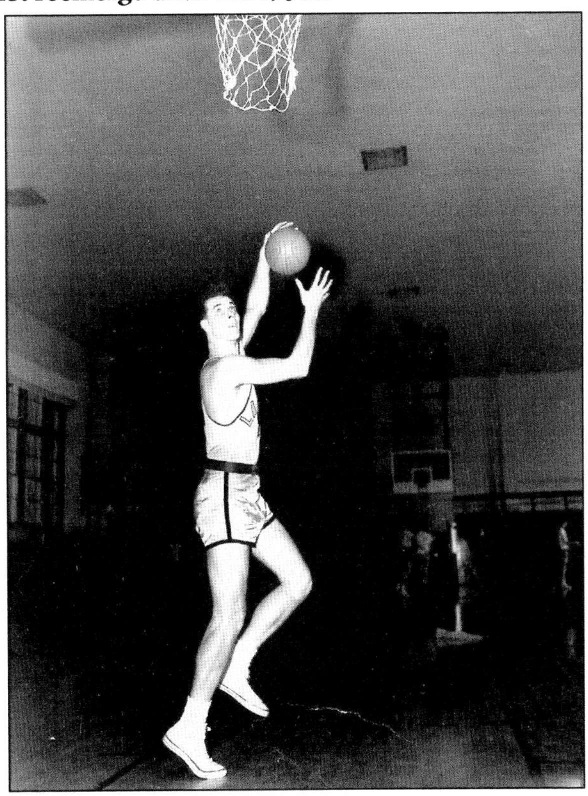

Larry Foust, from Painesville, Ohio, graduated from LaSalle College in 1950 and played in the NBA in Fort Wayne, Minneapolis, and St. Louis until 1962.

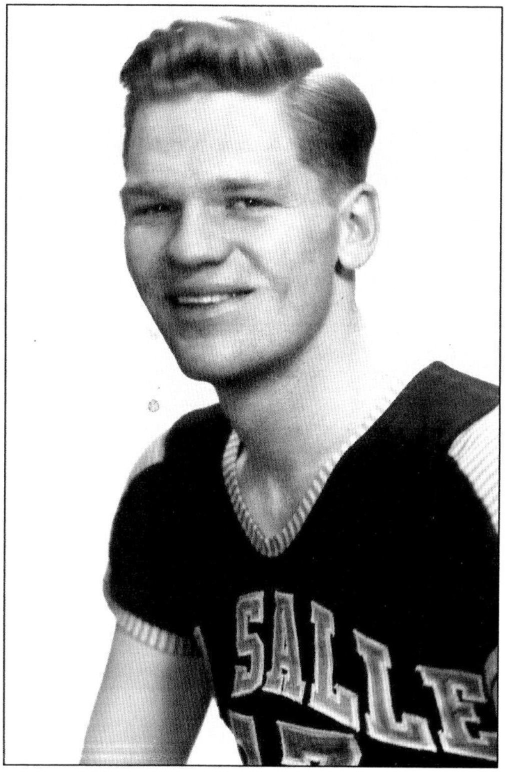

Jack George, from Swissvale, Pennsylvania, graduated in 1953 and played in the NBA in Philadelphia and New York until 1961.

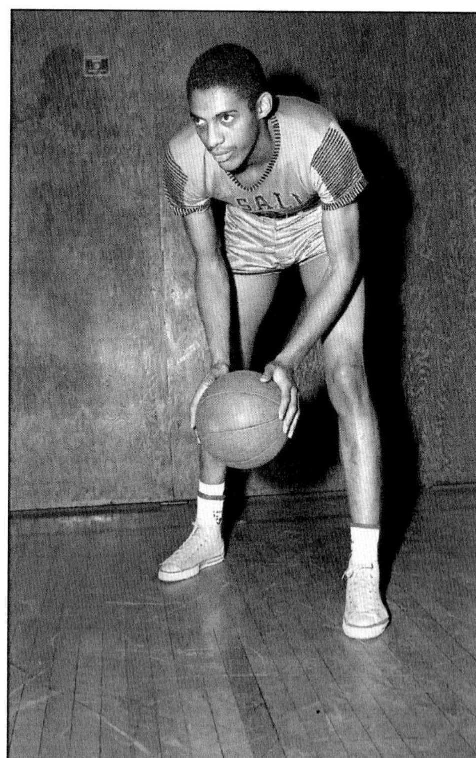

Jackie Moore's NBA career spanned from 1954 until 1957. He played in Syracuse, Milwaukee, and Philadelphia.

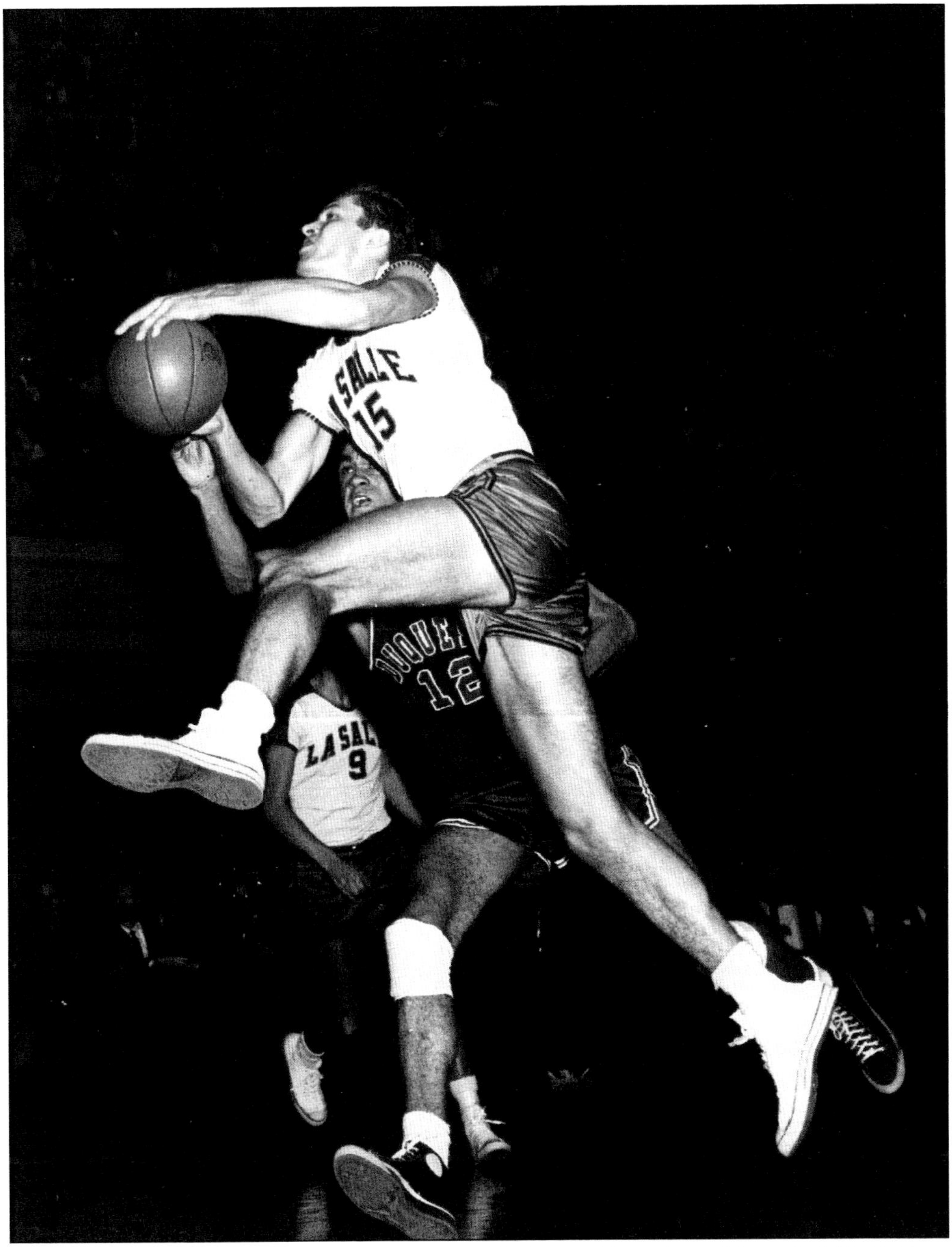

Philadelphia's Tom Gola, nicknamed "Mount All-Around," graduated from LaSalle College in 1955. He led the Explorers to a National Invitational Tournament Championship in 1952, a NCAA Championship in 1954, and was named MVP of the NCAA Tournament and Player of the Year in 1954. Gola set the NCAA record for rebounds with 2,201. He played in the NBA in Philadelphia, San Francisco, and New York until 1966 and is in the Basketball Hall of Fame. Gola later coached LaSalle's basketball team during its 23–1 season, served as controller of the city of Philadelphia, and sat in the Pennsylvania House of Representatives.

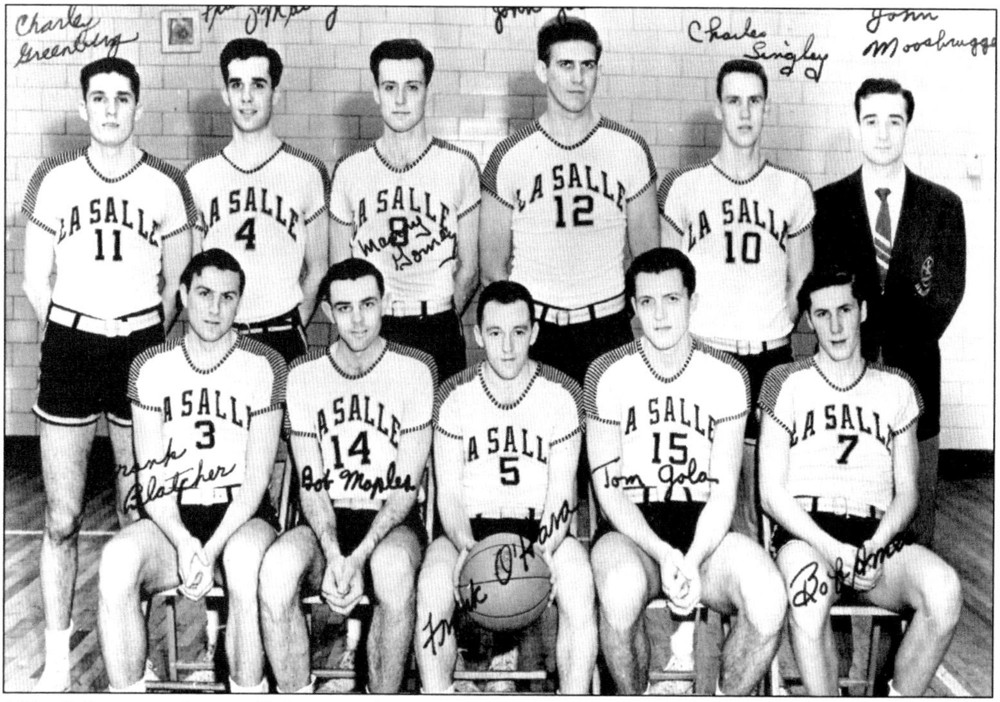

All of the members of the 1954 NCAA championship team hold a place in LaSalle University's Hall of Athletes. The LaSalle Explorers were the first college basketball team in the Philadelphia area to win a national title.

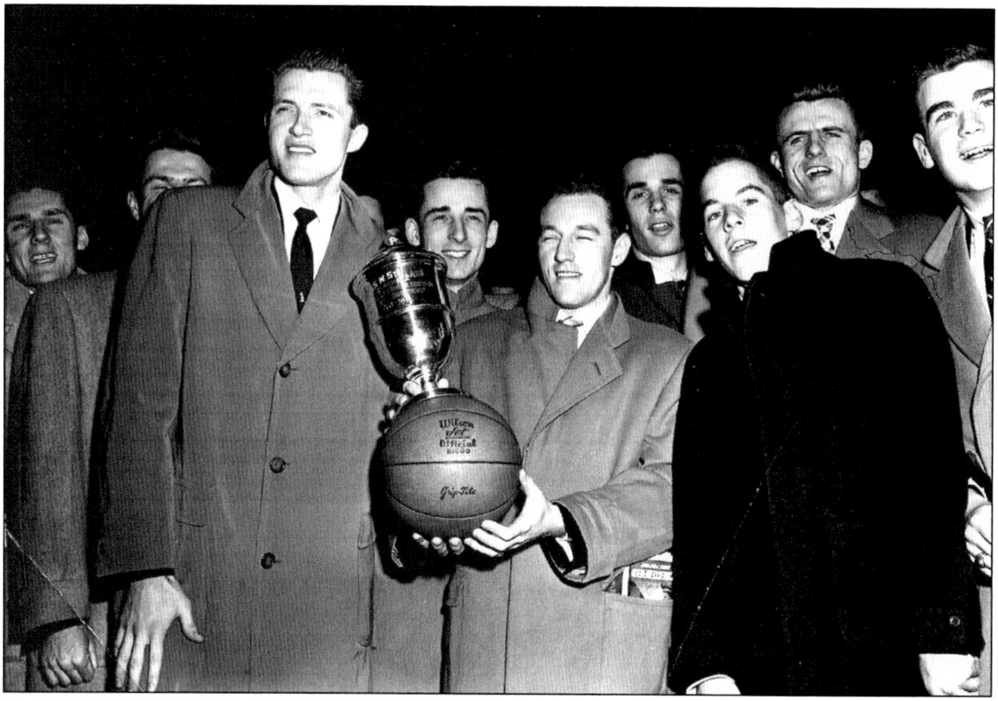

Tom Gola (front left) and his teammates returned from Kansas City, Missouri, with the NCAA tournament trophy in March of 1954.

Jim Phelan, a 1951 graduate, was captain of LaSalle's basketball team. He played in the NBA in Philadelphia from 1953 until 1954. Phelan was named College Division Coach of the Year in 1962 after leading Mount St. Mary's College to an NCAA title. He coached Mount St. Mary's basketball team for 49 years.

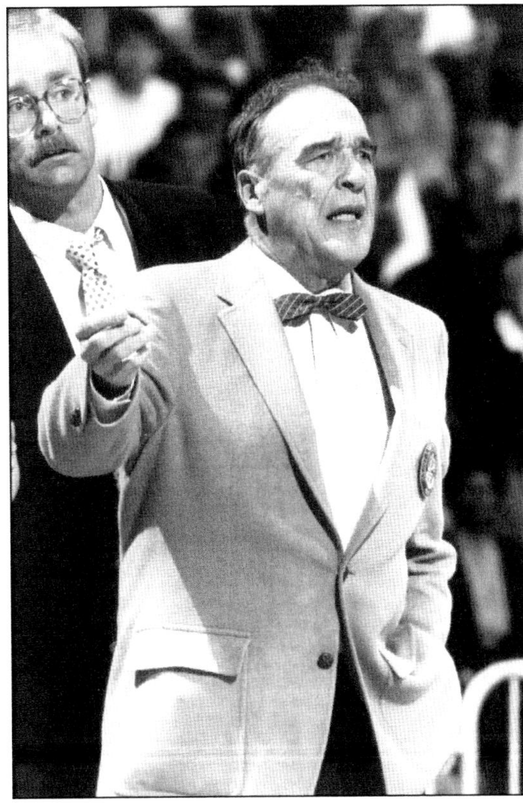

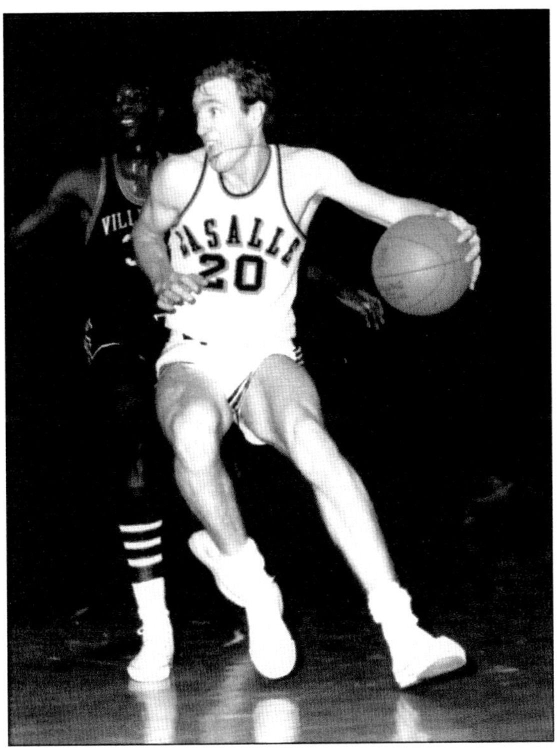

Larry Cannon, from Philadelphia, was a member of the Explorer's team that went 23–1 in 1969. He graduated that year and played in the NBA and ABA in Miami, Denver, Indiana, Memphis, and Philadelphia until 1974. Cannon was inducted into LaSalle's Hall of Athletes and the Big Five Hall of Fame.

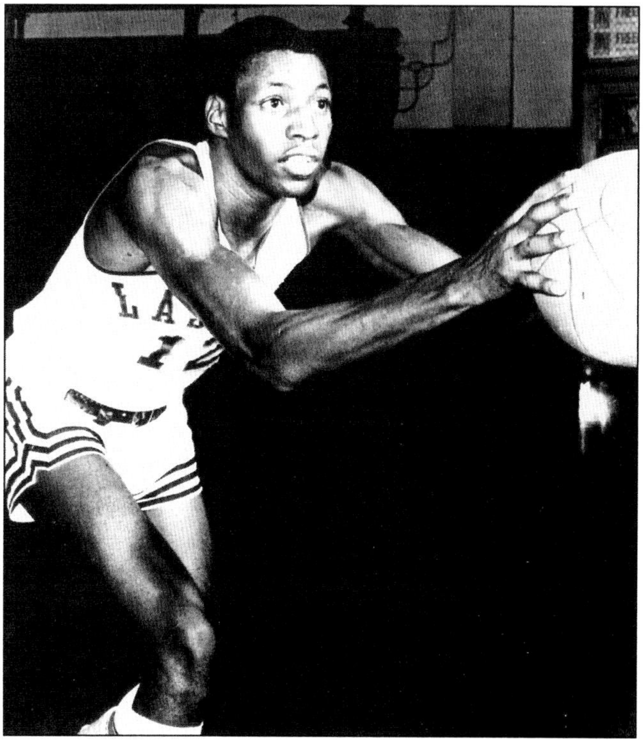

Bernie Williams, from Washington, D.C., graduated from LaSalle in 1969 and played in the NBA and ABA in San Diego and Virginia until 1974.

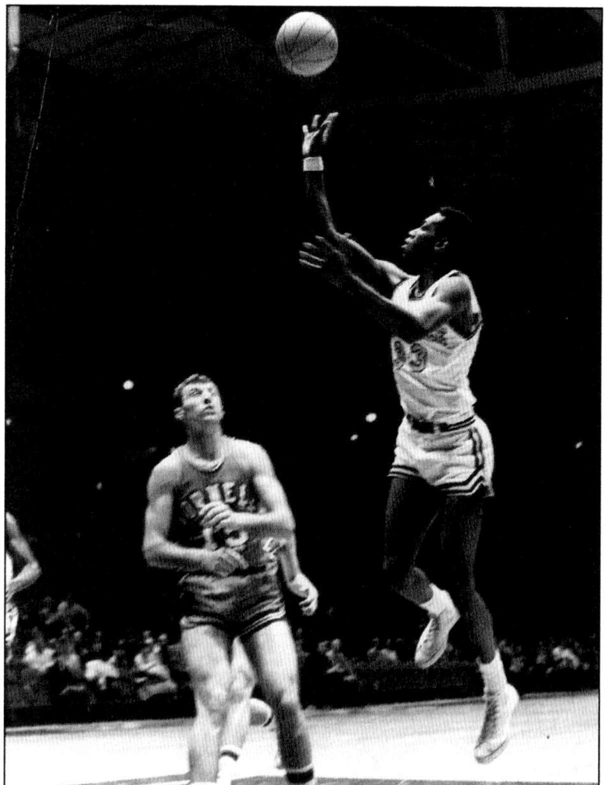

Ken Durrett, from Pittsburgh, Pennsylvania, was a 1971 graduate and played in the NBA in Cincinnati, Omaha, and Philadelphia until 1975.

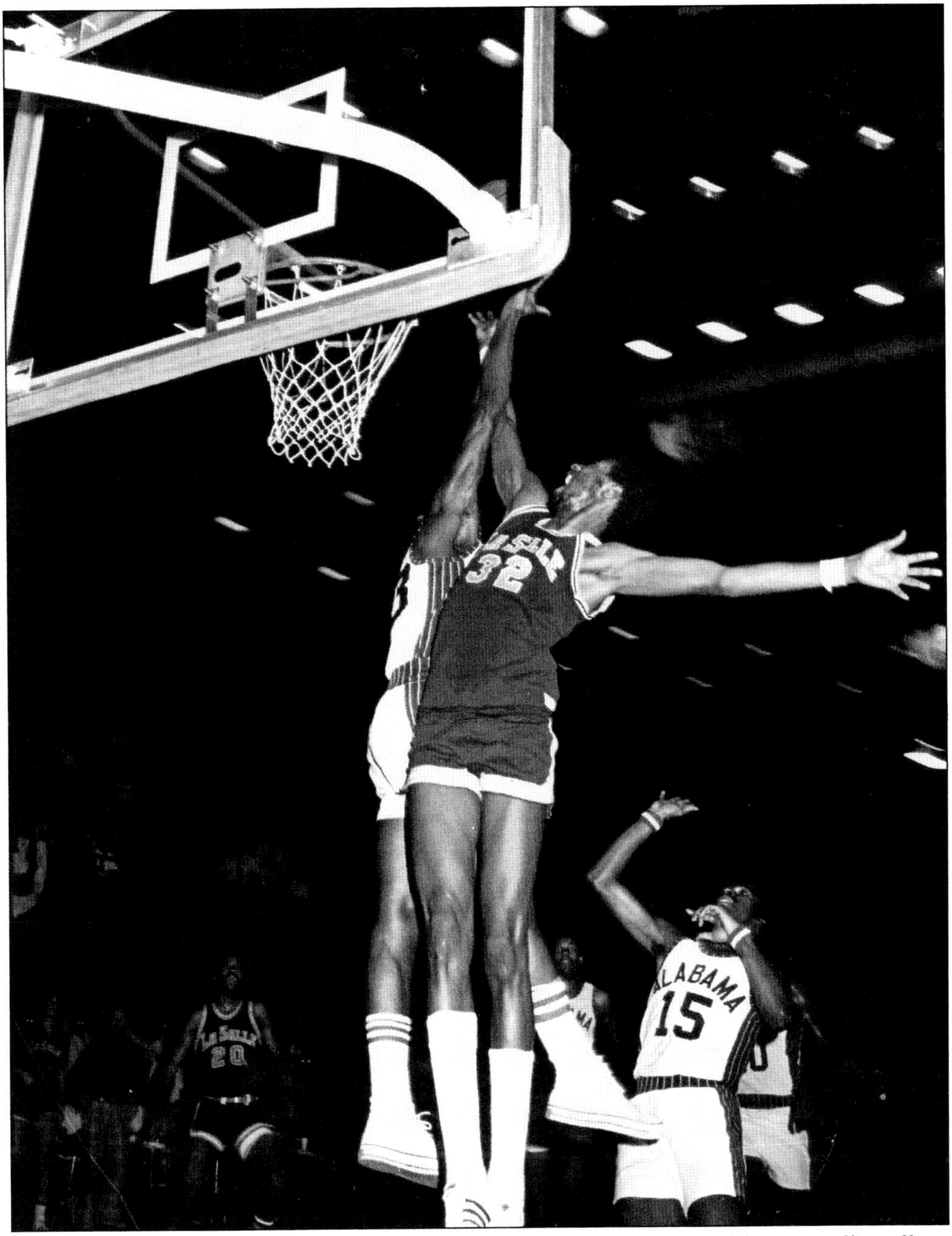

Philadelphia's Joe "Jellybean" Bryant, father of Kobe Bryant, graduated from LaSalle College in 1975 and played in the NBA in Philadelphia, San Diego, and Houston until 1983.

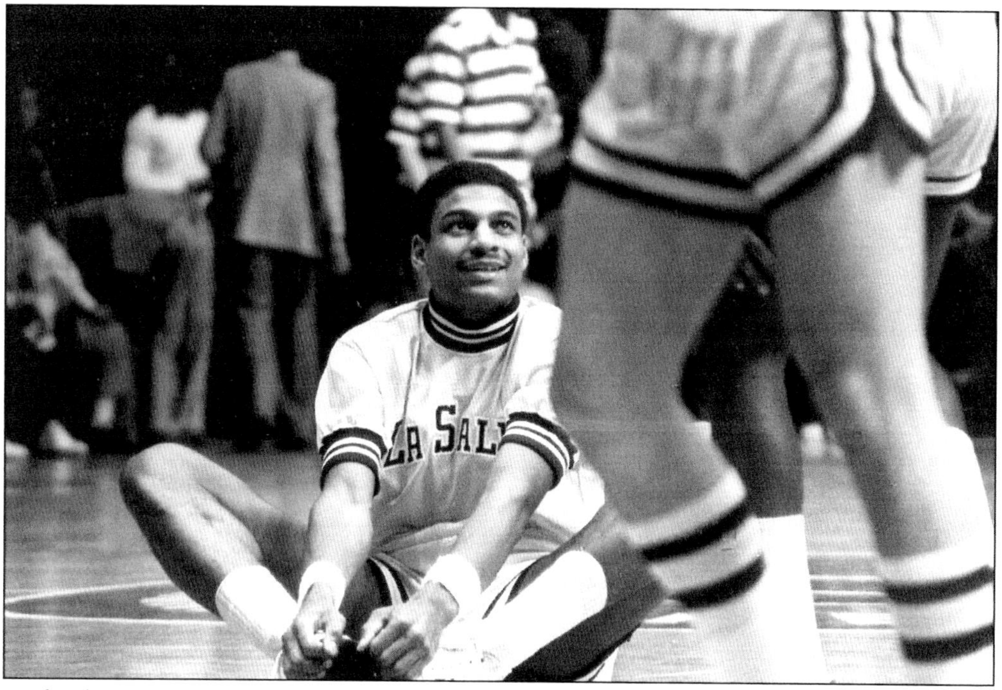

Michael Brooks, a 1980 LaSalle graduate from Philadelphia, was one of the Explorer's all-time scorers with 2,628 points. He was NCAA Player of the Year in 1980 and was chosen to be captain of the U.S. Olympic Basketball Team in 1980 when the United States boycotted the Summer Games in Moscow. Brooks played in the NBA in San Diego, Indiana, and Denver until 1988.

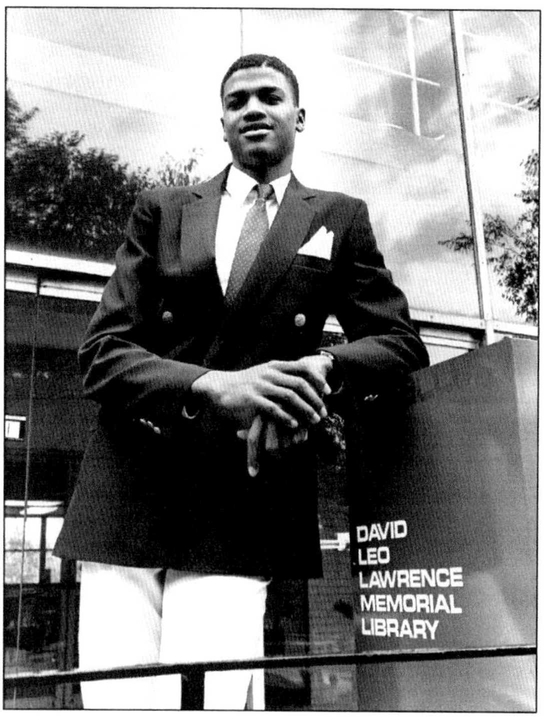

Philadelphia's Ralph Lewis graduated in 1985 and played in the NBA in Detroit and Charlotte from 1987 until 1990.

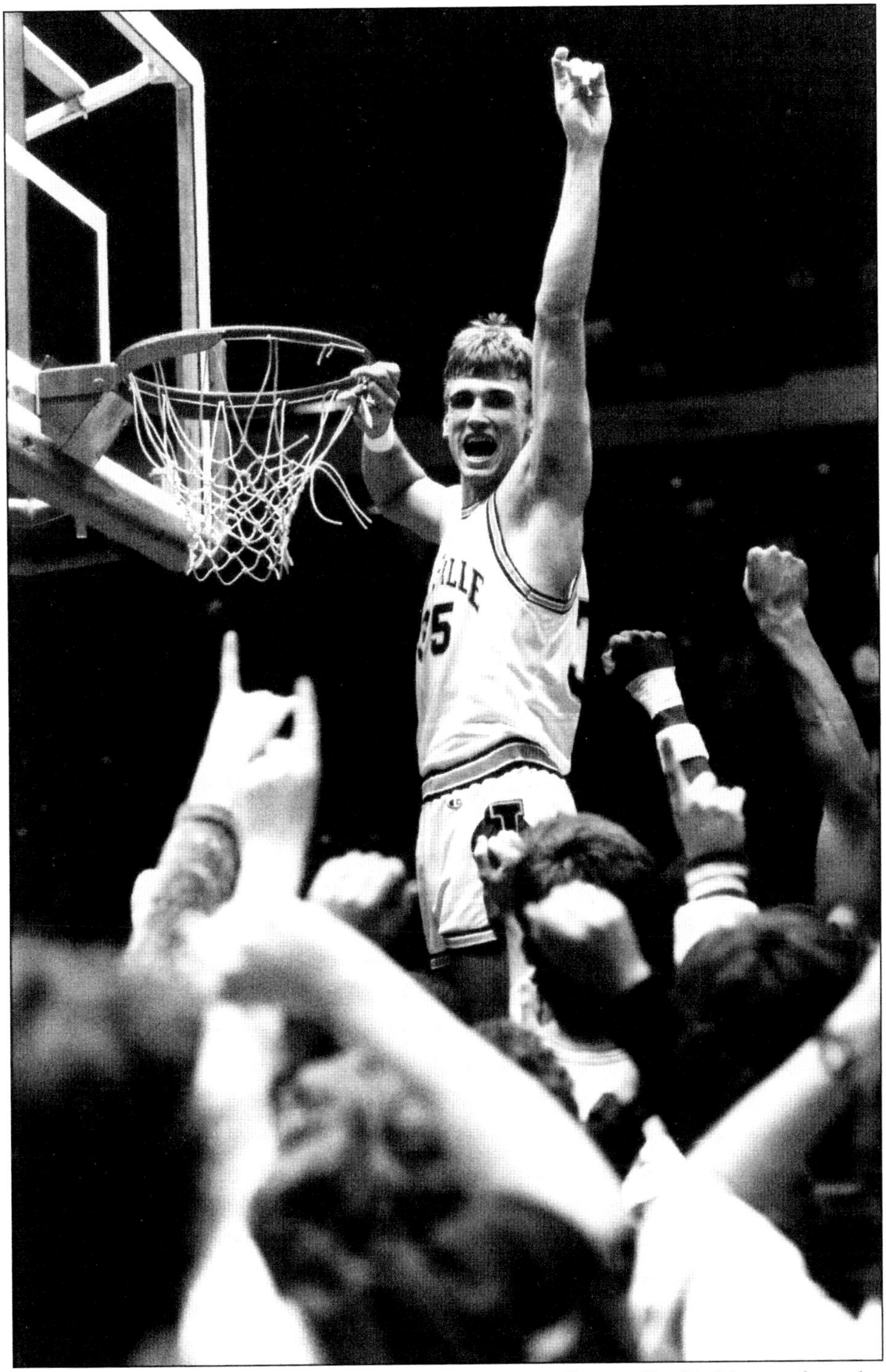

The class of 1988's Tim Legler was inducted into LaSalle's Hall of Athletes after playing 121 games in an Explorer uniform. He led the NBA in three-point shot percentage in 1996 and played in Phoenix, Denver, Utah, Dallas, Golden State, and Washington until 2000. He later became a basketball commentator for ESPN.

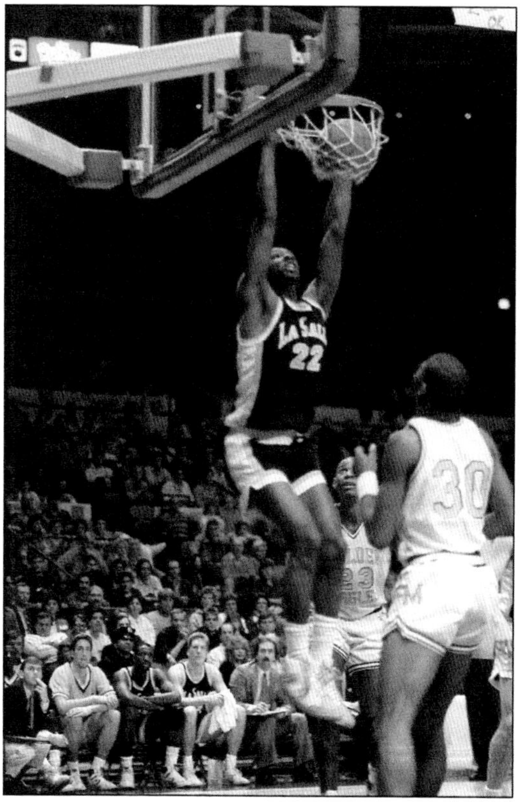

Nicknamed the "L-Train," Philadelphia's Lionel Simmons was the NCAA's third all-time scorer with 3,217 points. He graduated in 1990 and was chosen as NCAA Player of the Year. Simmons played in the NBA in Sacramento until 1997.

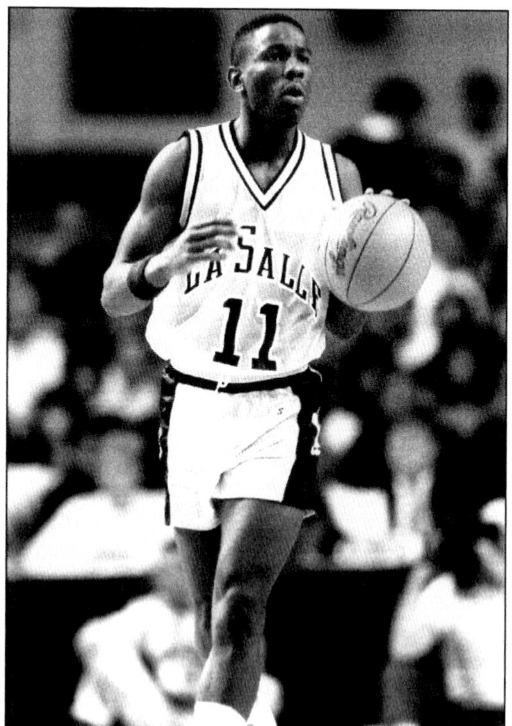

Doug Overton, from Philadelphia, graduated from LaSalle University in 1990 and played in the NBA in Washington, Denver, Philadelphia, Orlando, New Jersey, Boston, Charlotte, and Los Angeles (Clippers) from 1992 until 2002. He scored 1,795 points as an Explorer and was inducted into LaSalle's Hall of Athletes and the Big Five Hall of Fame.

Philadelphia's Randy Woods graduated in 1992 and played in the NBA in Los Angeles (Clippers) and Denver until 1996. Speedy Morris coached Woods during his time at LaSalle.

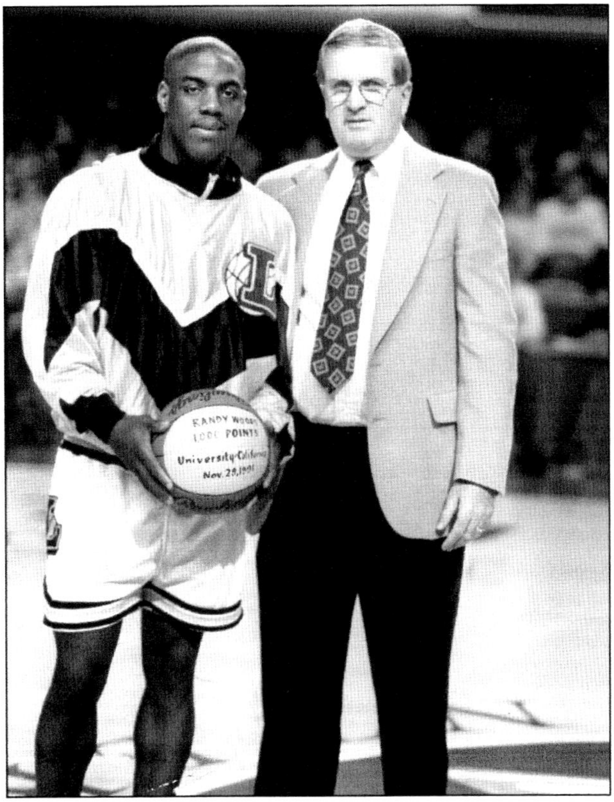

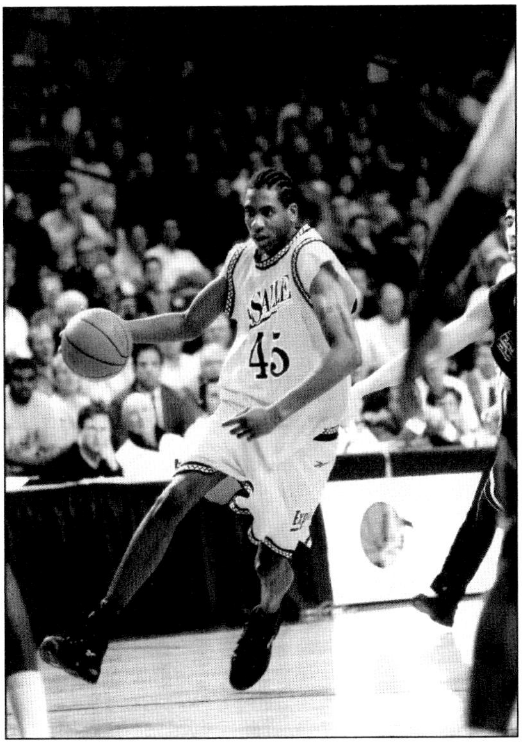

The class of 2002's Rasual Butler, from Philadelphia, went on to play in the NBA in Miami and New Orleans.

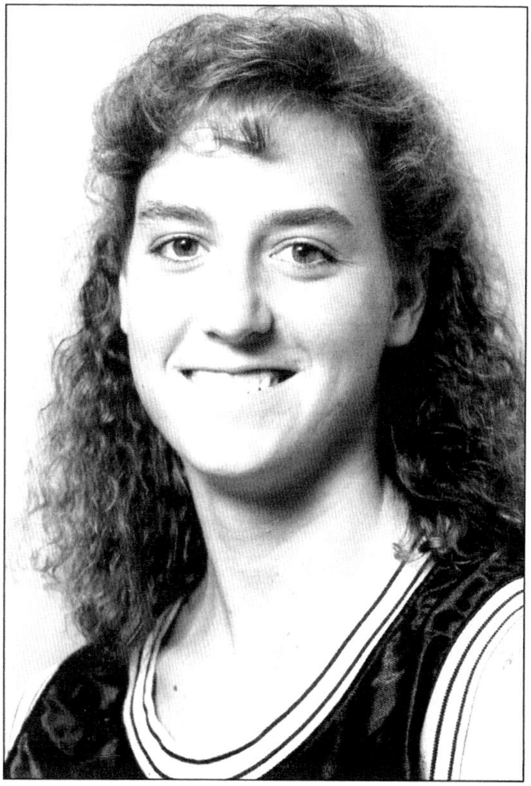

Jennifer Cole was LaSalle's first women's basketball player to have her number retired.

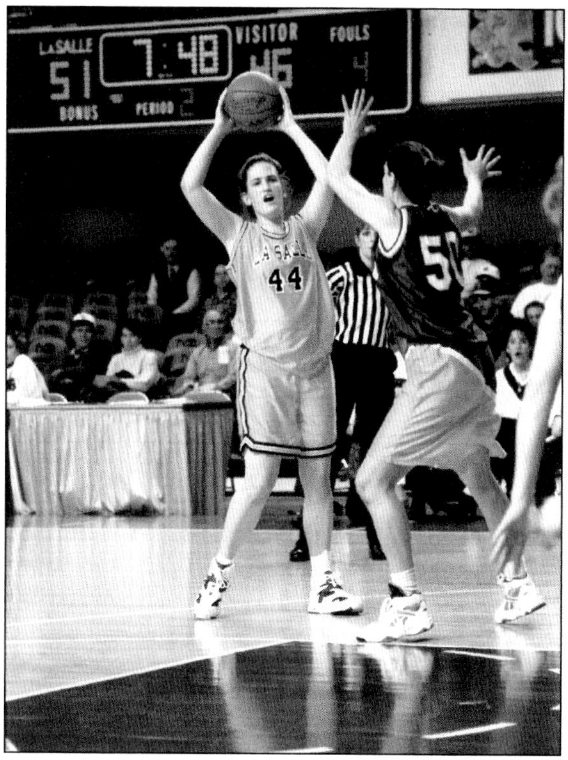

Chrissie Donahue graduated from LaSalle in 1997. She was LaSalle's first women's basketball player to start in every game that she played and was inducted into the Big Five Hall of Fame.

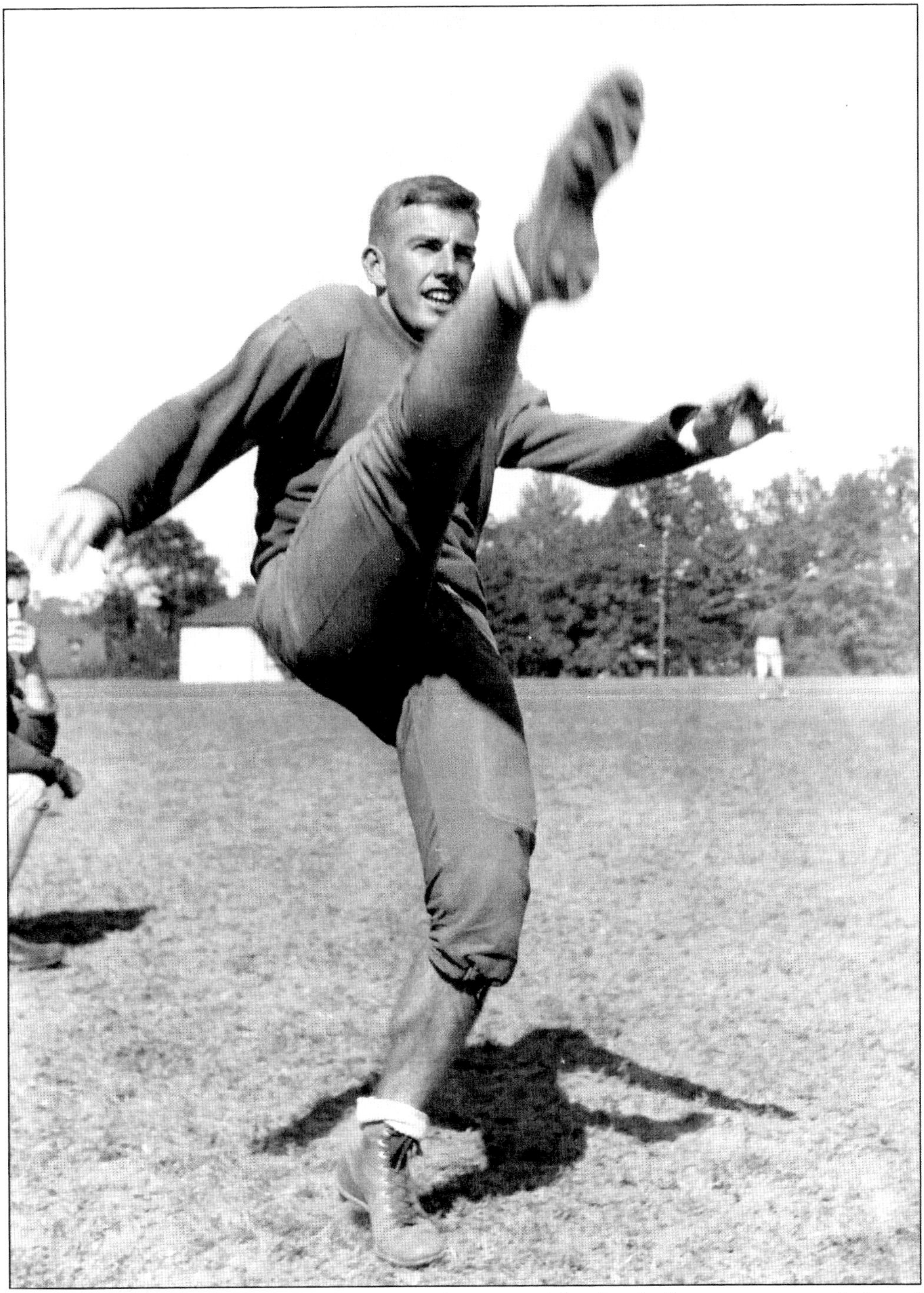

Paul Prettyman was LaSalle's punter in the 1930s. The football team went undefeated in 1934.

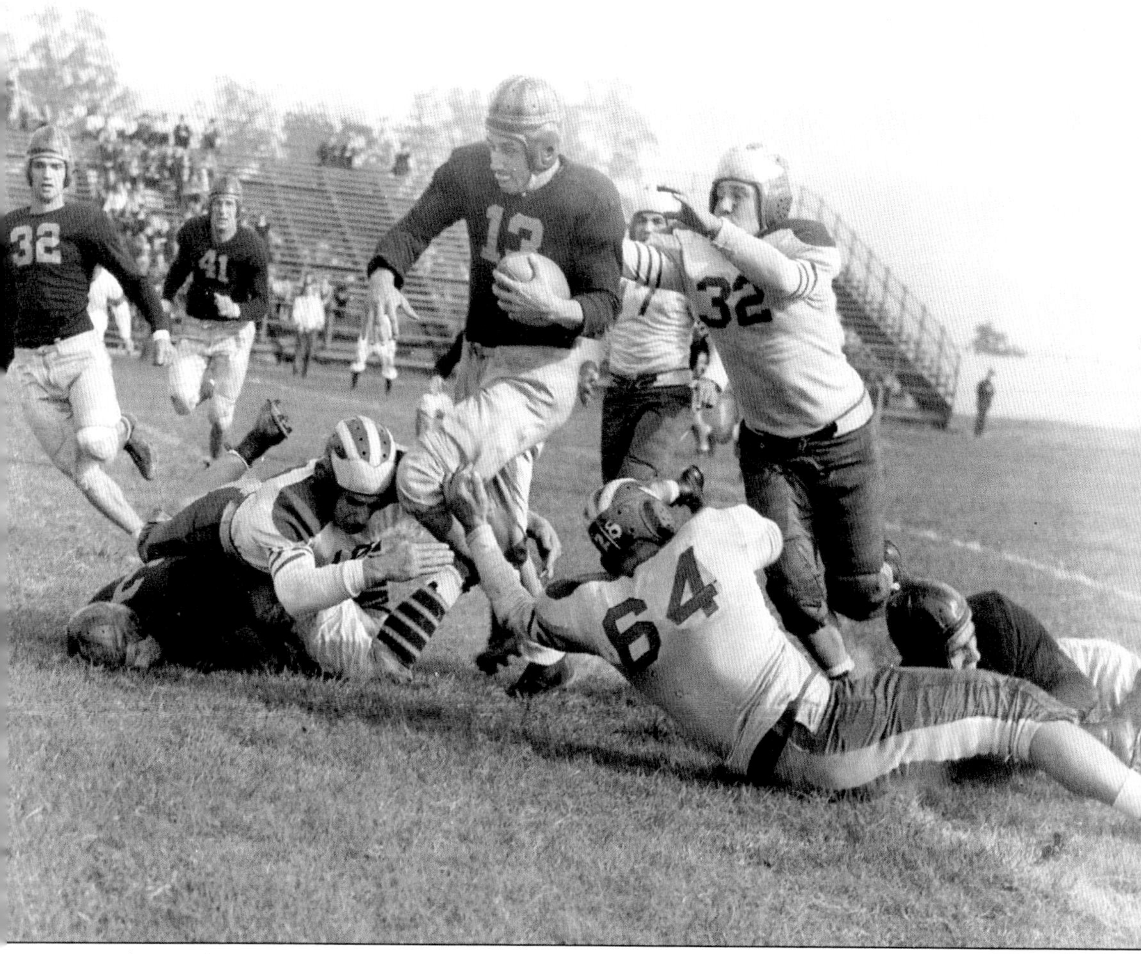

The Explorers played against Scranton in 1939.

George Somers, from St. Clair High School in Fountain Springs, Pennsylvania, graduated from LaSalle College in 1939 and played in the NFL in Philadelphia and Pittsburgh until 1942.

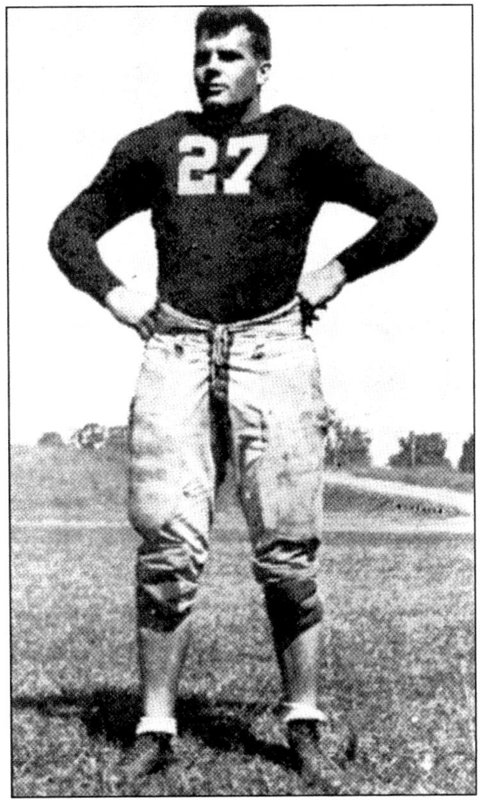

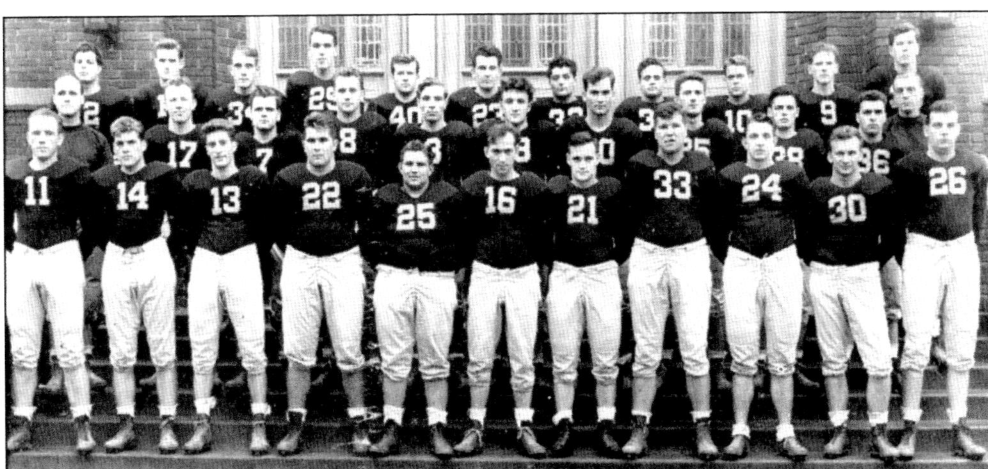

LaSalle's football program was cut due to low enrollment during the Second World War a year after this 1941 team photograph was taken.

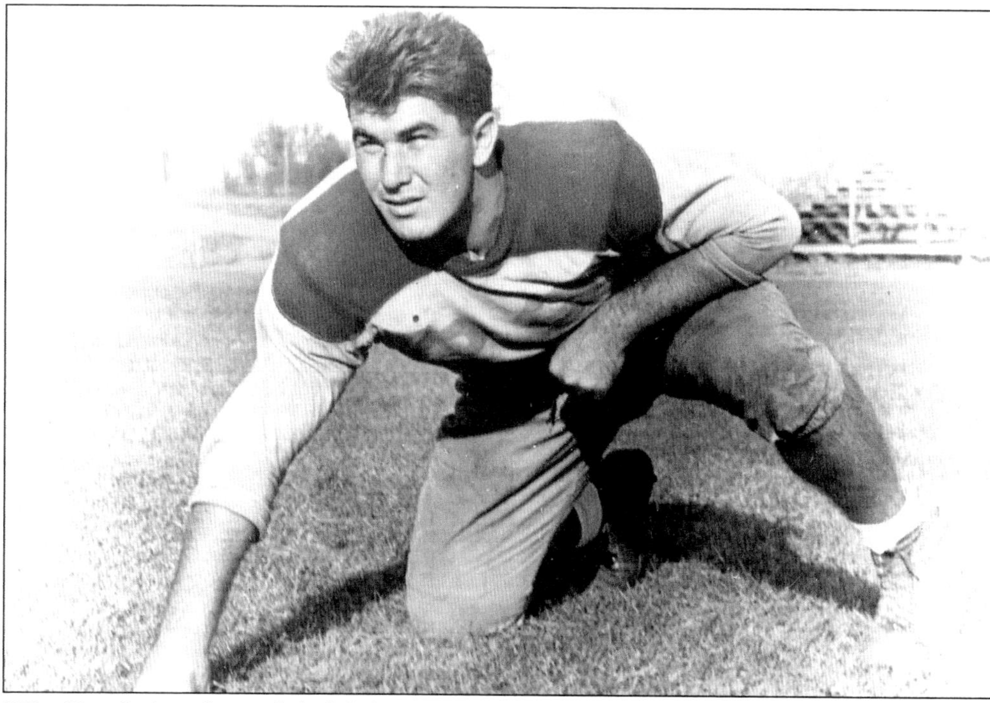

Mike Mandarino, from Philadelphia's West Catholic High School, graduated in 1942 and played center in the NFL in Philadelphia from 1944 until 1945.

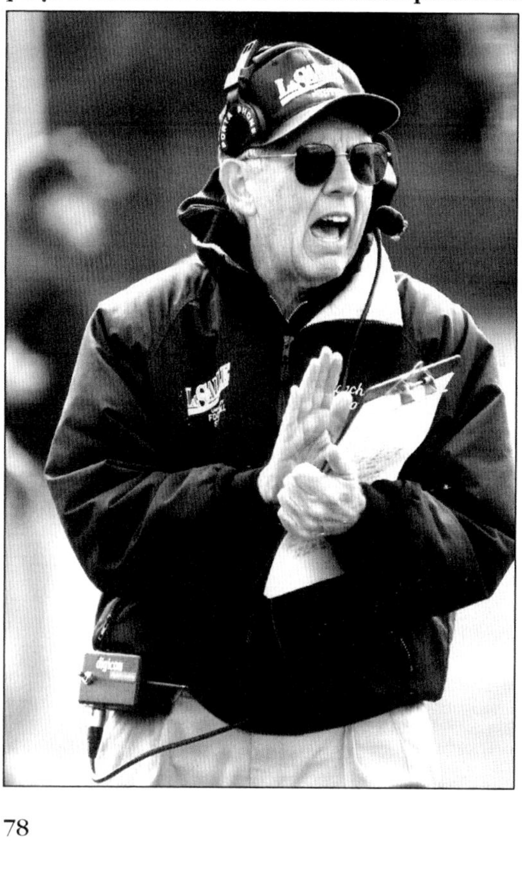

Bill Manlove coached LaSalle's football team when the program was reintroduced in 1997.

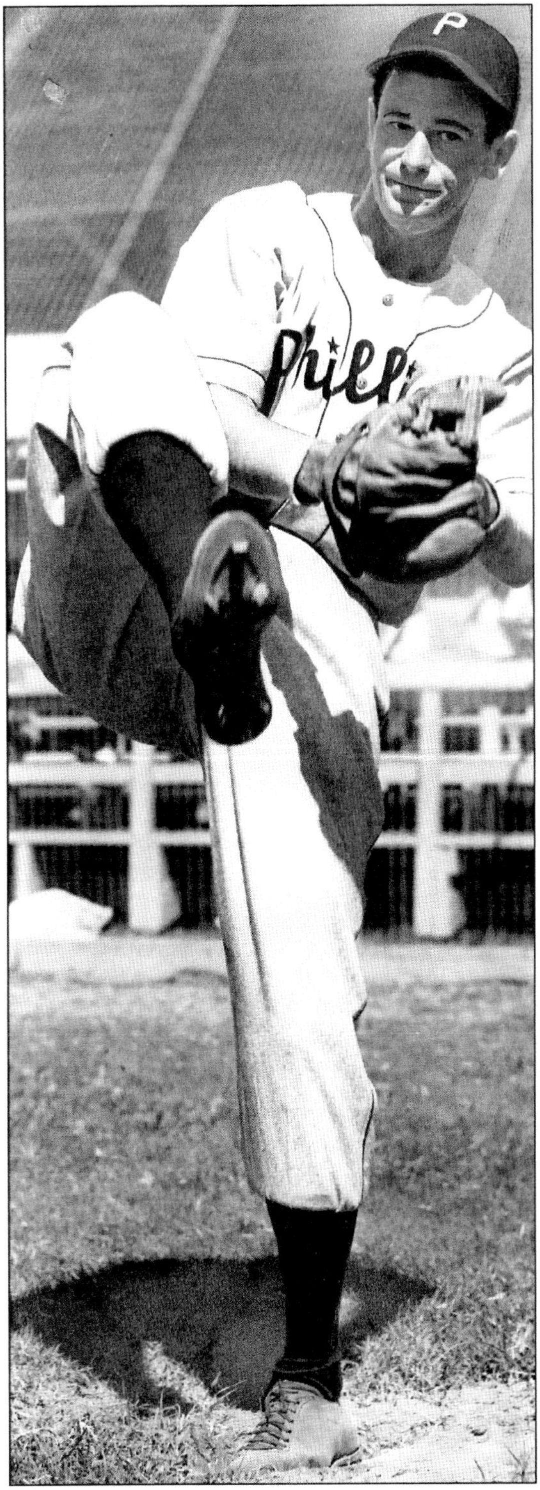

Philadelphia's Frank Hoerst graduated in 1939 and pitched in the major leagues in Philadelphia (Phillies) from 1940 until 1947.

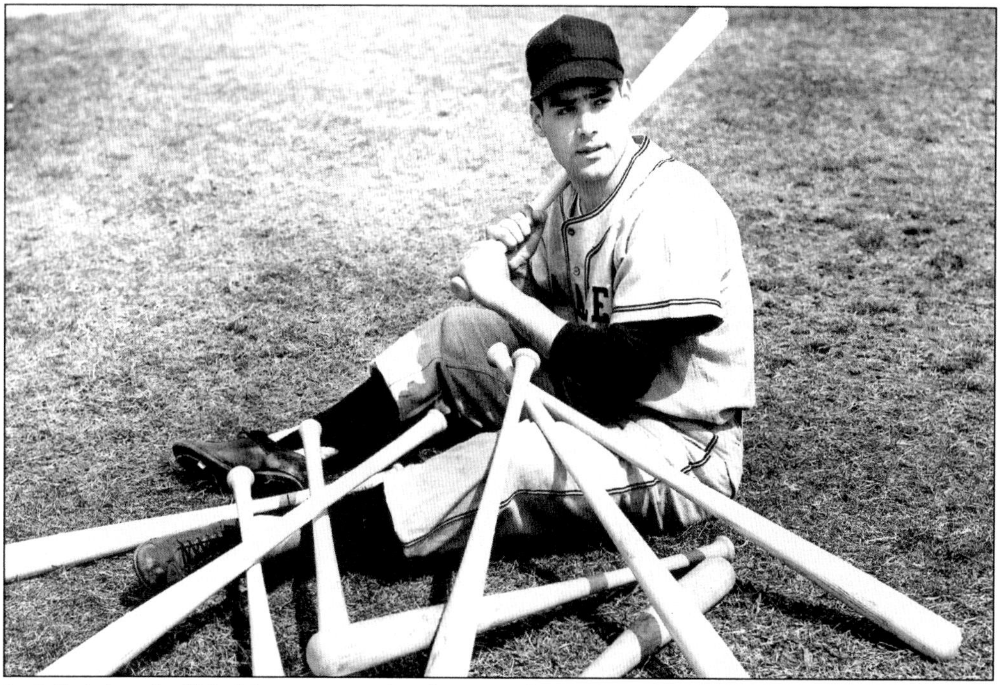

LaSalle's baseball field was named in honor of Dr. Hank DeVincent, a 1956 graduate.

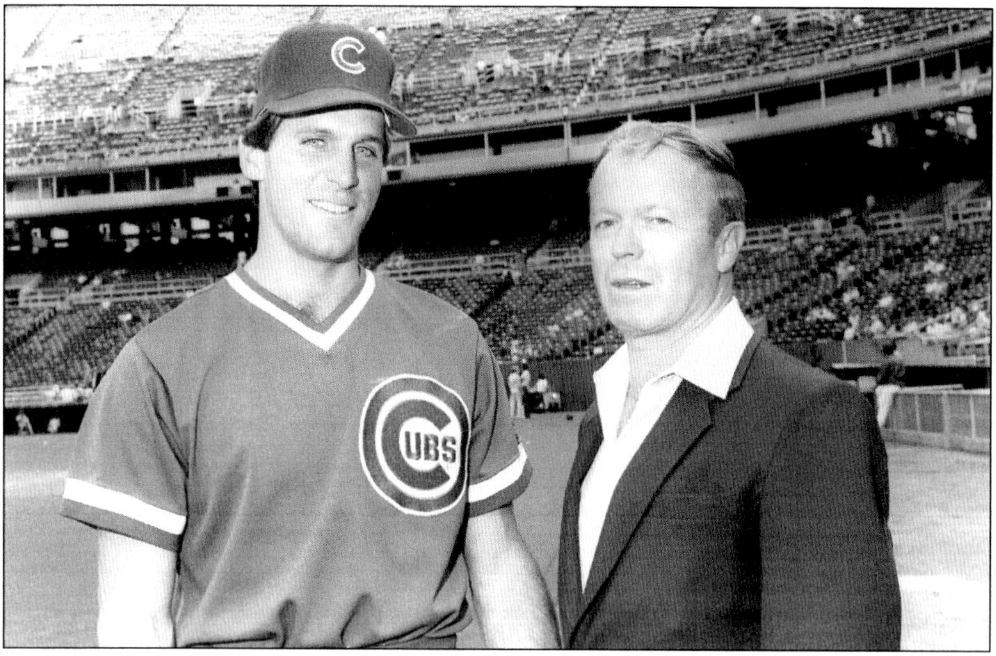

The class of 1978's Tom Filer, from Philadelphia, pitched in the major leagues in Chicago (Cubs), Toronto, Milwaukee, and New York (Mets) from 1982 until 1992. Gene McDonnell coached Filer during his time as an Explorer. He graduated from LaSalle in 1955, coached the baseball team for nearly 35 years, and won Big Five titles in 1965 and 1966. McDonnell was inducted into LaSalle's Hall of Athletes' Coaches' Corner in 1980, and his number was retired in 1990.

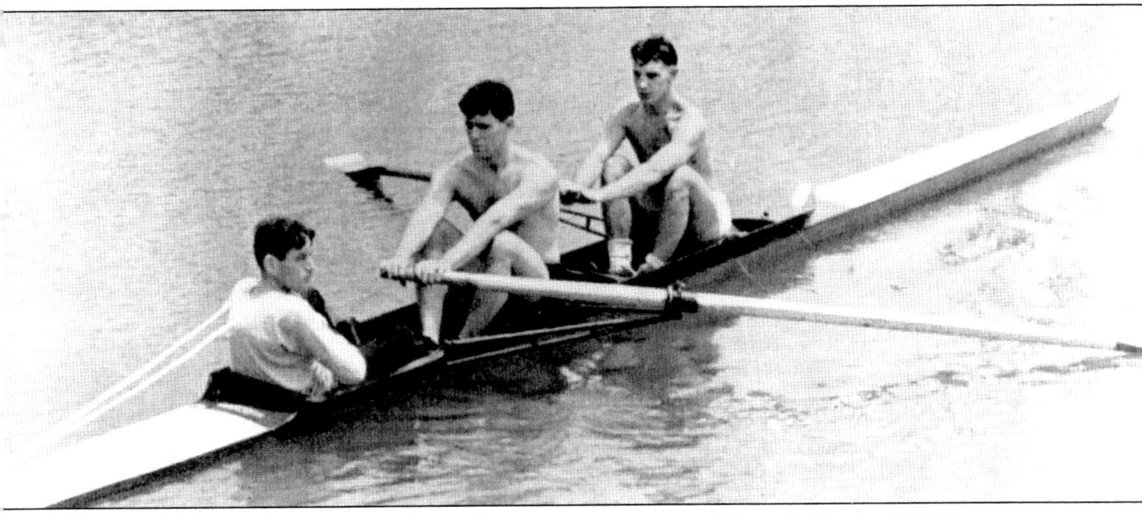

Charles M. Kieffer was LaSalle's first Olympian. He won a gold medal in the 1932 Summer Games in Los Angeles as a member of the U.S. Crew Team with Joseph A. Schauers and Edward F. Jennings.

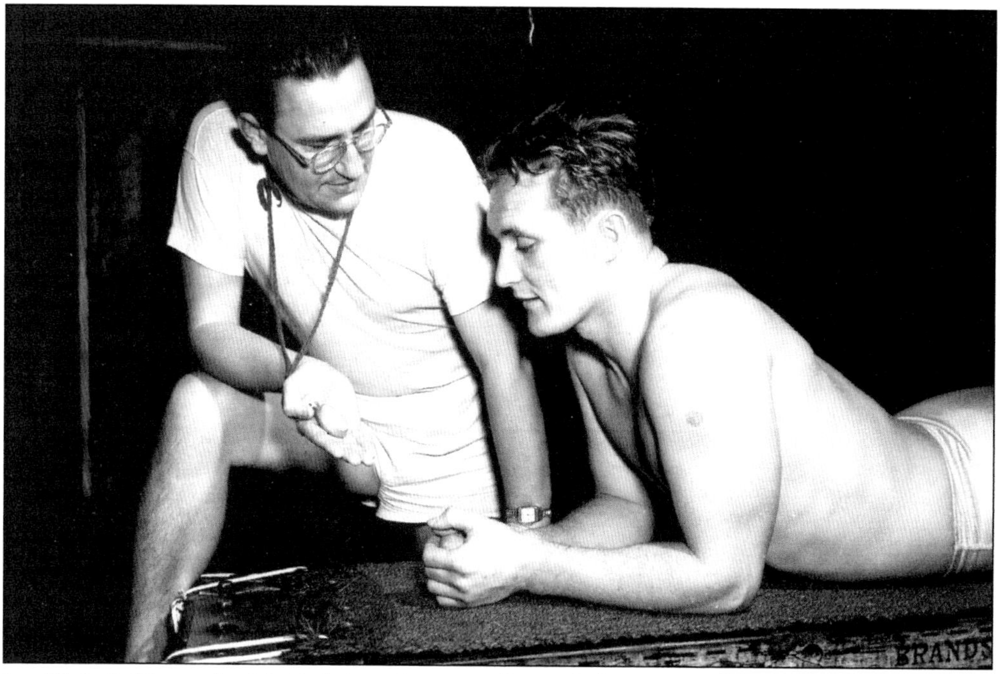

Joe Kirk (left) coached LaSalle's swim team from 1941 until 1967 and led the Explorers to an Eastern Catholic College Swimming Championship in 1947 and a Mid-Atlantic Conference title in 1957. Kirk was inducted into LaSalle's Hall of Athletes' Coaches' Corner, and the university's pool was named in his honor. He coached Olympic swimmer Joe Verdeur (right) during his time at LaSalle.

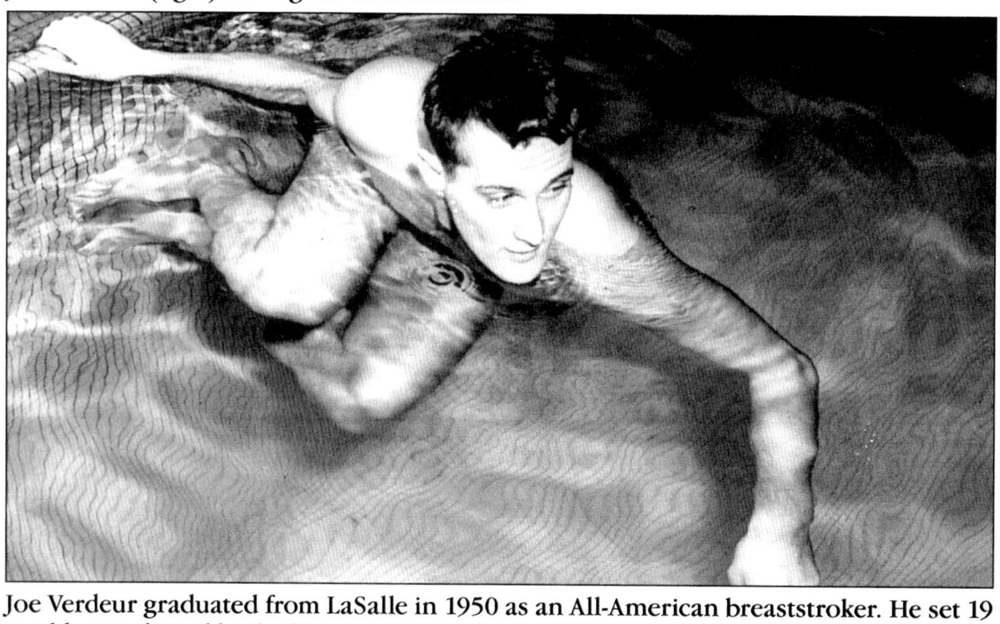

Joe Verdeur graduated from LaSalle in 1950 as an All-American breaststroker. He set 19 world records and broke his own records in the 200-yard and 200-meter breaststrokes. Verdeur won a gold medal in the 200-meter butterfly in the 1948 Summer Games in London as a member of the U.S. Swim Team and was inducted into the International Swimming Hall of Fame.

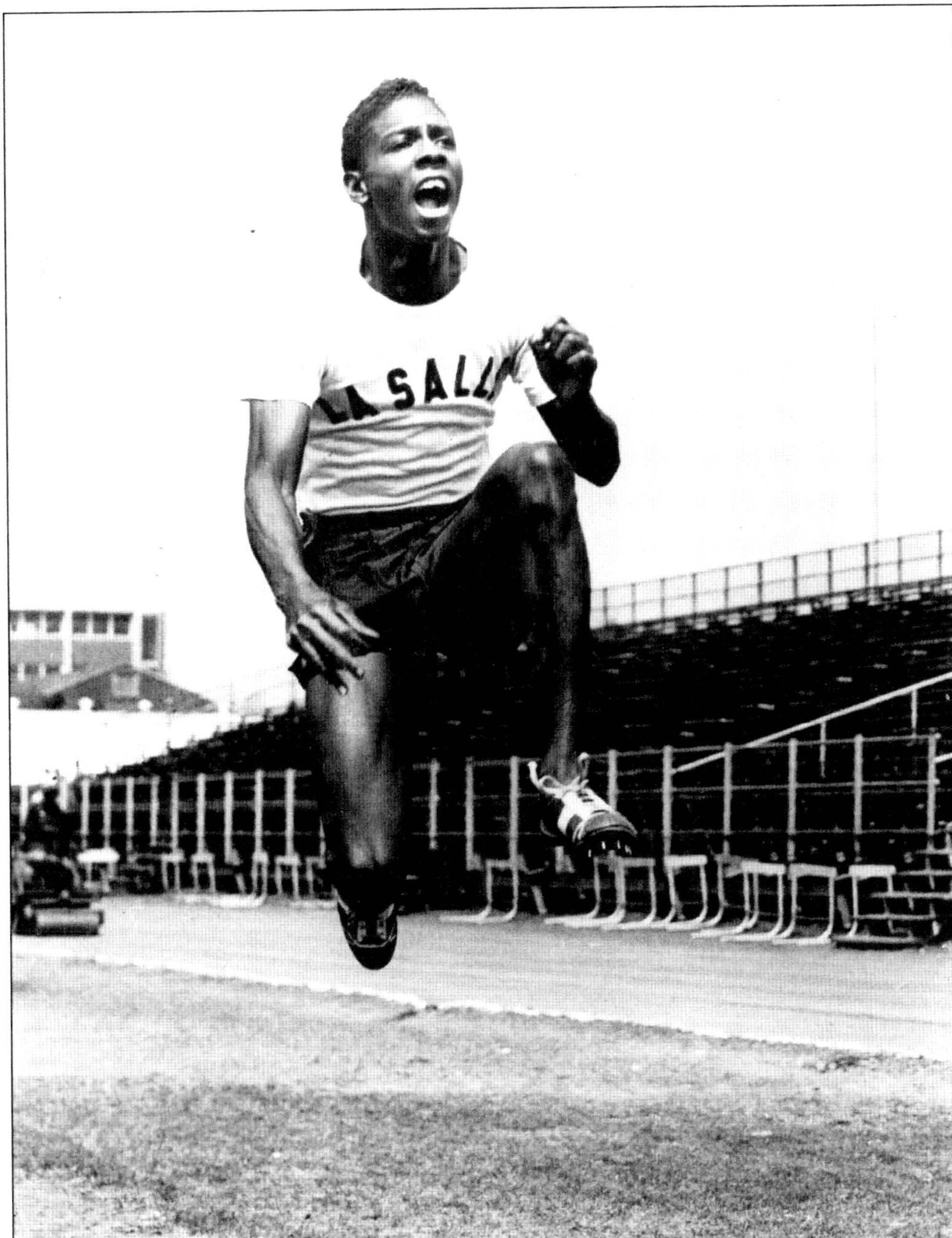

Ira Davis graduated in 1958 and coached LaSalle's track team. He appeared in the 1956 Summer Games in Melbourne, the 1960 Summer Games in Rome, and the 1964 Summer Games in Tokyo as a member of the U.S. Track and Field Team. Davis, Frank Loughney, Al Cantello, Tom Gola, and Joe Verdeur were the charter members of LaSalle's Hall of Athletes in 1961.

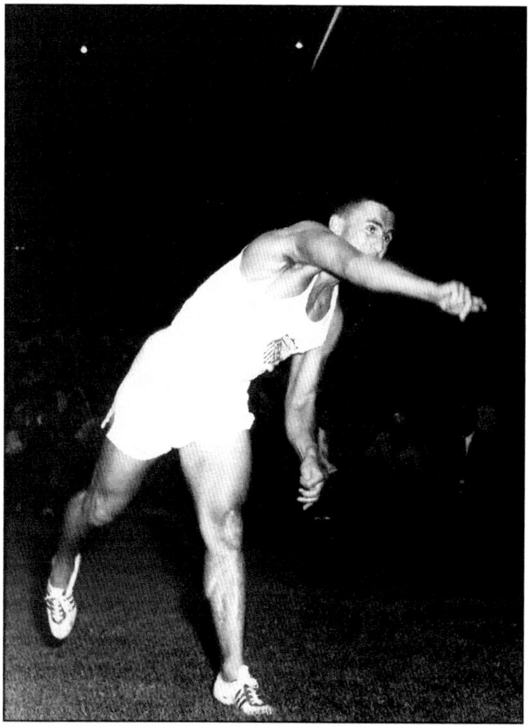

The Class of 1955's Al Cantello, from Norristown, Pennsylvania, participated in the 1960 Summer Games in Rome as a member of the U.S. Track and Field Team.

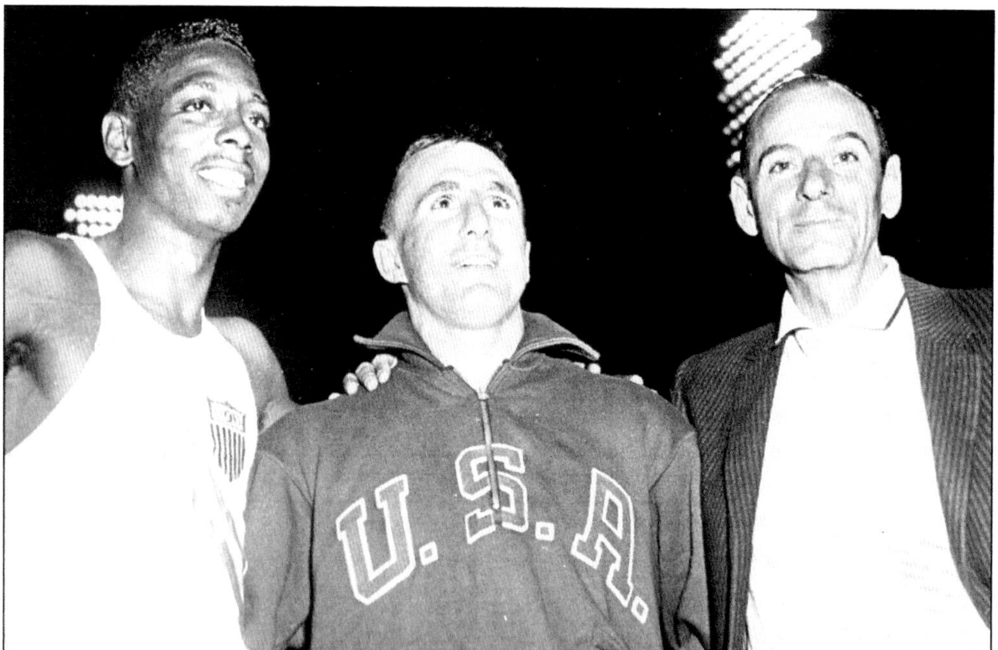

Frank Wetzler (right) was LaSalle College's track and field coach from 1949 until 1969 and won 14 titles. He served as president of the Intercollegiate Association of Amateur Athletes of America and as a member of the NCAA Rules and Games committees. Olympians Ira Davis (left) and Al Cantello were coached by Wetzler during their time at LaSalle.

Hugh Foley and Stan Cwiklinski were members of the U.S. Crew Team that won a gold medal at the 1964 Summer Games in Tokyo. Both men graduated from LaSalle College in 1966.

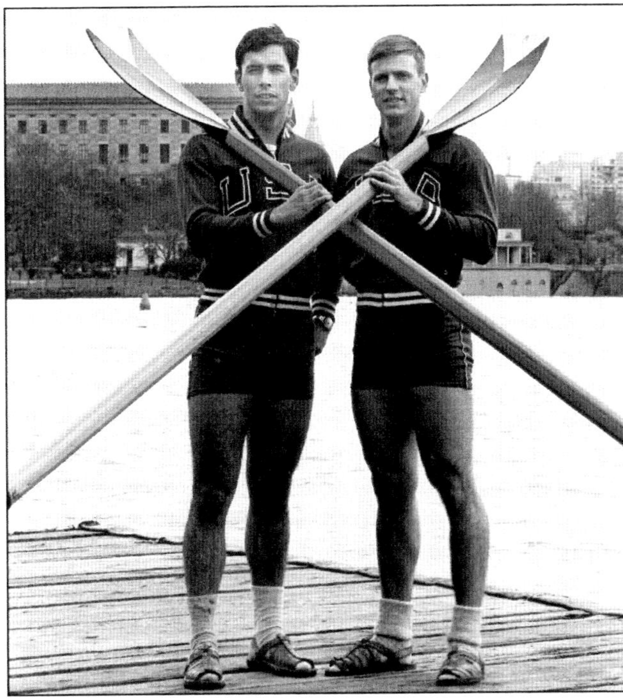

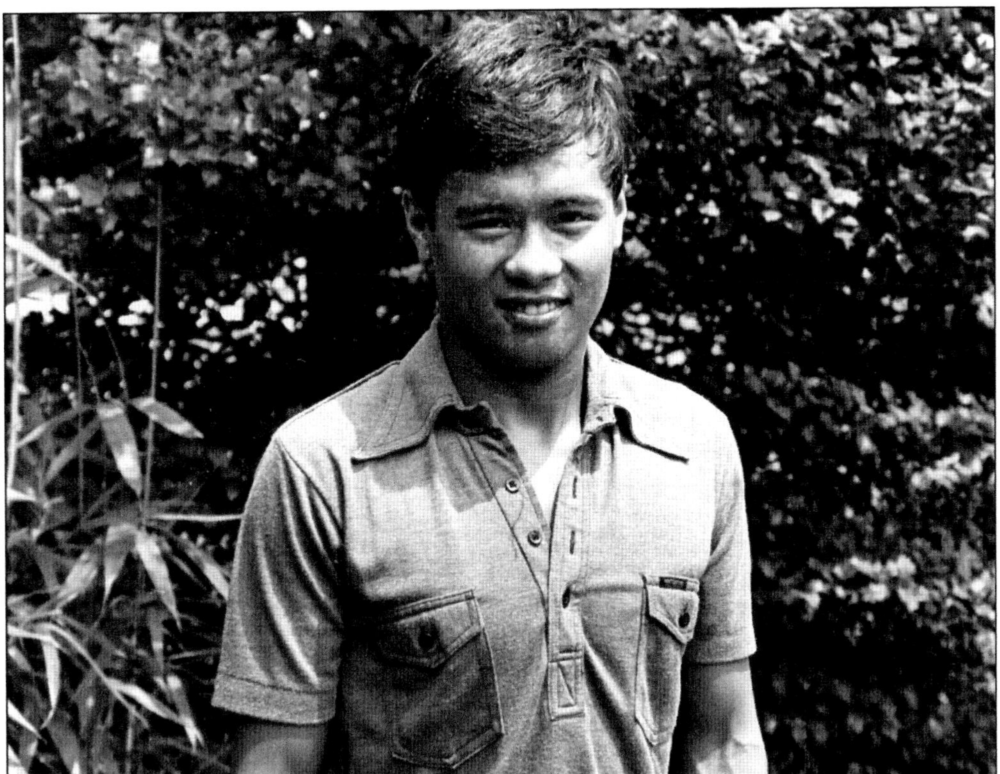

Edwin Borja participated in the 1976 Summer Games in Montreal as a member of the Philippine Swim Team. He graduated in 1980.

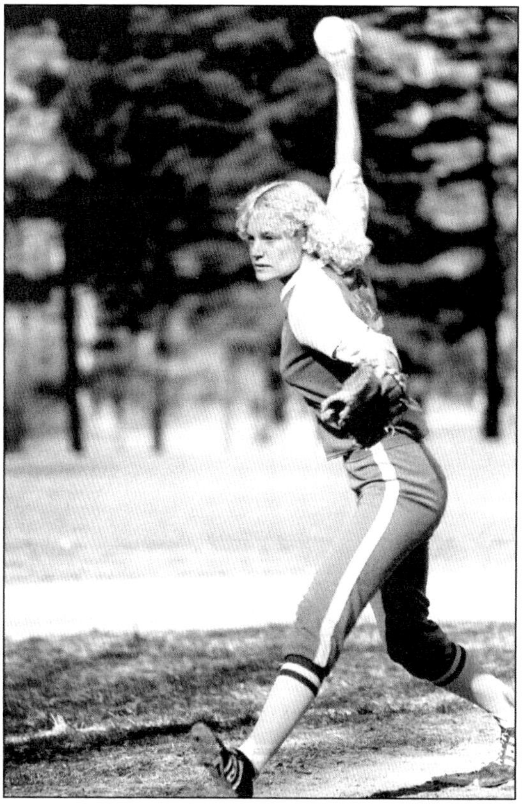

Laura Frieze would have played on the U.S. Field Hockey Team in the 1980 Summer Games in Moscow if it had not been for the American boycott. She also played softball at LaSalle.

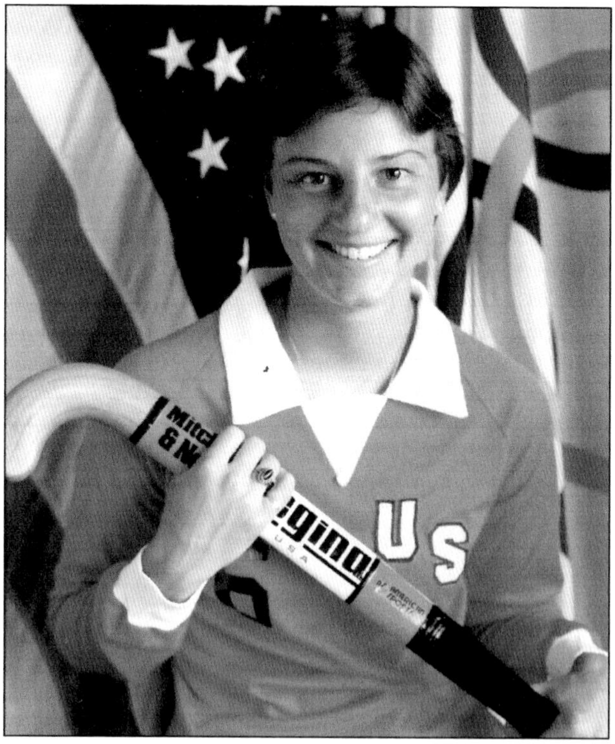

Diane Moyer graduated in 1980 and won an Association for Intercollegiate Athletics for Women (AIAW) National Championship with LaSalle's field hockey that year. She too would have played in the 1980 Summer Games in Moscow. Moyer was on the U.S. Field Hockey Team during the 1984 Summer Games in Los Angeles and won a bronze medal. She became the first woman athlete to be inducted into LaSalle's Hall of Athletes.

The class of 1993's Frank Lescas was a member of the Albanian Swim Team during the 1992 Summer Games in Barcelona.

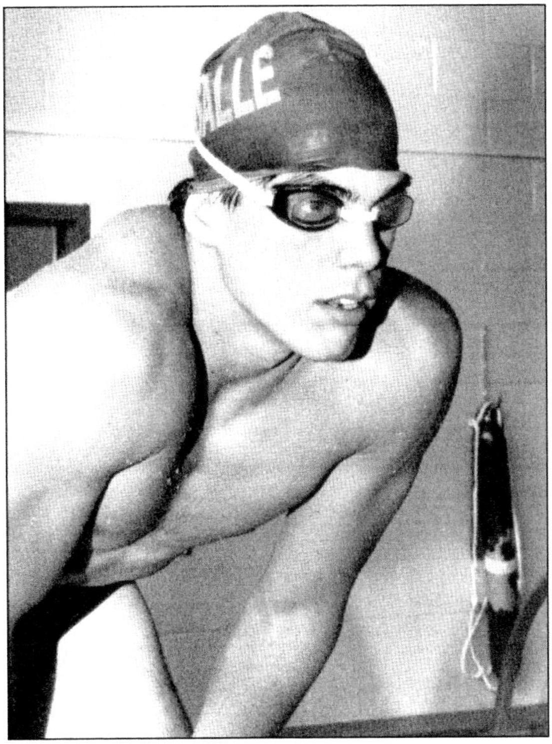

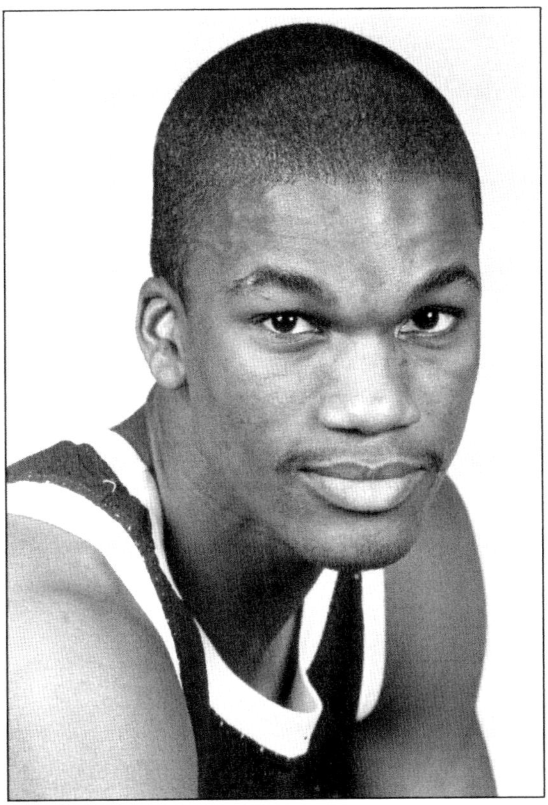

Derek Brown graduated in 1993 and was a member of the U.S. Handball Team during the 1996 Summer Games in Atlanta.

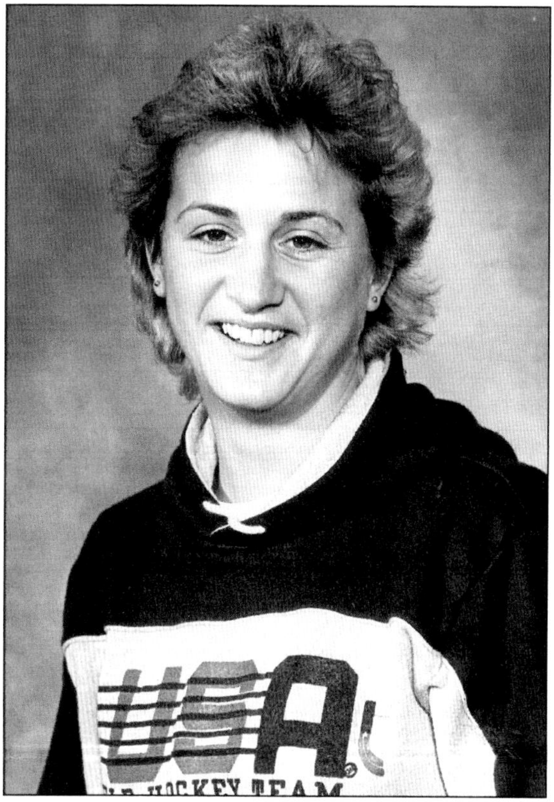

Kathy McGahey played on LaSalle's AIAW National Championship Field Hockey Team in 1980 and graduated in 1982. McGahey won a bronze medal with the U.S. Field Hockey Team in the 1984 Summer Games in Los Angeles and was inducted into LaSalle's Hall of Athletes.

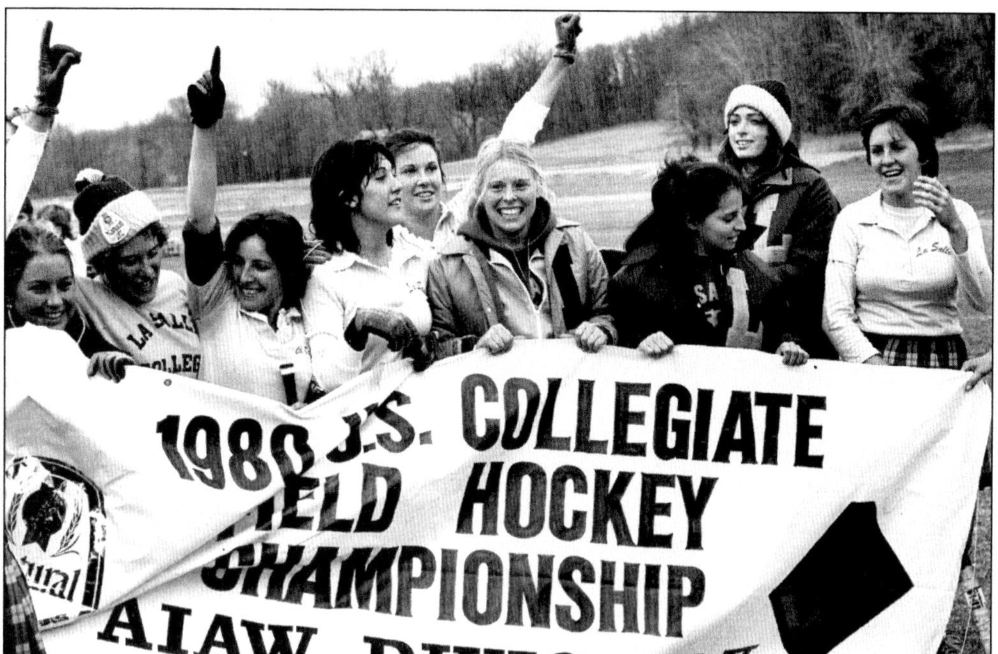

LaSalle's field hockey team celebrated an AIAW National Championship after defeating Southwest Missouri State in 1980.

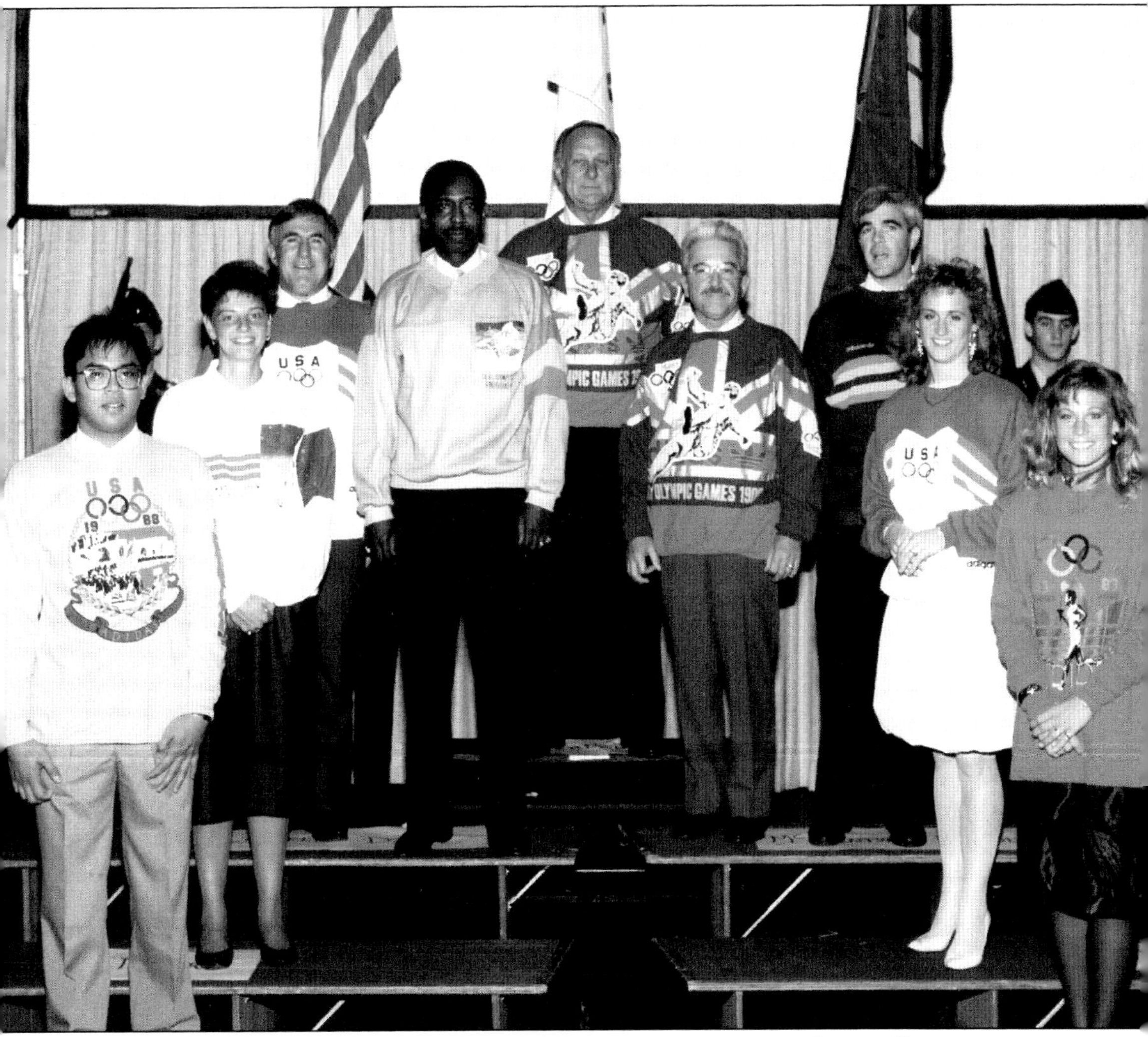

LaSalle Olympians, from left to right, Eric Buhain, Diane Moyer, Al Cantello, Ira Davis, Joe Verdeur, John McIntyre, Bill Belden, Kathy McGahey, and Diane Bracalente gathered in 1988 to commemorate the 40th anniversary of Verdeur's gold medal victory. Eric Buhain swam for the Philippines in the 1988 Summer Games in Seoul and graduated from LaSalle University in 1991. The Class of 1950's John McIntyre was a member of the U.S. Crew Team at the 1948 Summer Games in London. Bill Belden graduated in 1970 and was a member of the U.S. Crew Team during the 1976 Summer Games in Montreal and the abortive 1980 Summer Games in Moscow. Diane Bracalente was assistant director of the LaSalle Student Union and a member of the 1988 U.S. Field Hockey Team.

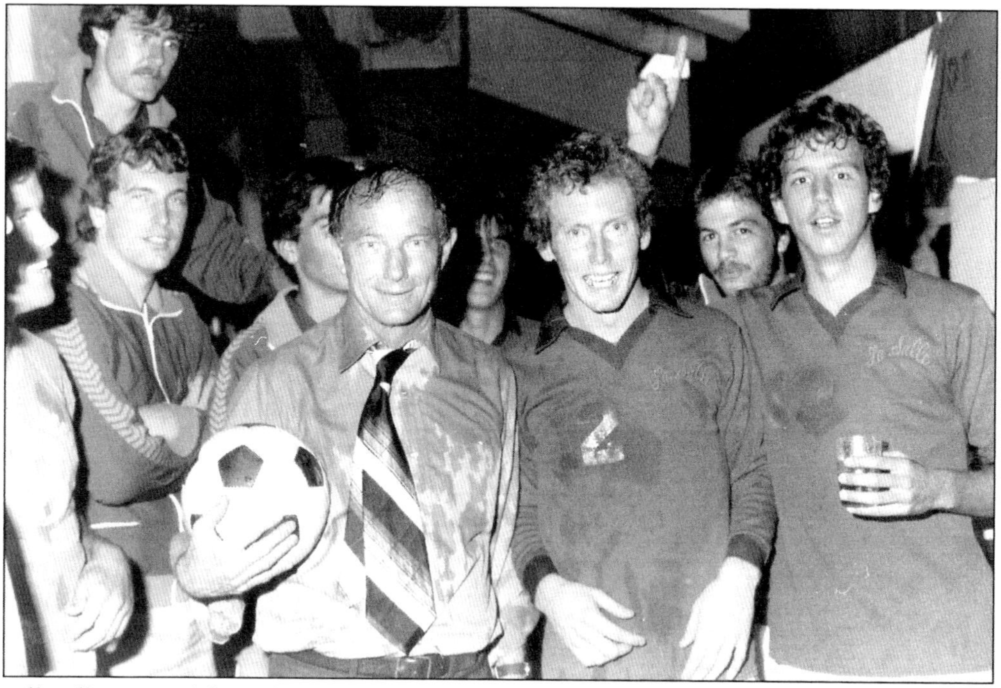

Bill Wilkinson celebrated his 100th victory while coaching the Explorers in 1981. LaSalle's soccer team went 10–3–2 that year.

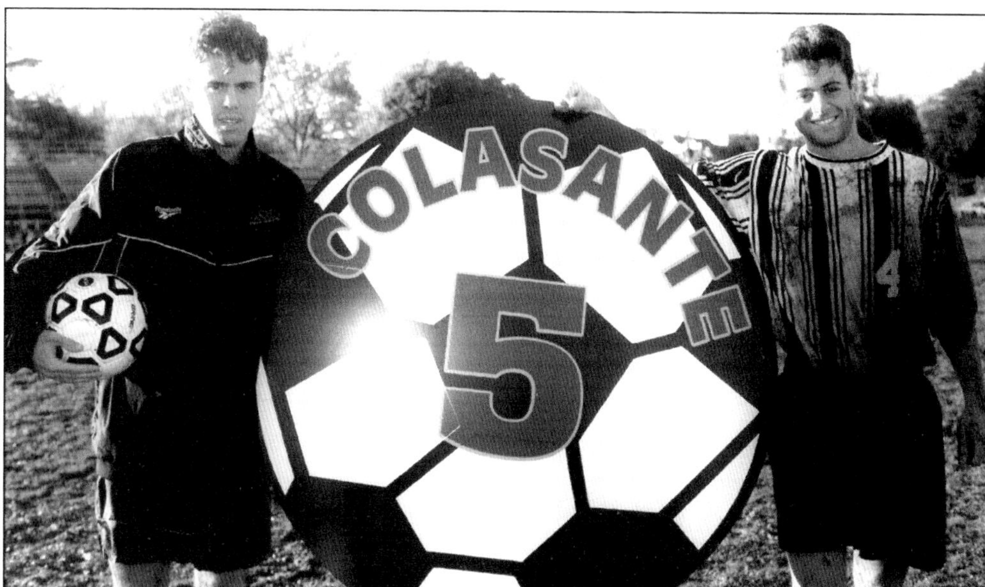

Soccer player Cesidio Colasante's number was retired in 1997. Colasante (left) went on to play professional soccer in Philadelphia.

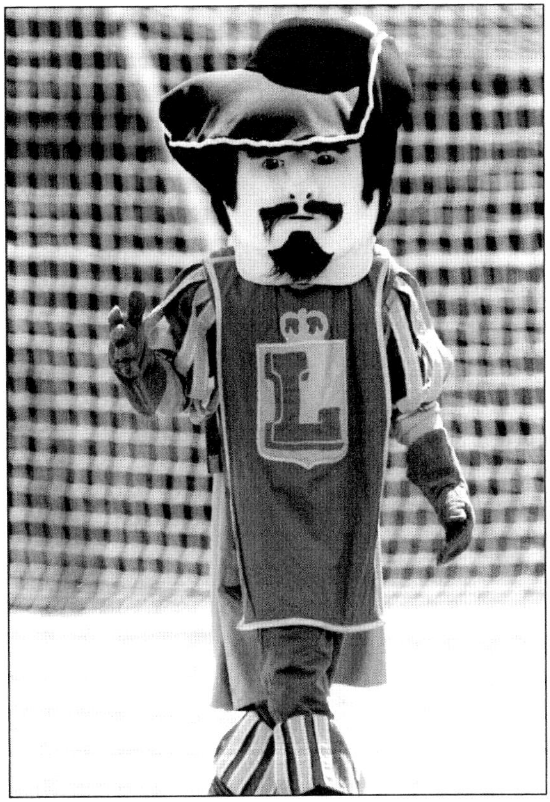

The students of LaSalle College chose Explorers as the name of their sports teams in 1932. The mascot was originally a French cavalier in the mid-1950s. The Explorer appeared as an astronaut in the 1960s and the 1970s.

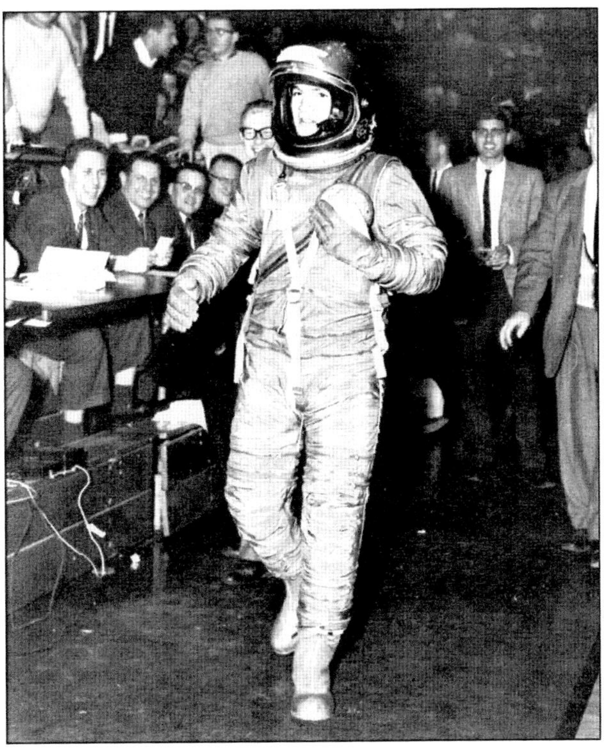

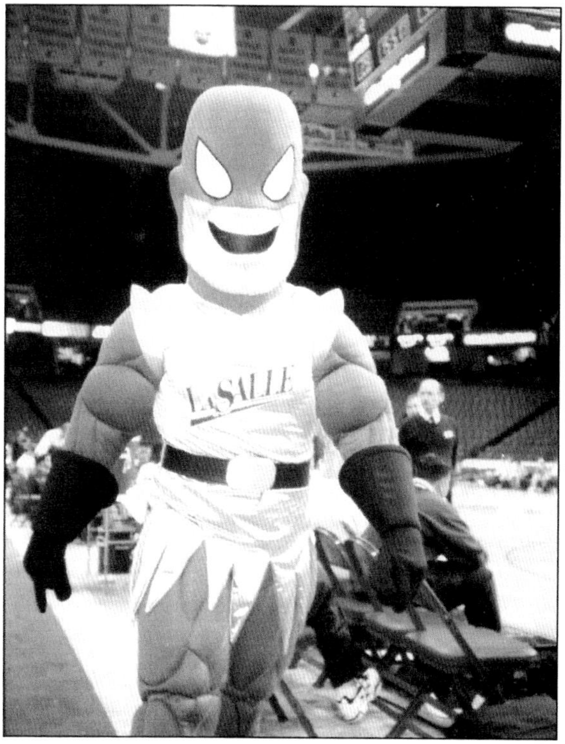

The Mascot became a superhero in the 1990s and reemerged as a cavalier in 2002. Ironically, there is no correlation between the French explorer Rene-Robert Cavelier de LaSalle and the founder of the Christian Brothers.

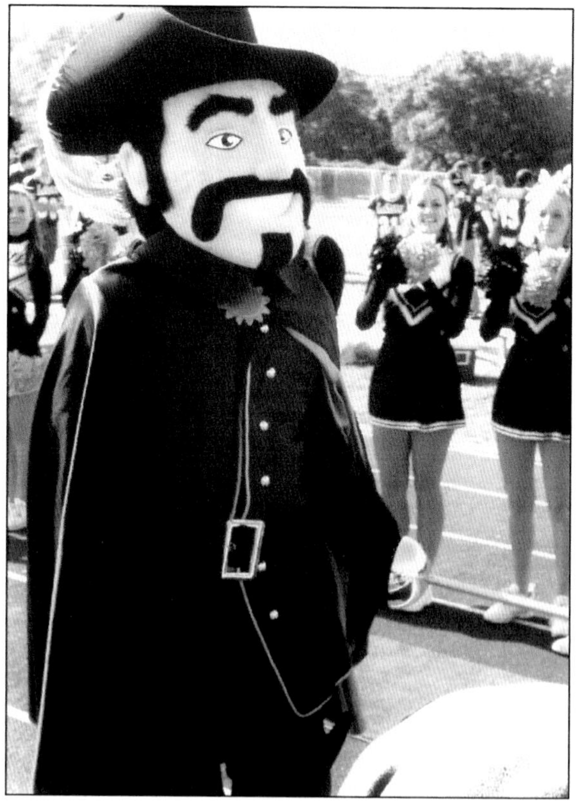

Four

LaSalle through the Years

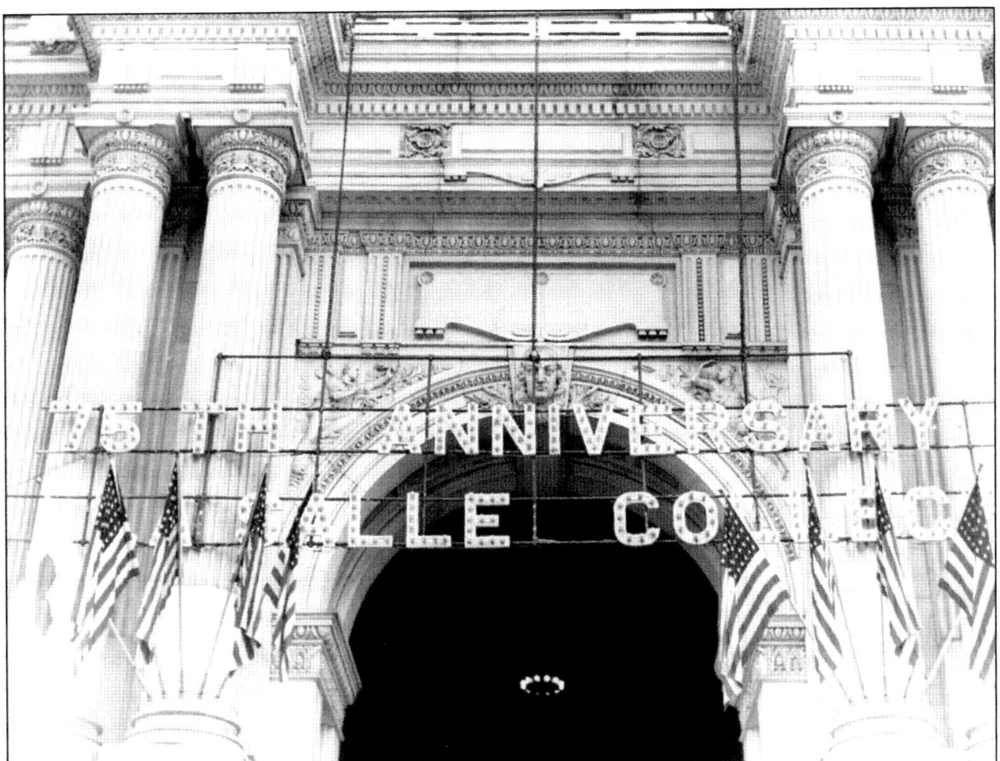

An electric sign commemorating LaSalle College's 75th anniversary was displayed outside of Philadelphia's City Hall in 1938.

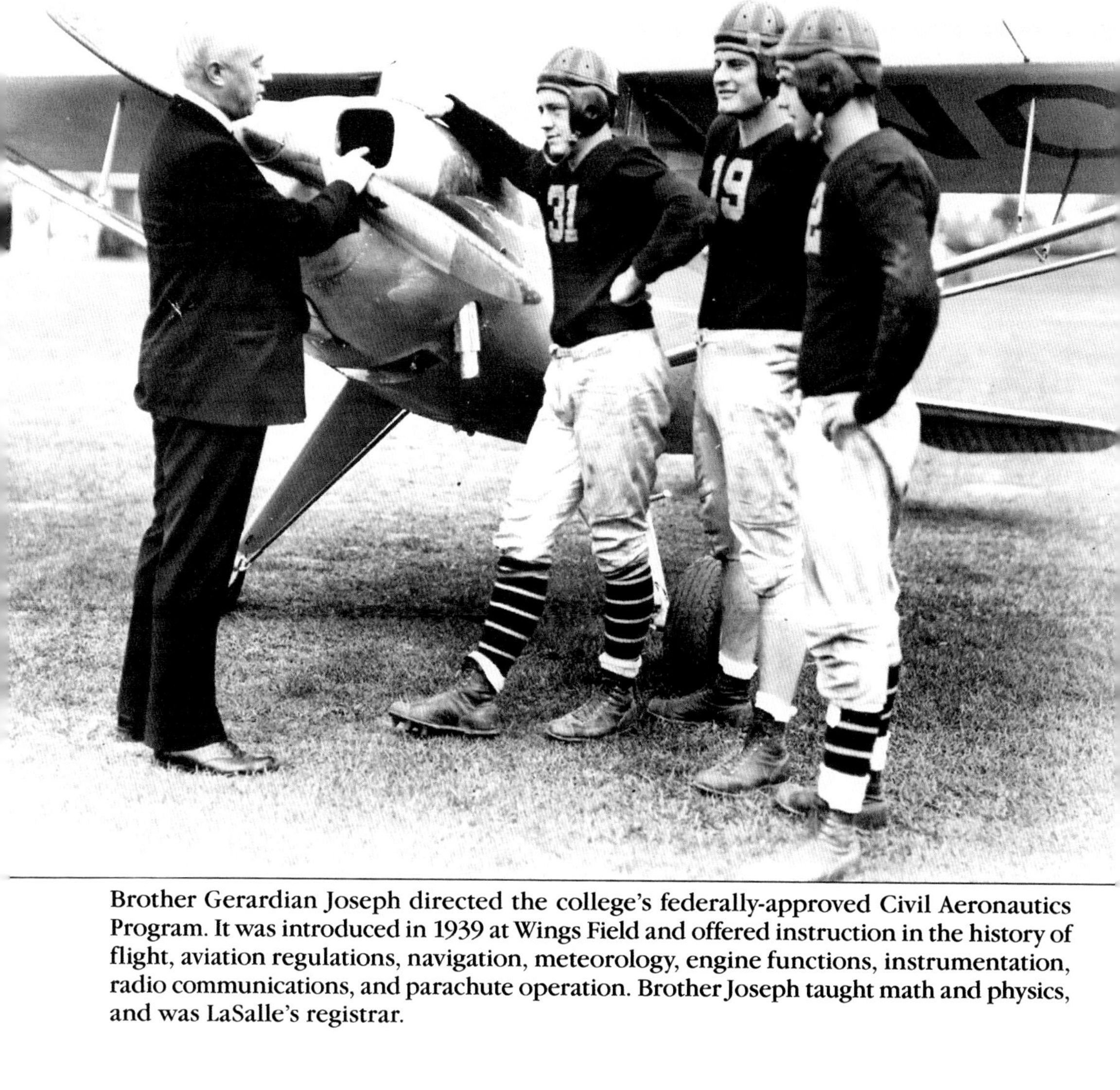

Brother Gerardian Joseph directed the college's federally-approved Civil Aeronautics Program. It was introduced in 1939 at Wings Field and offered instruction in the history of flight, aviation regulations, navigation, meteorology, engine functions, instrumentation, radio communications, and parachute operation. Brother Joseph taught math and physics, and was LaSalle's registrar.

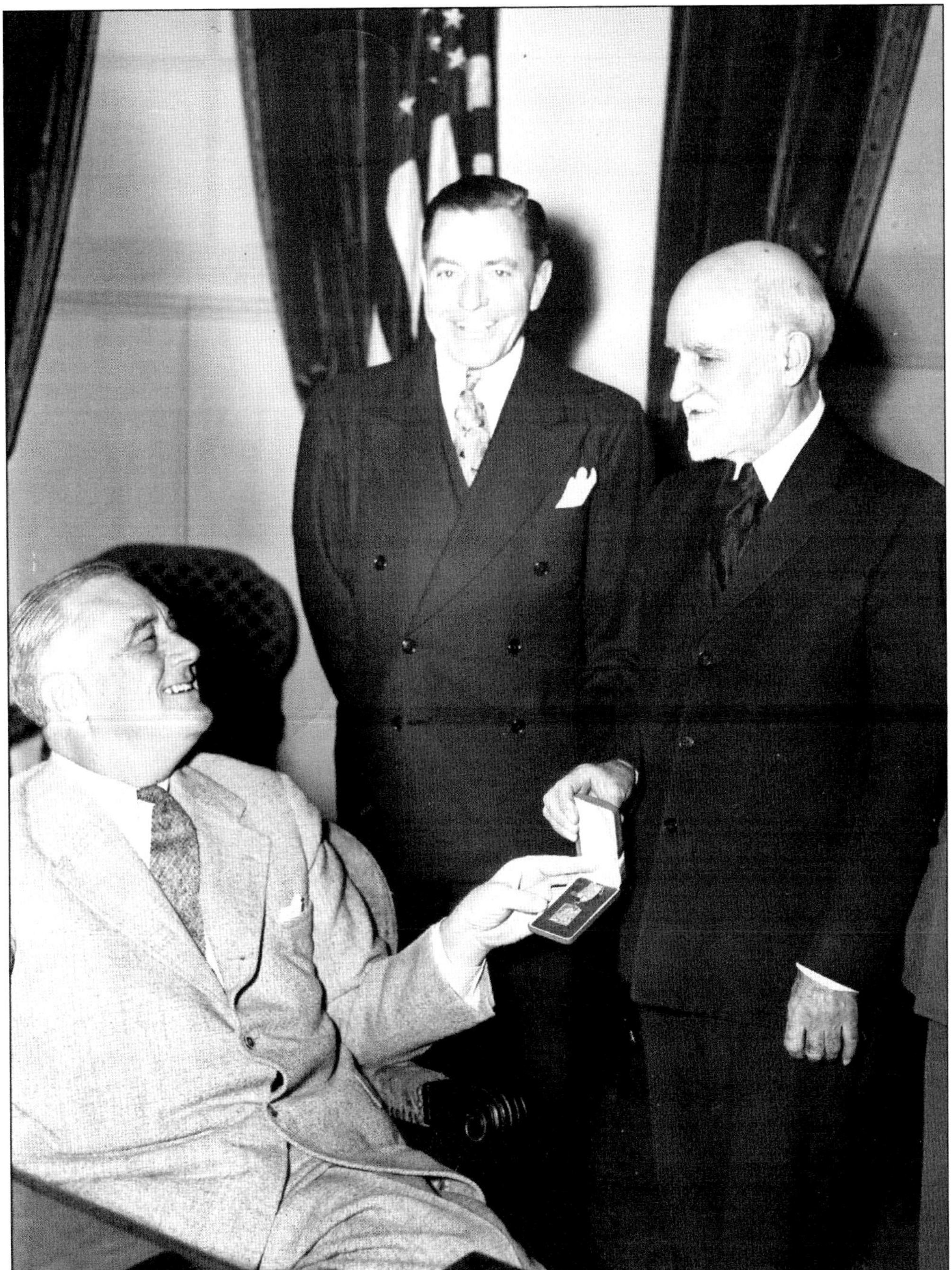

LaSalle's president from 1928 until 1932, Brother Elzear Alfred presented Pres. Franklin Delano Roosevelt with the De LaSalle Medal for Distinguished Service in the Cause of Peace and Social Security in January 1941. United States Representative James P. McGranery attended the ceremony. After his term as president, Brother Alfred ran the Sunday Labor Management School promoting cooperation between labor, industry, and government in Philadelphia during the Depression.

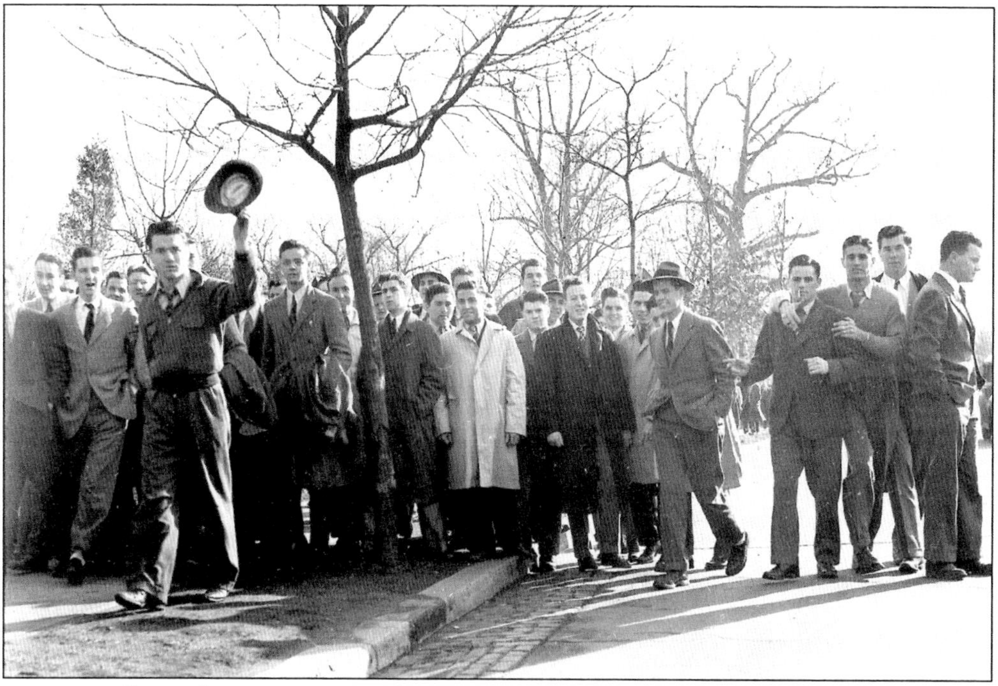

Many LaSalle students participated in the Hale America Program. This physical fitness regiment was initiated by football coach Jim Henry in order to prepare the young men for military service during the Second World War. Henry also taught economics.

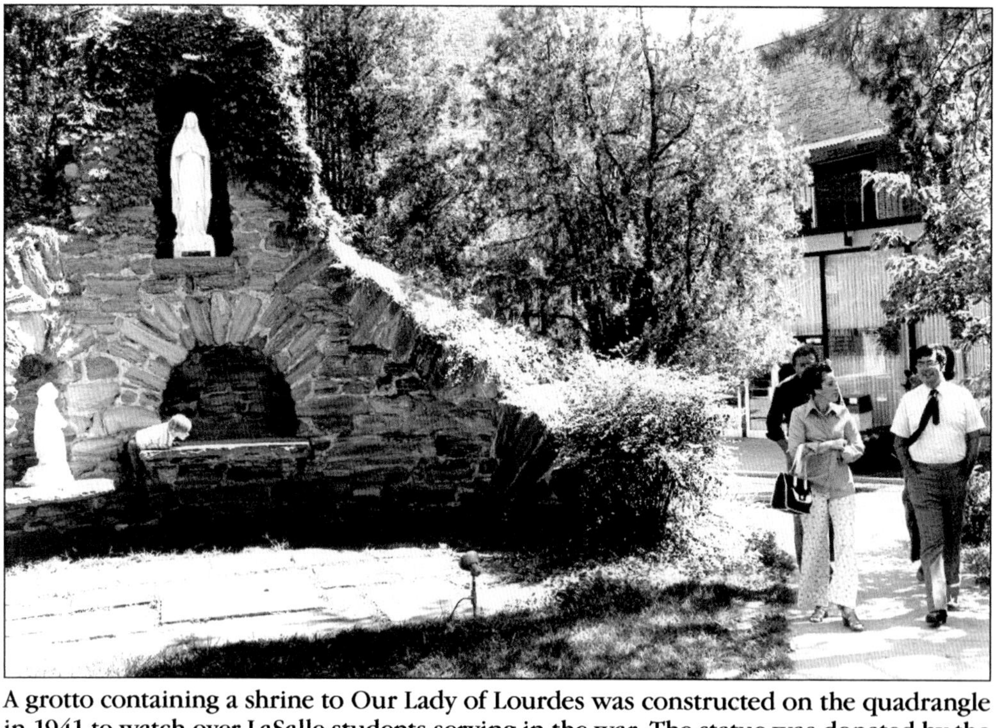

A grotto containing a shrine to Our Lady of Lourdes was constructed on the quadrangle in 1941 to watch over LaSalle students serving in the war. The statue was donated by the parents of Martin Hickey, a LaSalle College High School sophomore who died that year.

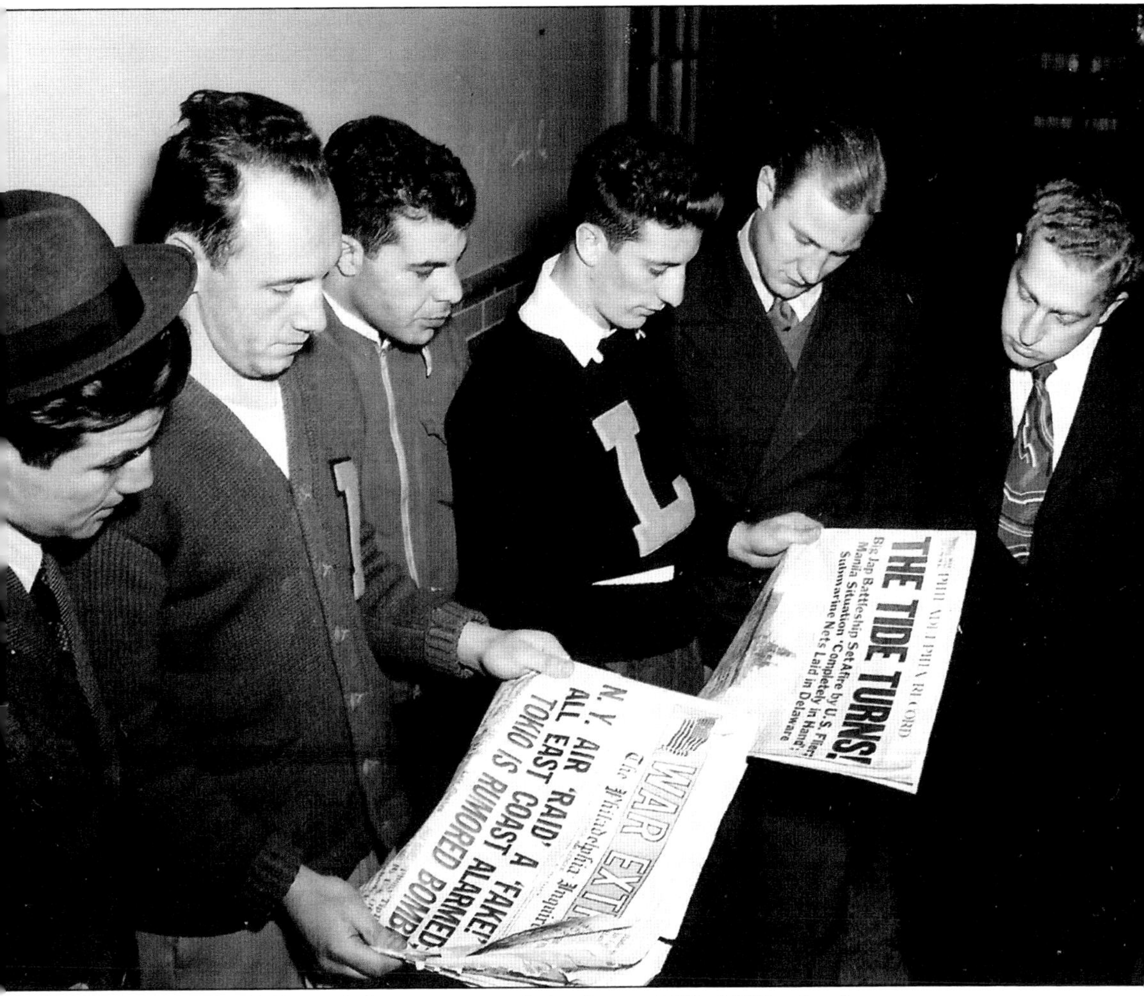

LaSalle students followed the progress of the Second World War in the newspapers.

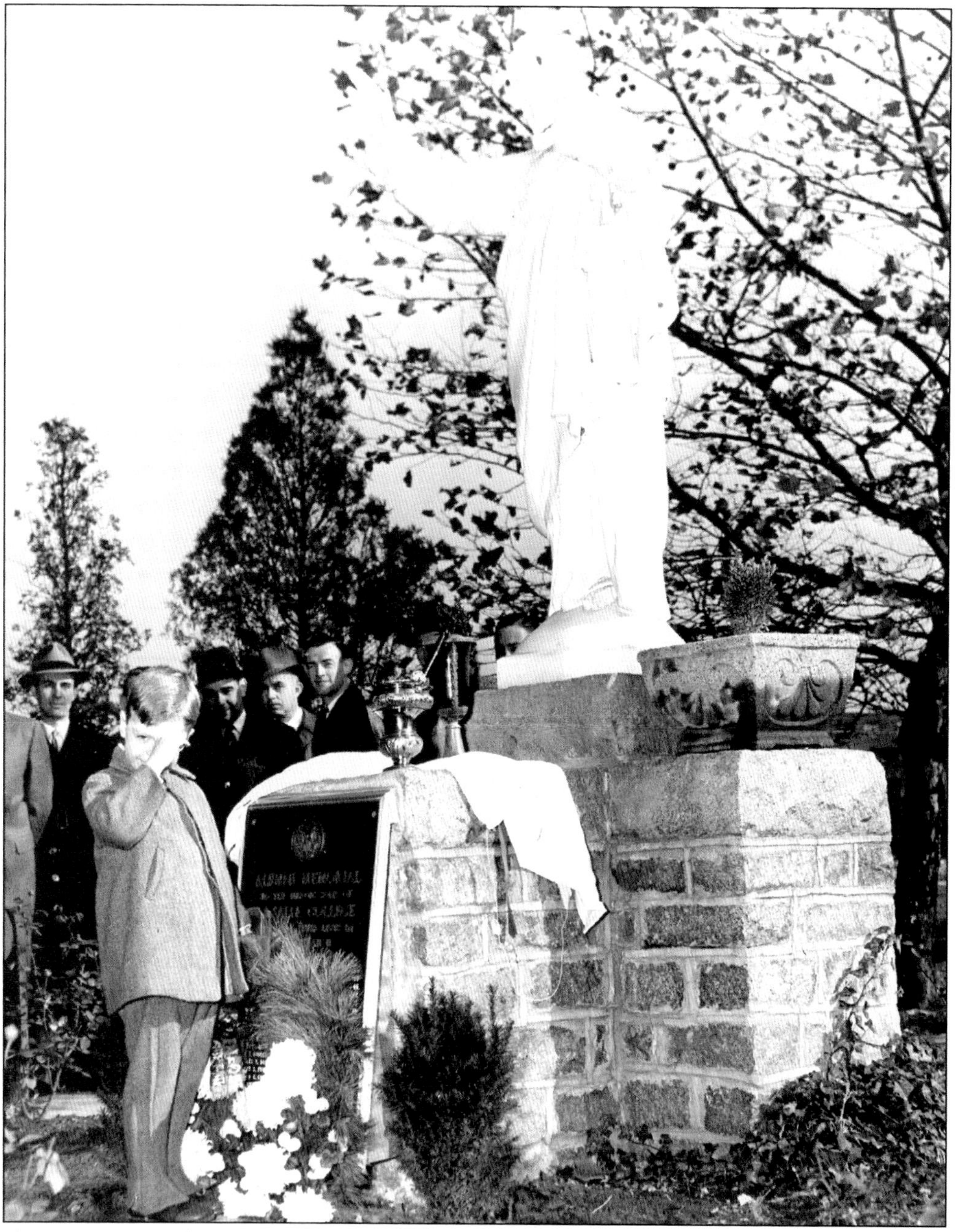

Tommy Cunningham, whose father, James, was the first LaSalle alumnus to be killed in the Second World War, unveiled the college's World War II memorial in 1946.

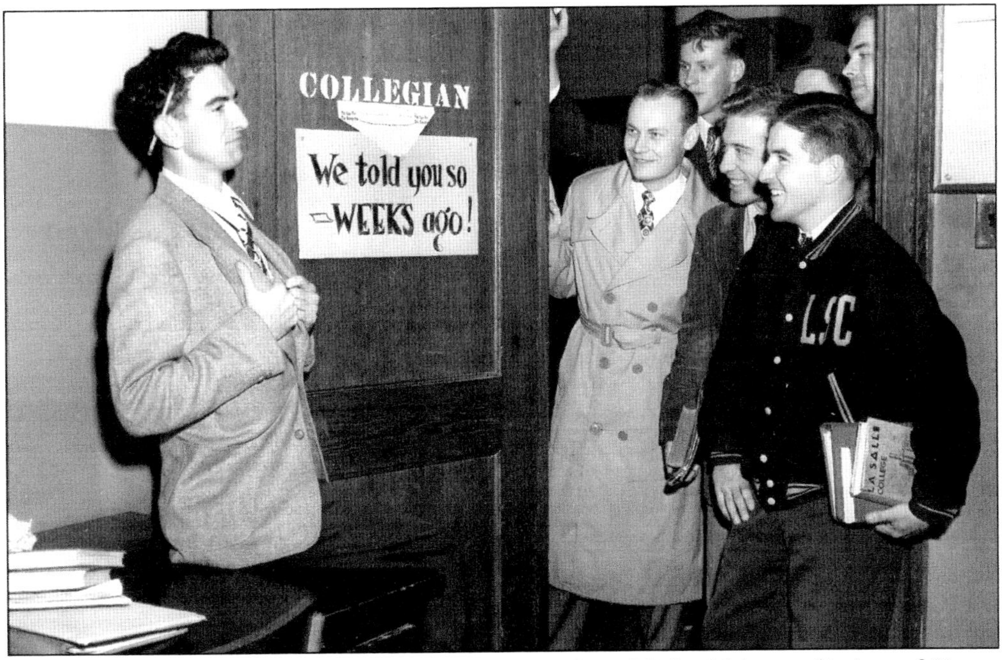

Editor of the school newspaper Walter J. Brough published his prediction of Harry Truman's presidential victory in the LaSalle *Collegian* in 1948. Publication of the *Collegian* began in 1931.

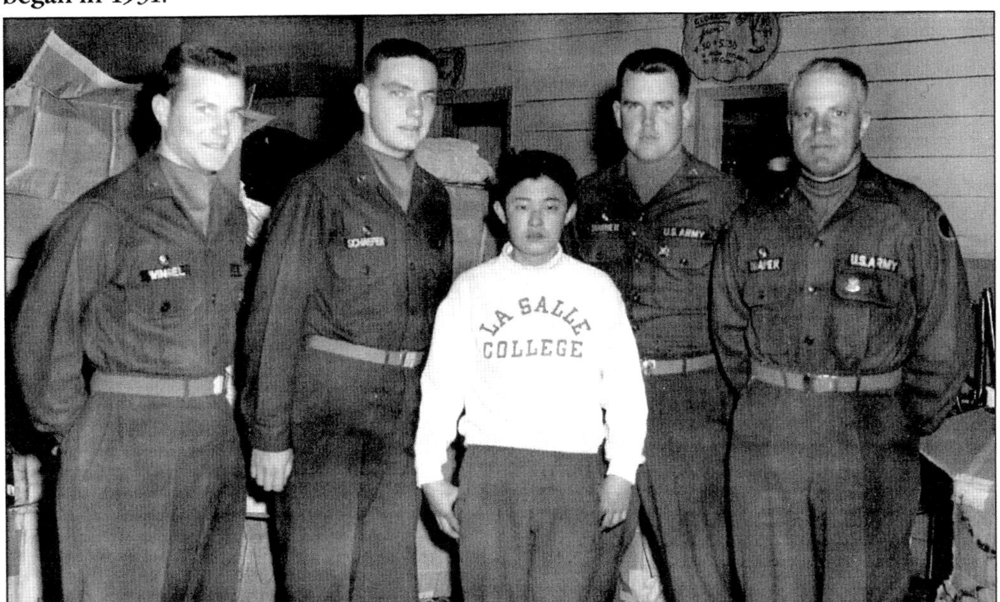

The class of 1954's Lt. Robert Schaefer (second from left) was serving in the United States Army with fellow alumni William Wingel (left) and Robert Bonner (second from right) in South Korea in 1955, when he wrote a letter to LaSalle College describing the privations faced by children in post-war Korea. The college responded with Operation: Person to Person, a clothing drive that sent 140 boxes of clothes to South Korea, including LaSalle sweatshirts.

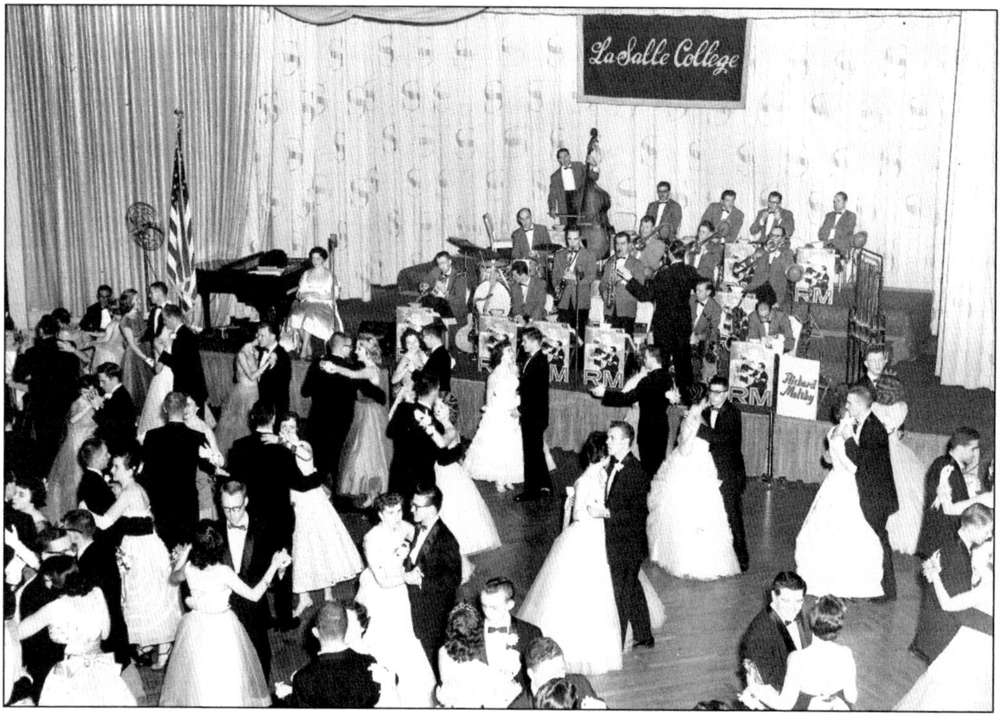

Richard Maltby's band performed at LaSalle College's Annual Blue and Gold Ball in 1958 at the Sheraton Hotel. Over 200 couples attended the event.

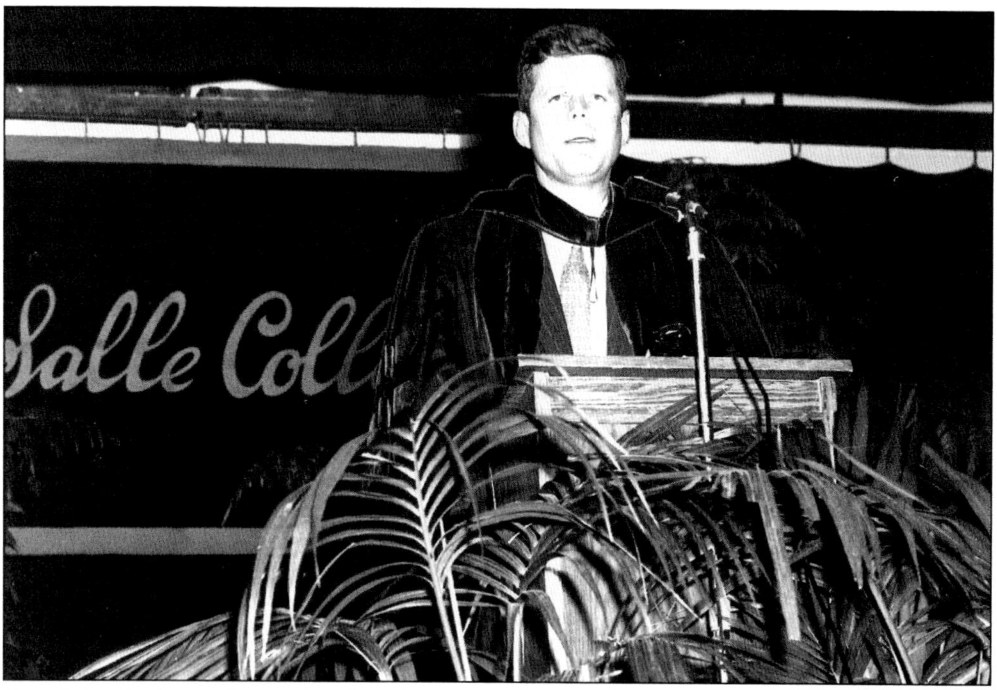
Sen. John F. Kennedy received an honorary degree from LaSalle in 1958. The degree was awarded to him in the auditorium in College Hall that was later converted into the De LaSalle Chapel.

German rocket scientist Dr. Wernher von Braun spoke at LaSalle and met with Pres. Brother Daniel Bernian in 1961.

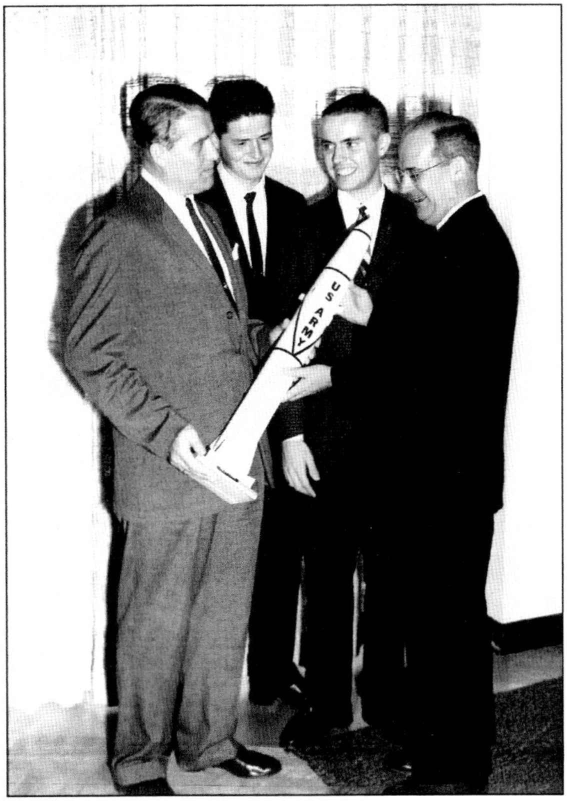

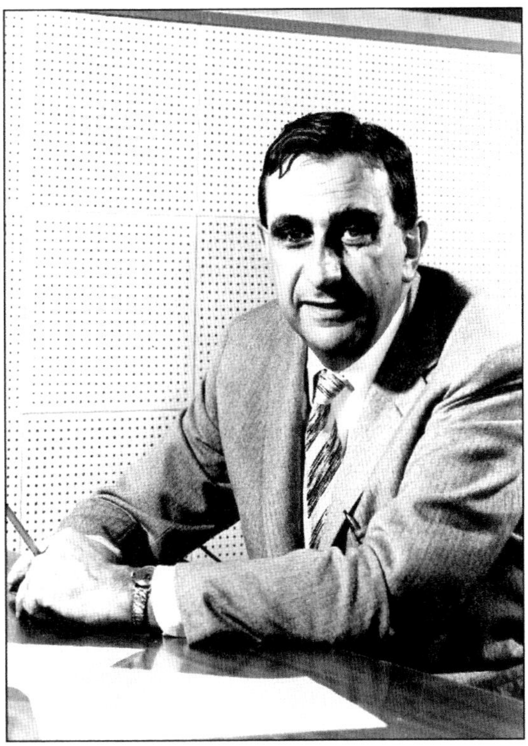

Dr. Edward Teller gave a lecture on the military possibilities of space travel in 1962. He had helped to develop the first hydrogen bomb 10 years earlier.

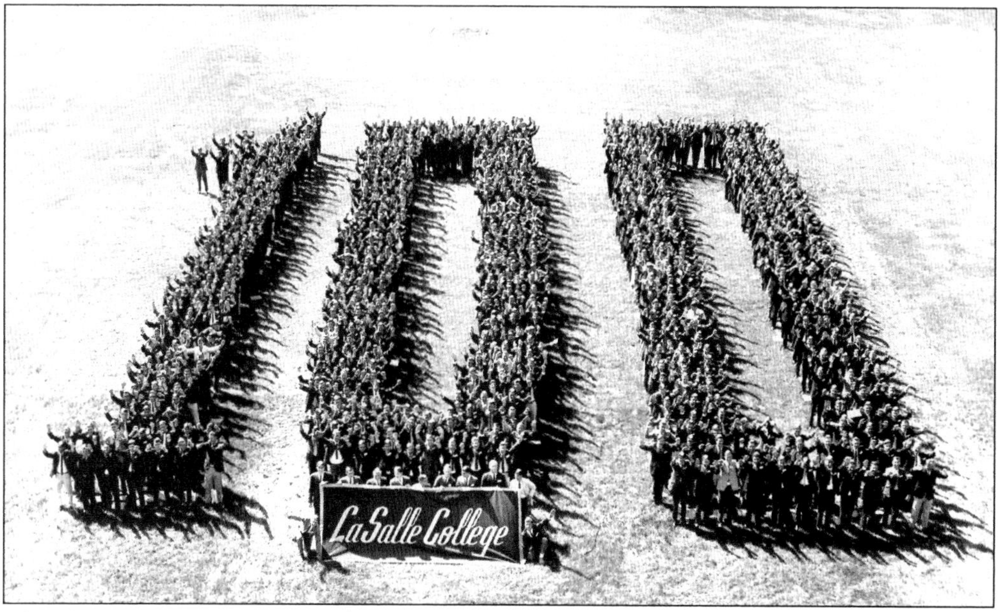

The freshmen class of 1962 gathered for an aerial photograph celebrating LaSalle's centennial.

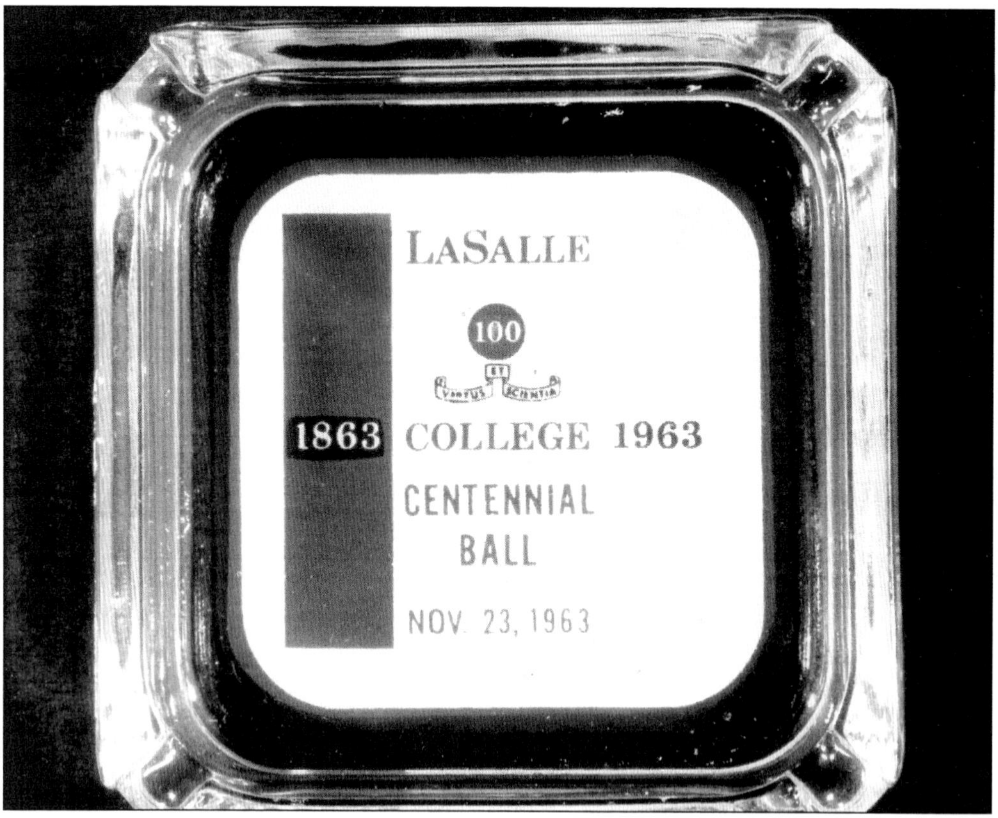

Ashtrays were made as favors for LaSalle College's Centennial Ball in November 1963. The engagement was cancelled due to the assassination of President Kennedy.

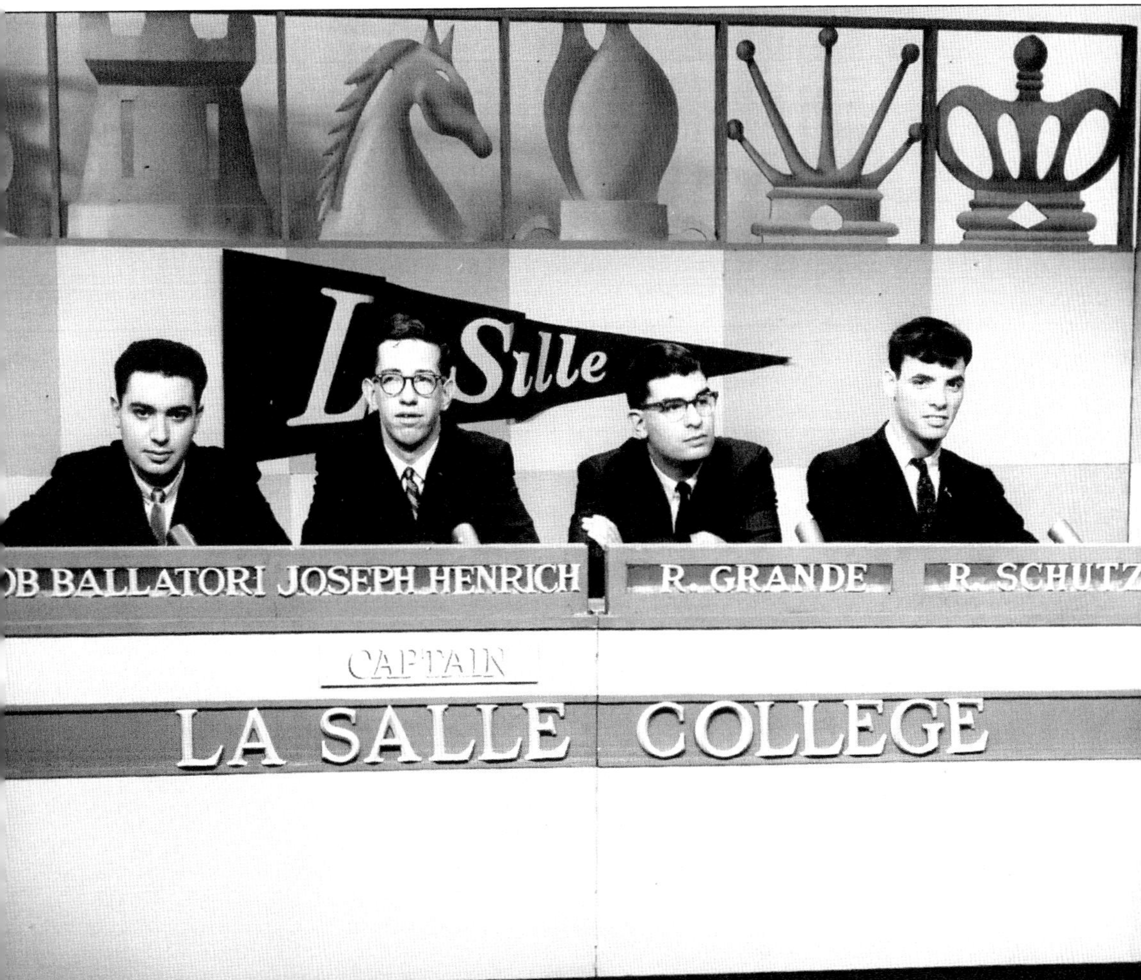

Students Bob Ballatori, Joseph Henrich, Richard Grande, and Richard Schutz represented LaSalle College on NBC's G.E. College Bowl in 1964. Their opponents were from Arizona State.

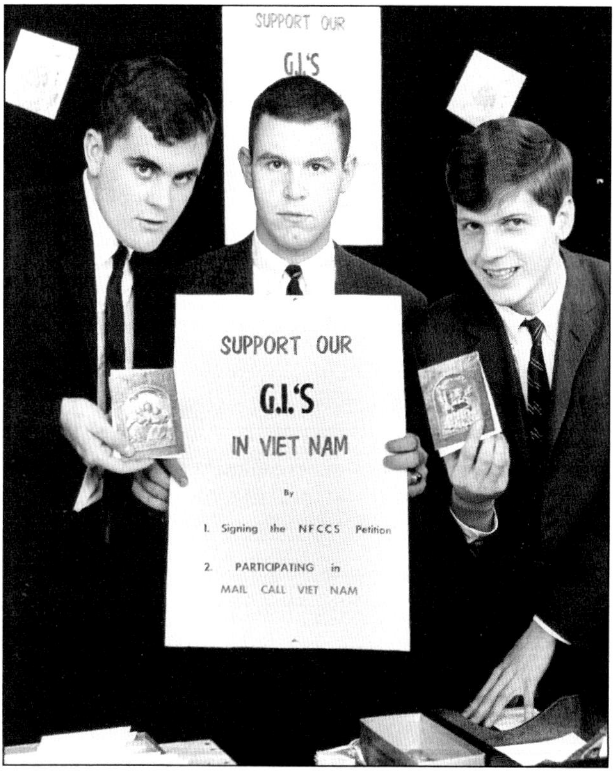

Many LaSalle students supported the troops in Vietnam in the mid-1960s.

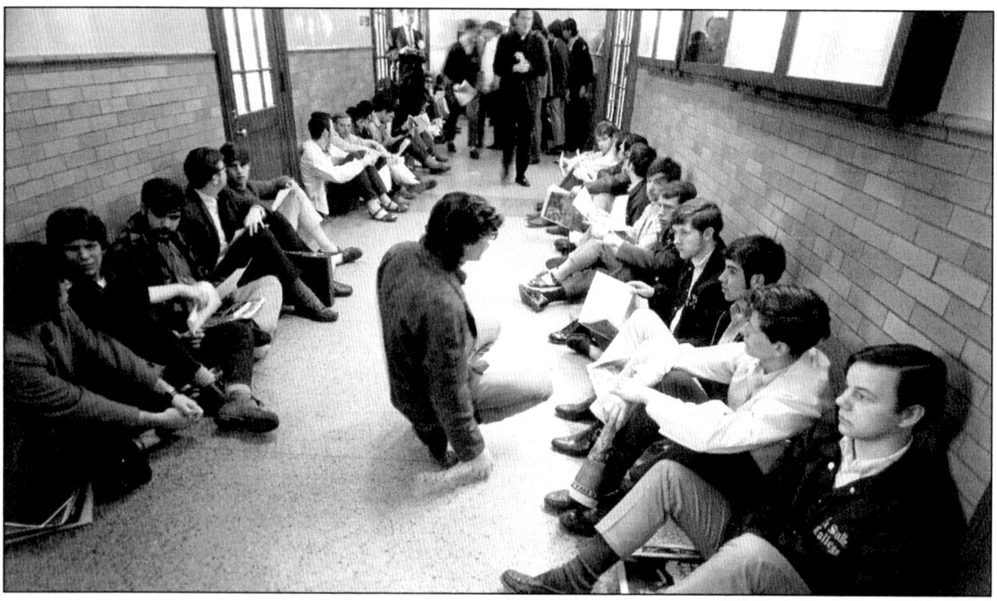

Students staged a demonstration in College Hall in 1969 to protest required ROTC training for freshmen. Three hundred students participated in the sit-in over a four day period, and a petition bearing 1,750 signatures was presented to the administration. ROTC was made voluntary through negotiations with Pres. Brother Daniel Bernian. For many, the incident represented a change in attitude toward the Vietnam War among students in the late 1960s.

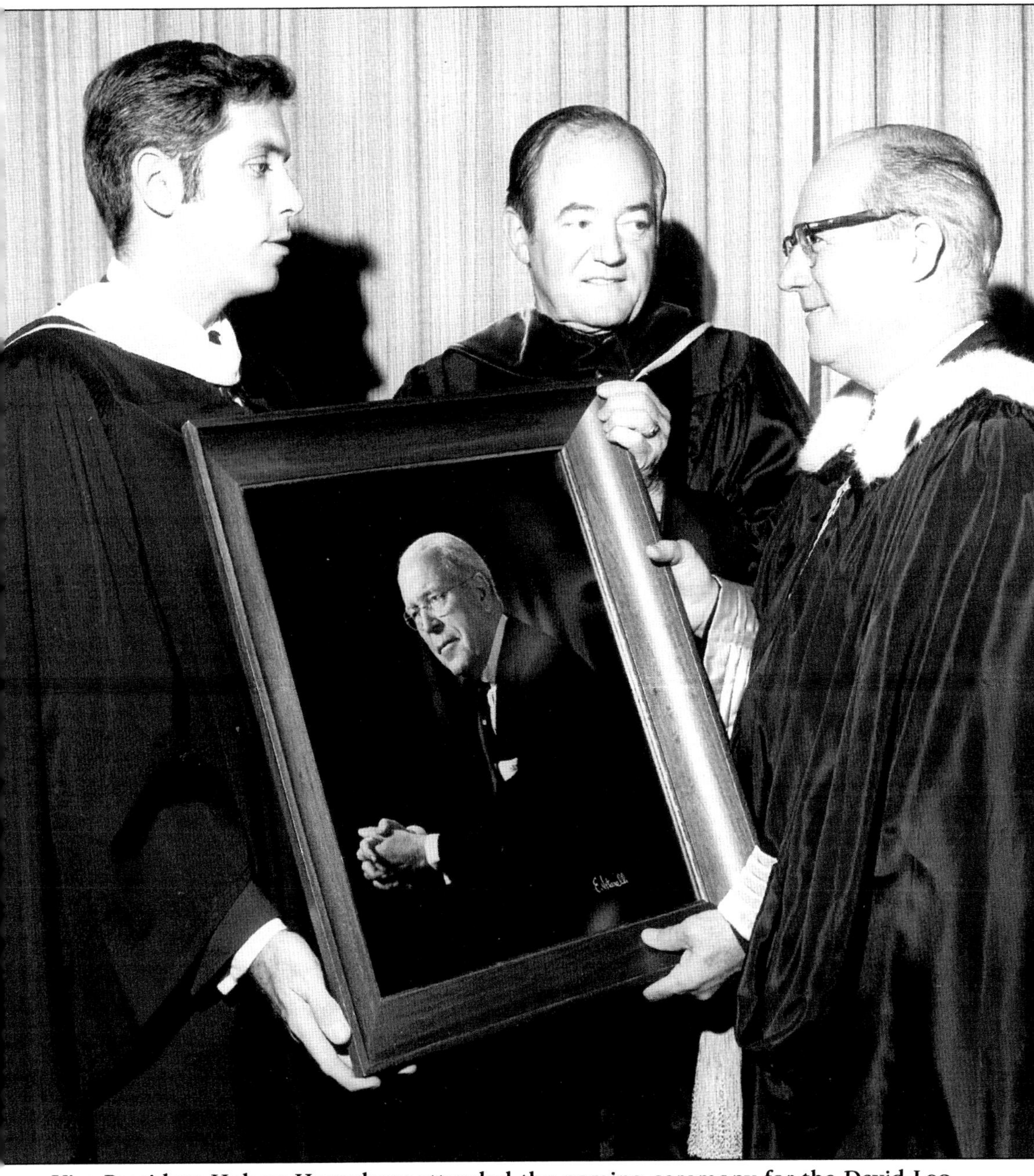

Vice-President Hubert Humphrey attended the naming ceremony for the David Leo Lawrence Library in 1969. Gerald Lawrence presented Pres. Brother Daniel Bernian with a portrait of his father Pennsylvania governor David Leo Lawrence.

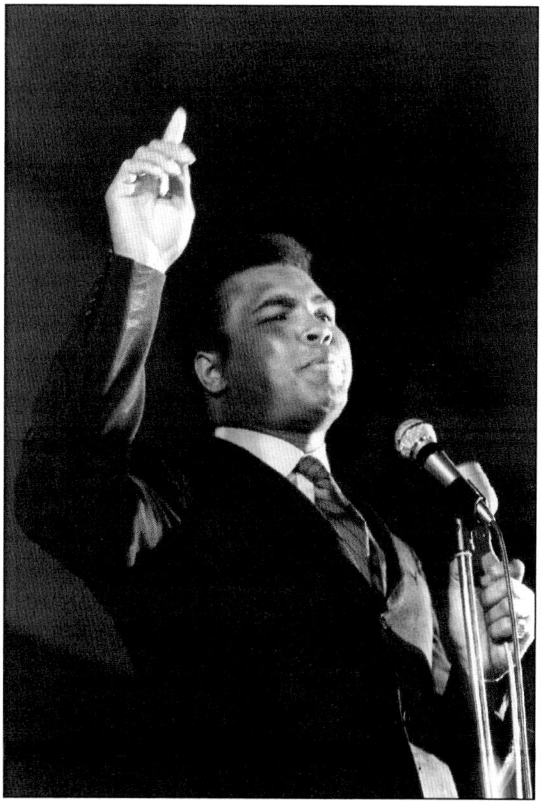

Muhammed Ali and Sammy Davis Jr. spoke at an African American Arts Festival held in Wister Hall's gymnasium in 1969. The event was sponsored by LaSalle's Black Student Union, the Black Coalition, and the Urban Studies Center. Money raised by the event went toward providing scholarships for African Americans in Philadelphia.

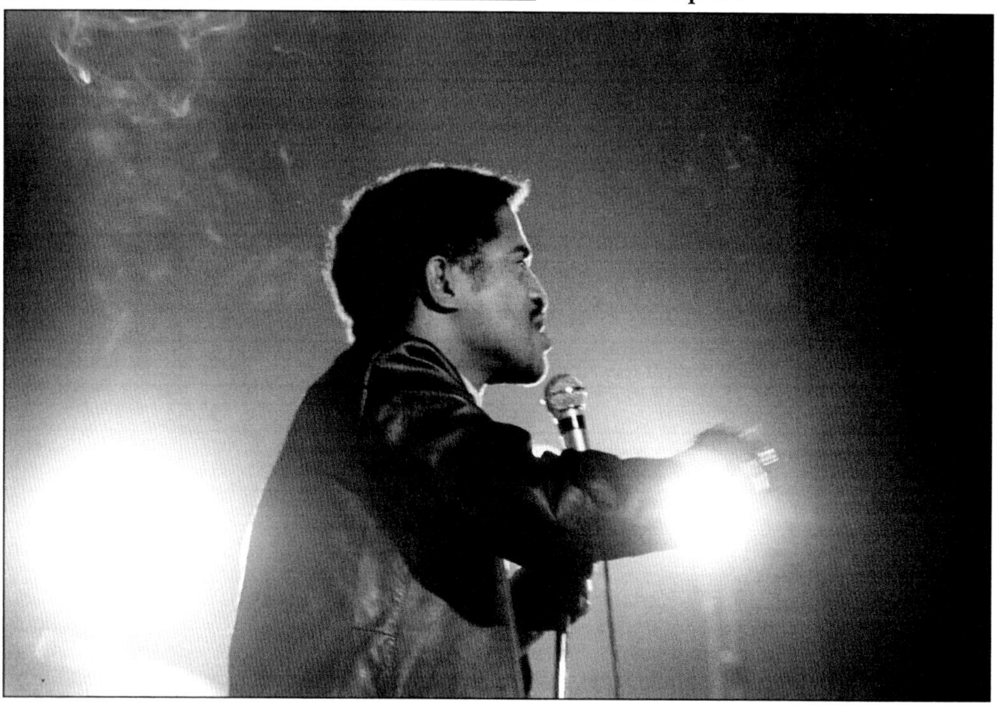

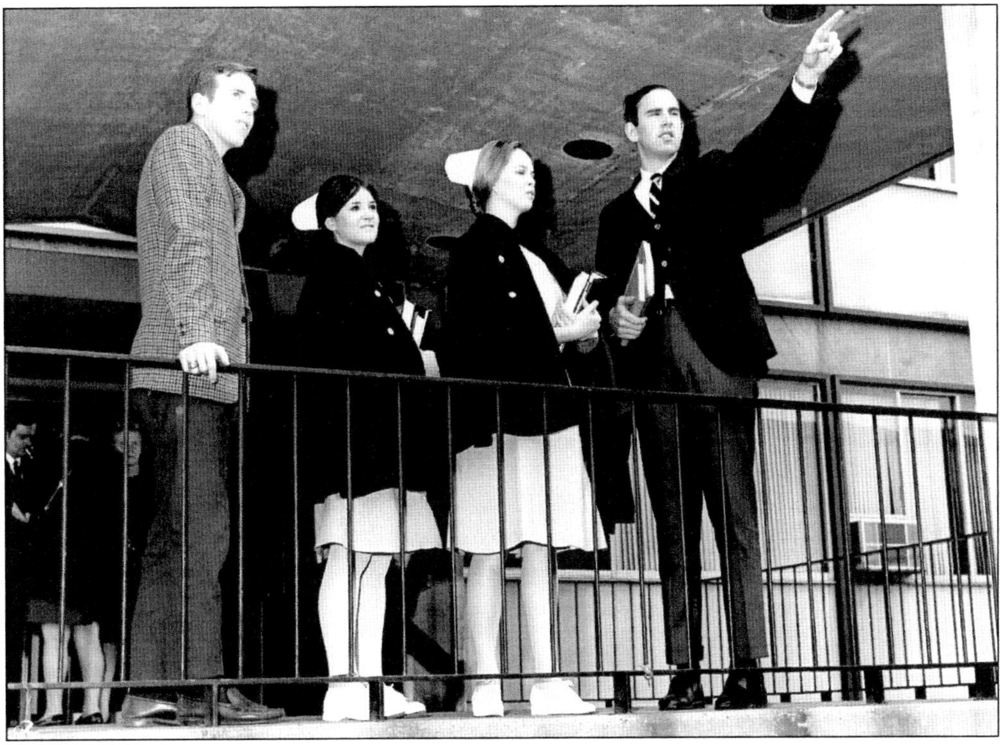

In 1969, nursing students from nearby Germantown Hospital became the first women permitted to attend day classes at LaSalle College. The college became coeducational a year later. Women had been taking evening courses, and the Teaching Sisters of the Archdiocese of Philadelphia had been attending summer workshops at LaSalle since the mid-1960s.

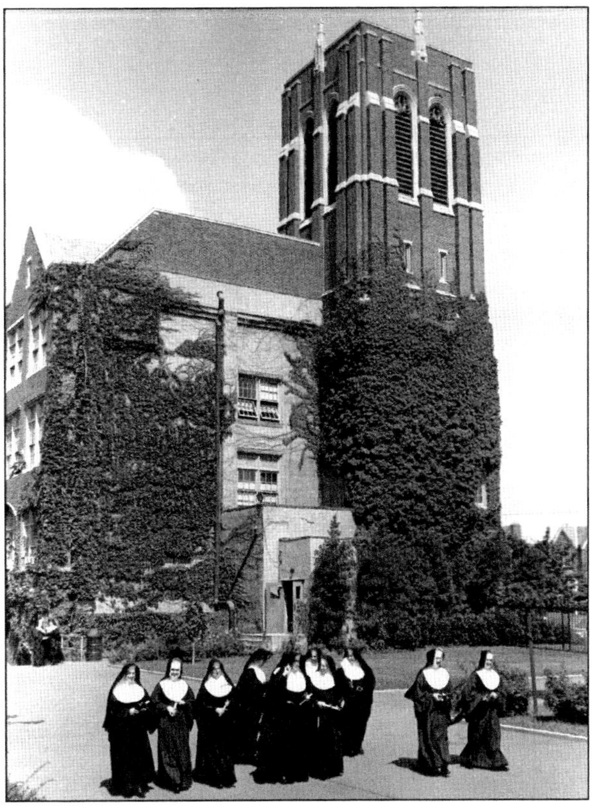

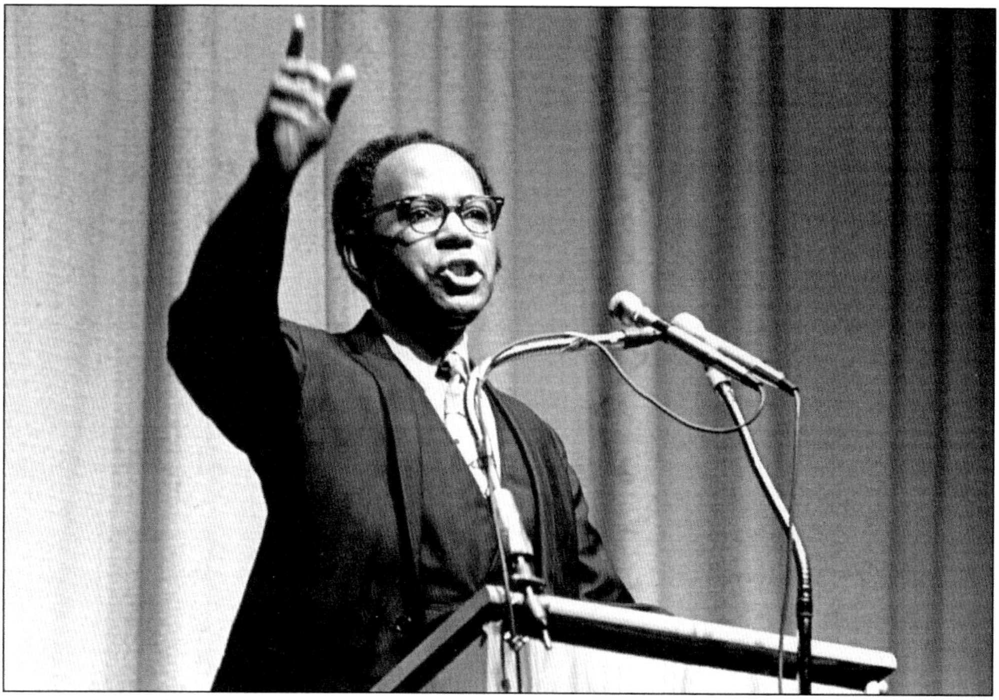

James Meredith was the first African American to attend the University of Mississippi in 1962. He spoke at LaSalle in 1970.

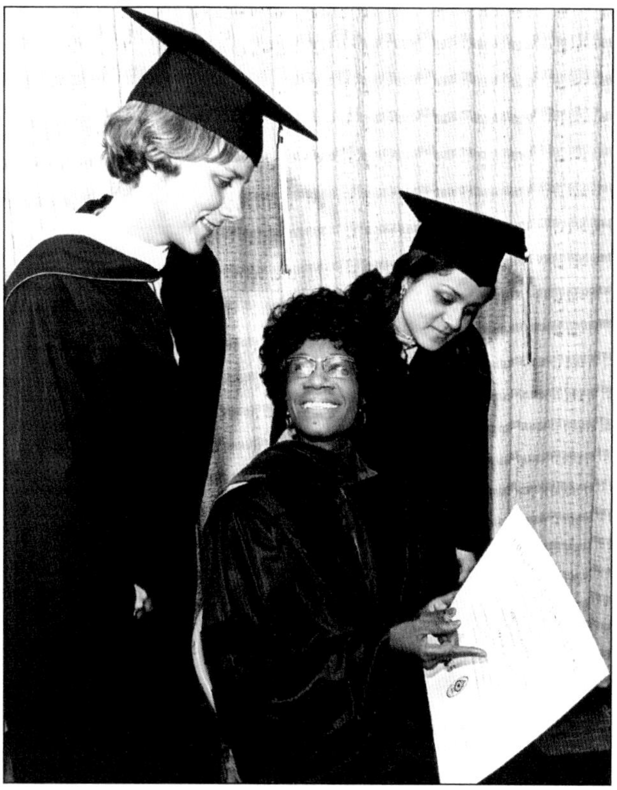

United States representative Shirley Chisholm, from Brooklyn, New York, was awarded an honorary degree from LaSalle in 1971. She was the first African American woman to win a seat in Congress. Chisholm ran for president of the United States in 1972.

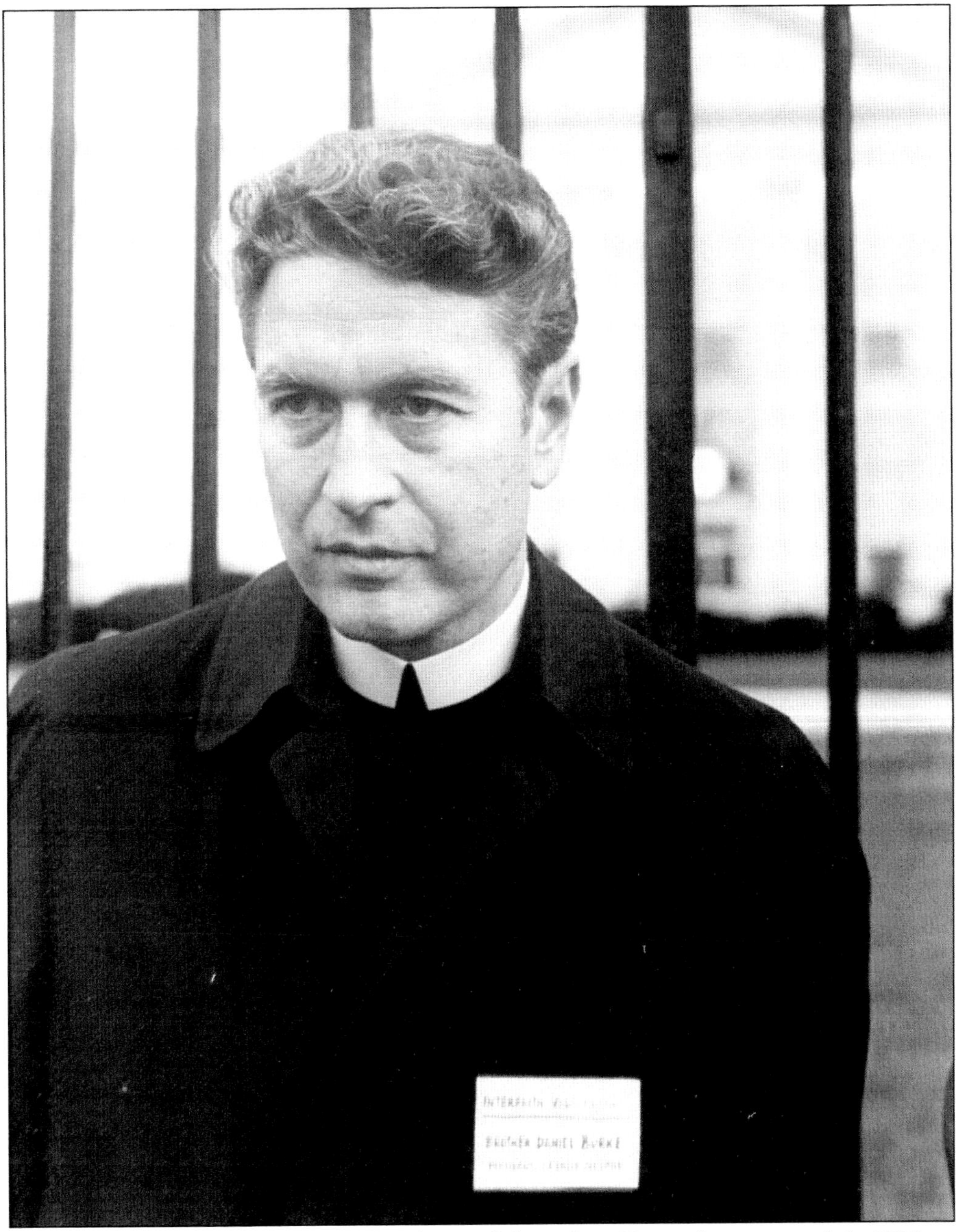

Pres. Brother Daniel Burke fasted in front of the White House for one week in 1971 to protest the Vietnam War.

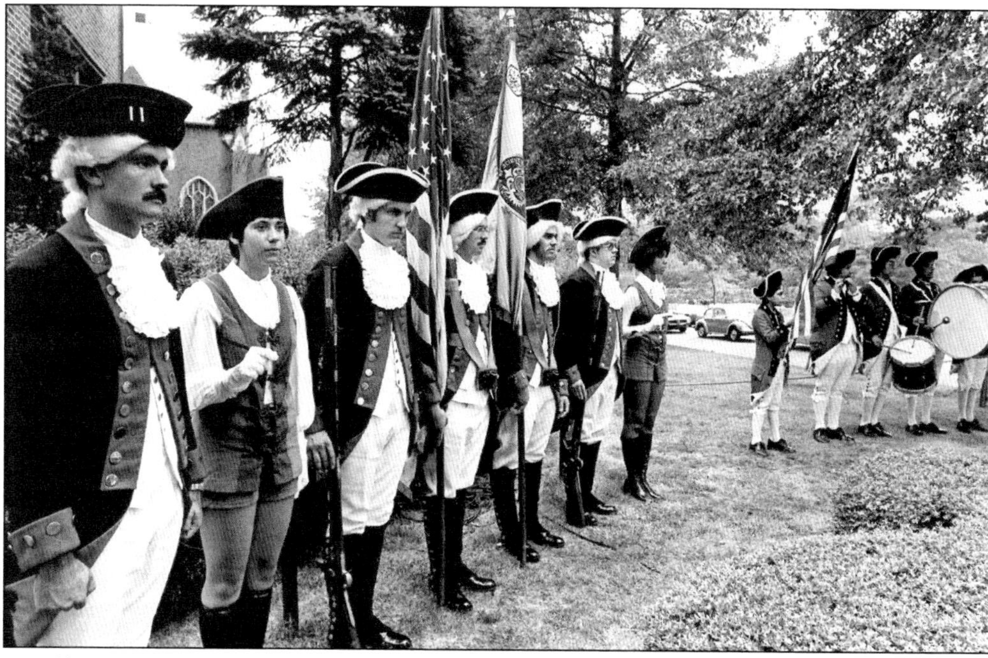

LaSalle's ROTC Color Guard and a fife and drum corps celebrated the flag-raising during the Bicentennial in 1976. LaSalle was recognized as an American Revolution Bicentennial College. Activities included a colonial soldier encampment, a performance of the play *1776*, and a lecture series featuring Dr. John White of the Religion Department, Dr. John Seydow of the English Department, and Dr. Joseph O'Grady of the History Department.

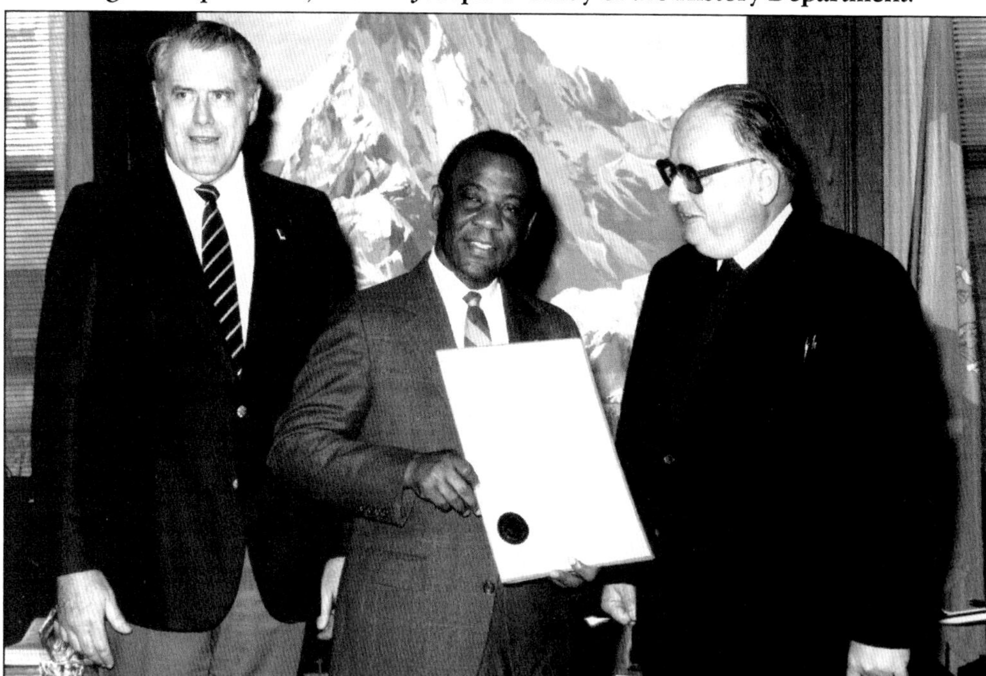

Philadelphia mayor Wilson Goode presented Pres. Brother Patrick Ellis with a plaque recognizing LaSalle University's 125th anniversary in 1988.

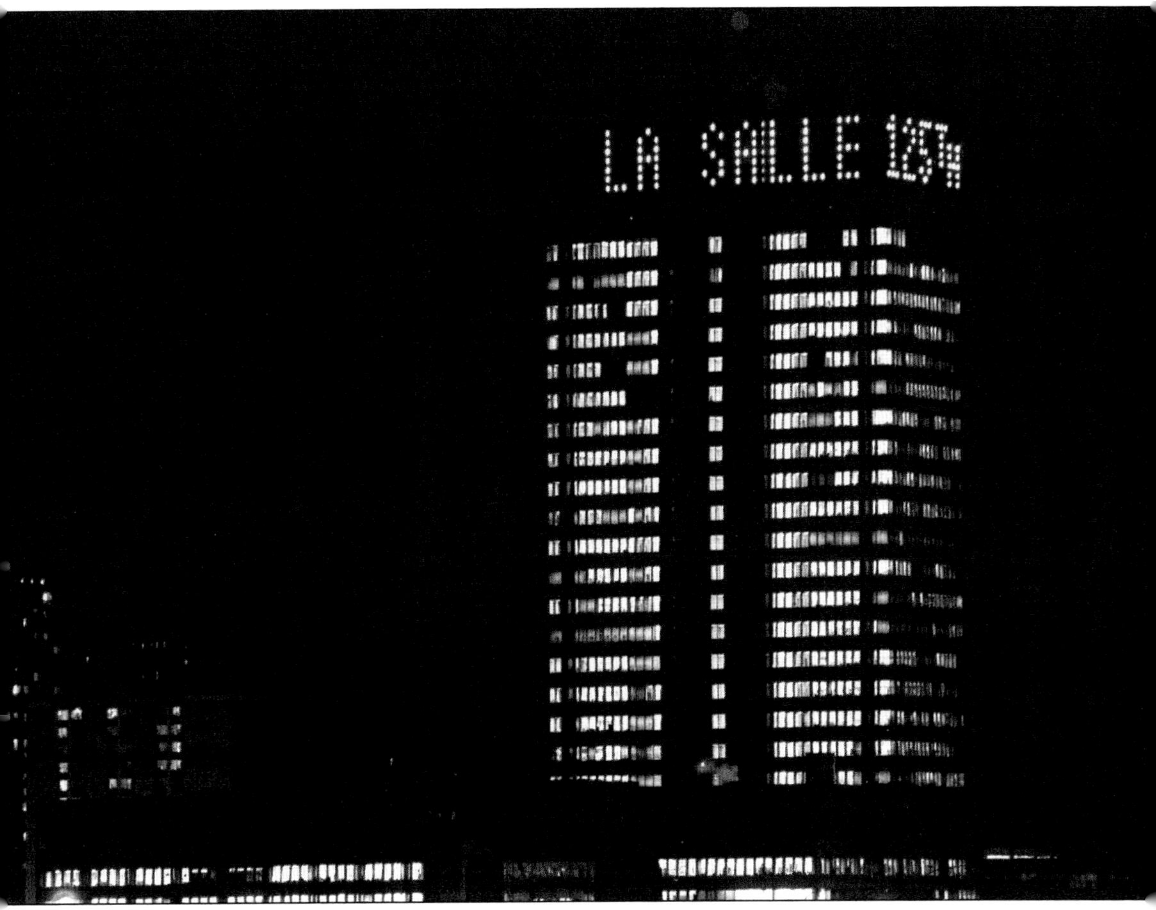

A sign atop the Philadelphia Electric Company Building announced LaSalle's 125th anniversary in 1988.

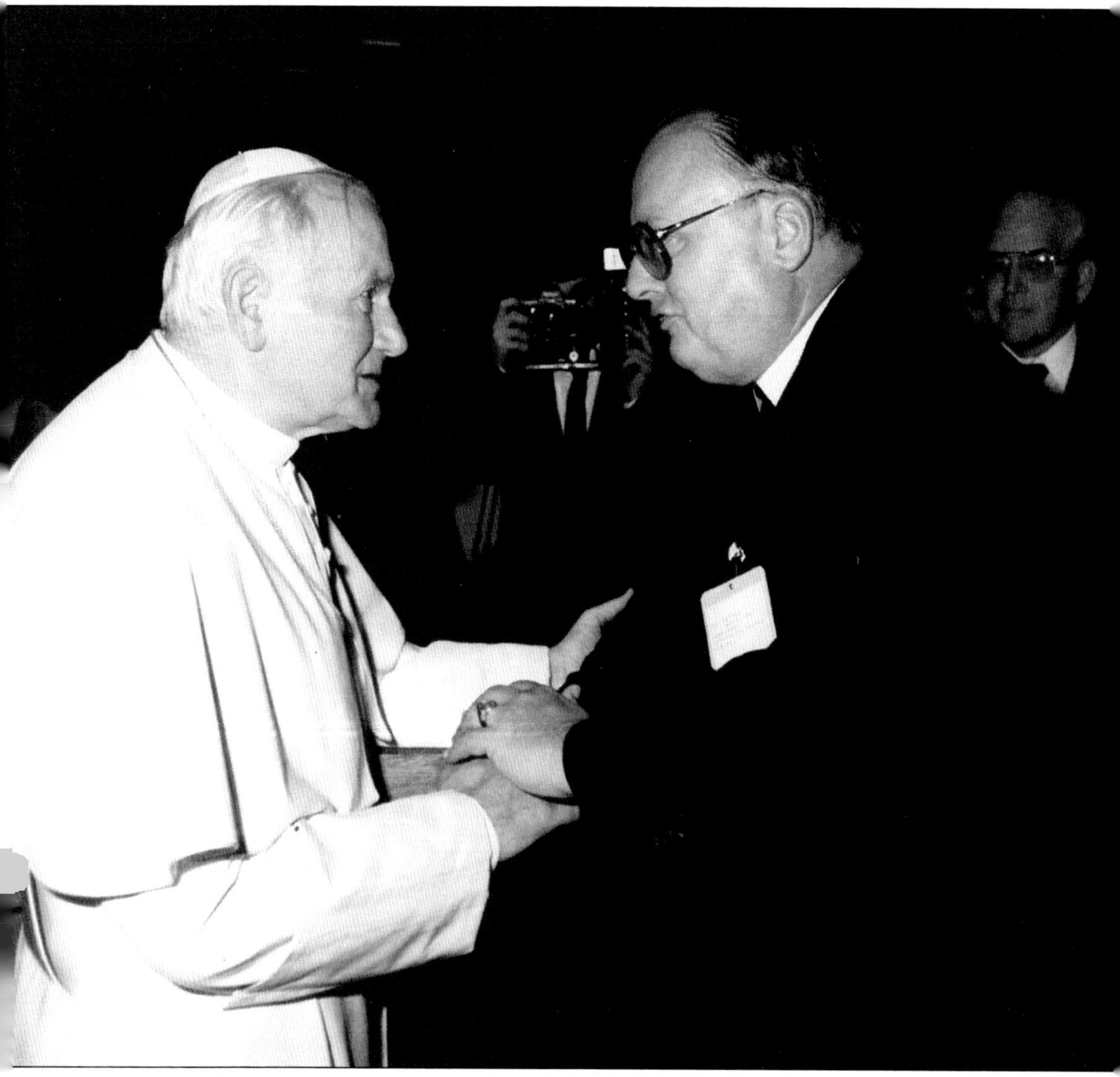

Pres. Brother Patrick Ellis met with Pope John Paul II in Rome while attending a conference addressing the role of the Vatican in Catholic higher education in 1989.

Philadelphia mayor Edward Rendell played basketball in a cancer research fund-raiser while visiting LaSalle University in 1996. He went on to become governor of Pennsylvania. Rendell gave his first political speech ever at LaSalle while running for district attorney of Philadelphia in 1977.

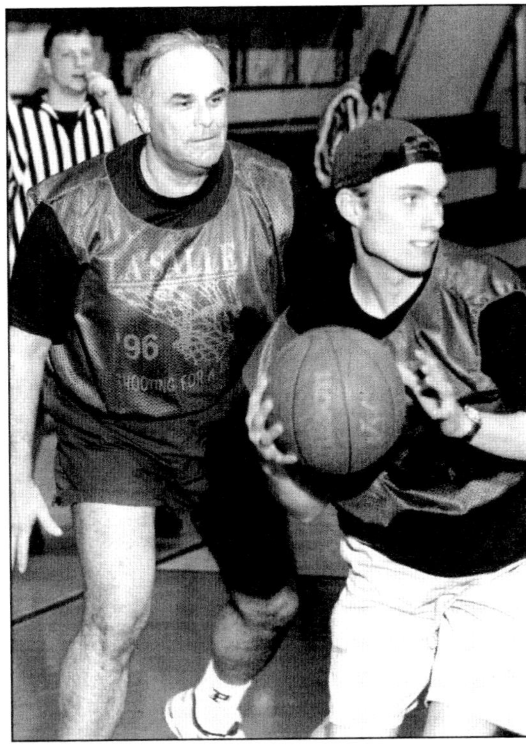

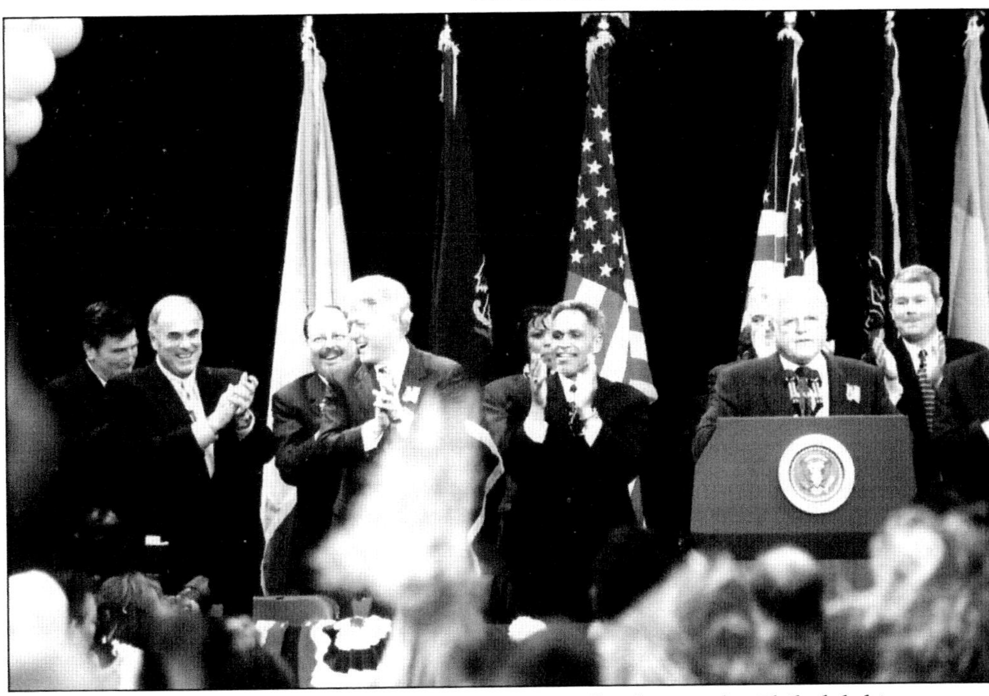

Pres. Bill Clinton came to LaSalle in 1999 for a rally during the Philadelphia mayoral election. He appeared in the Hayman Center with Mayor Edward Rendell, United States representative Chaka Fattah, city council member John Street, and Massachusetts senator Edward Kennedy. John Street won the election and became mayor of Philadelphia.

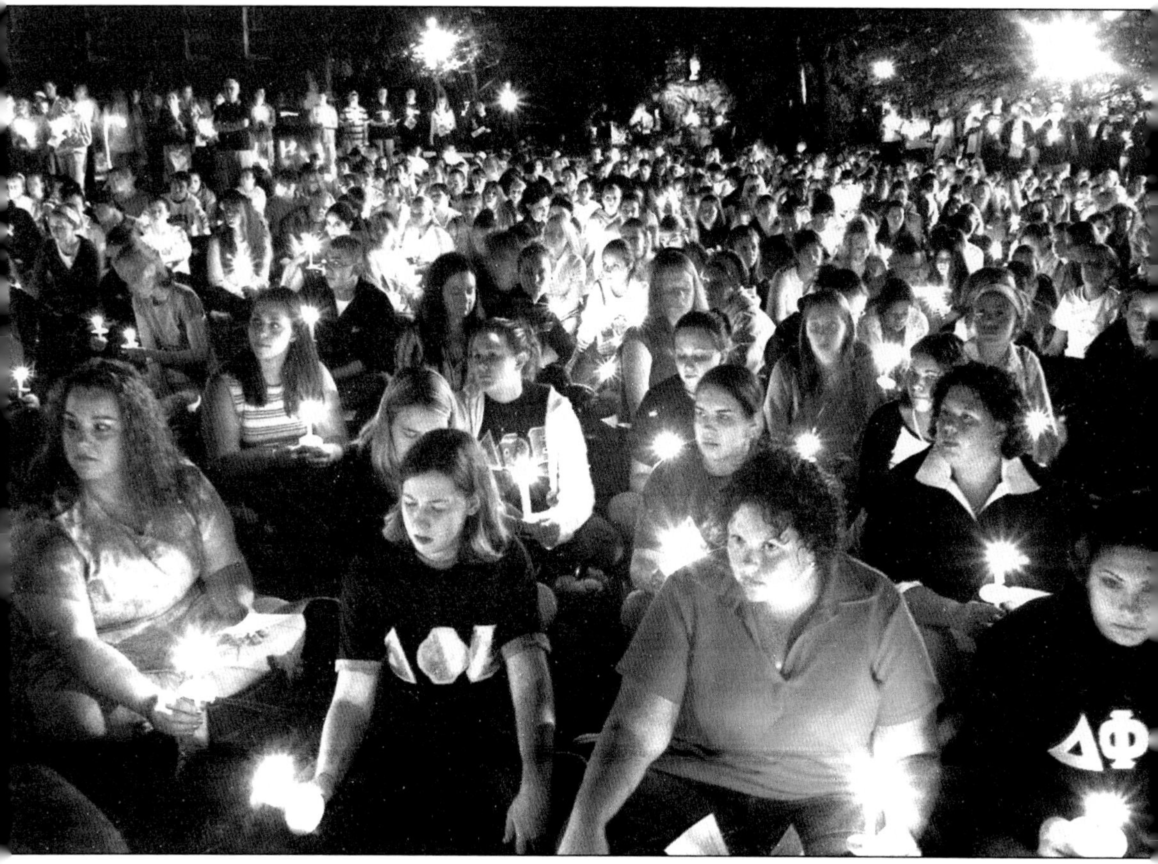

LaSalle University held a vigil after the September 11, 2001, terrorist attacks.

Five

PROMINENT LASALLIANS

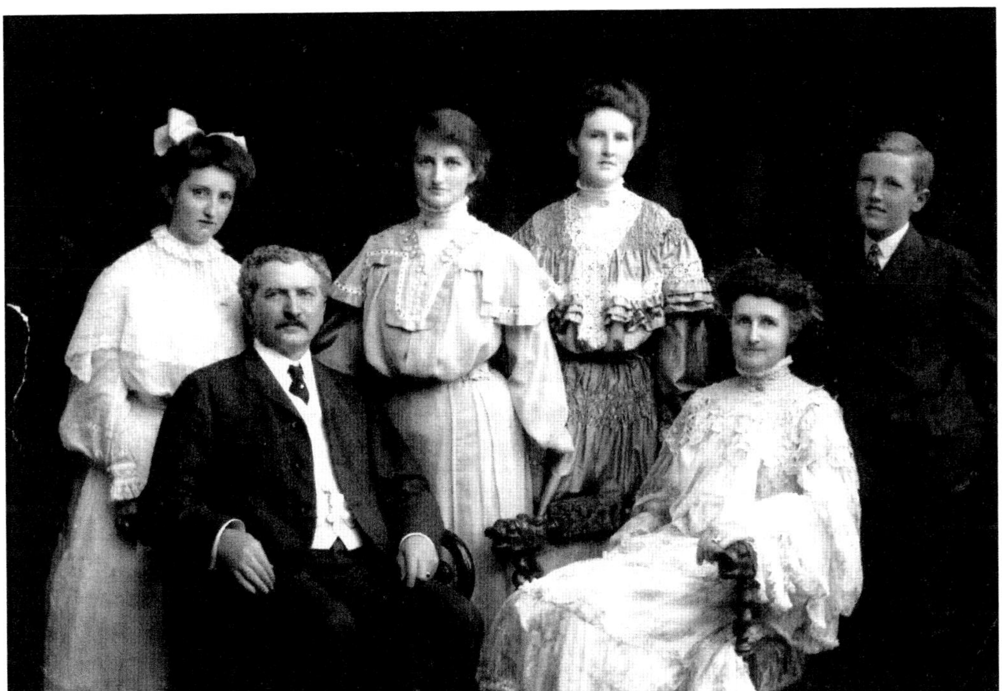

William F. Harrity received a bachelor's degree from LaSalle College in 1869 and a master's degree in 1871. After teaching math and Latin at LaSalle, he became Chairman of the Democratic City Committee of Philadelphia in 1882. Harrity became National Chairman of the Democratic Party in 1892 and helped Pres. Grover Cleveland get elected to a second term.

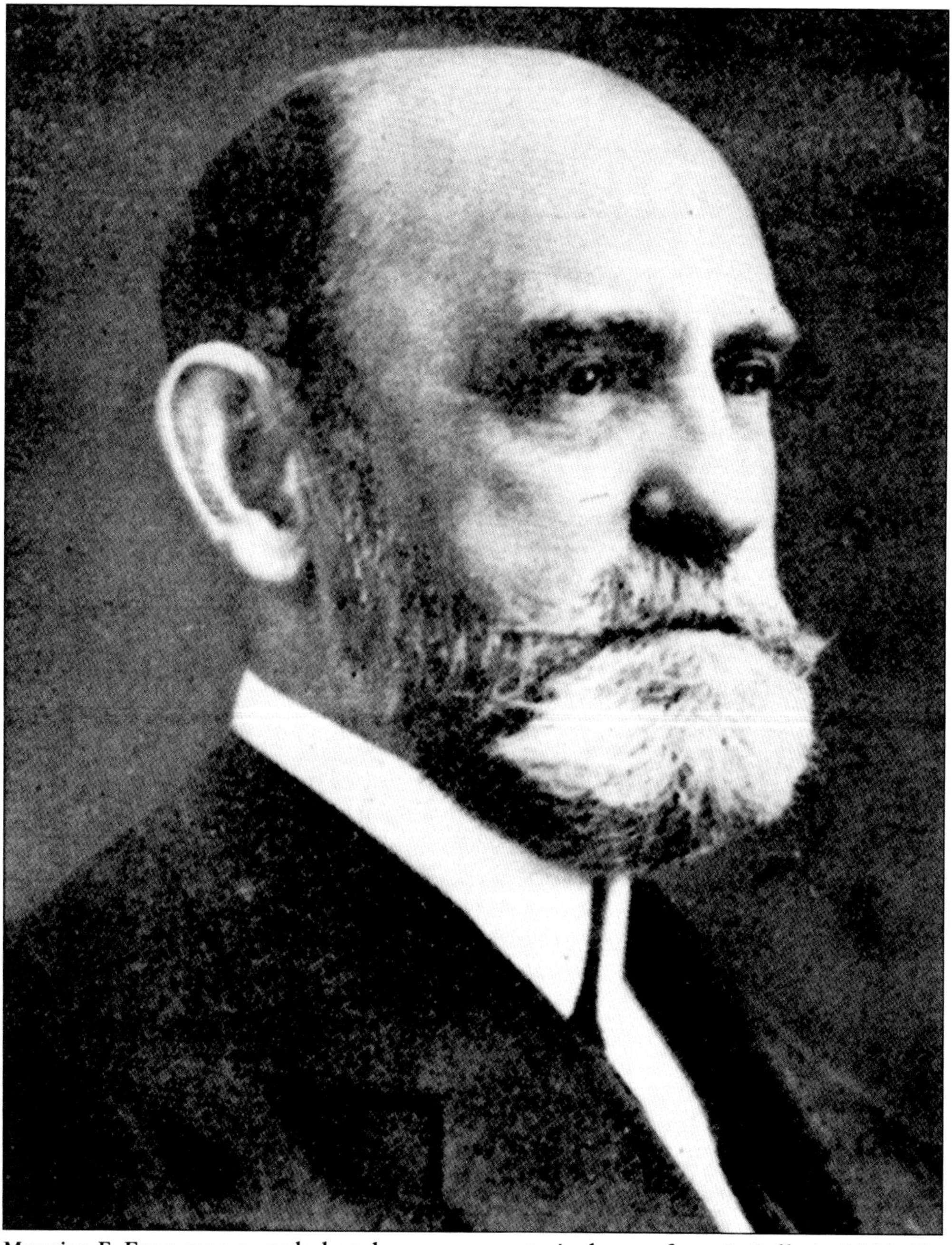

Maurice F. Egan was awarded an honorary master's degree from LaSalle in 1880. He taught English at the University of Notre Dame and Catholic University of America and wrote over 30 books. Egan was U.S. ambassador to Denmark from 1907 until 1918 and negotiated the purchase of the Virgin Islands.

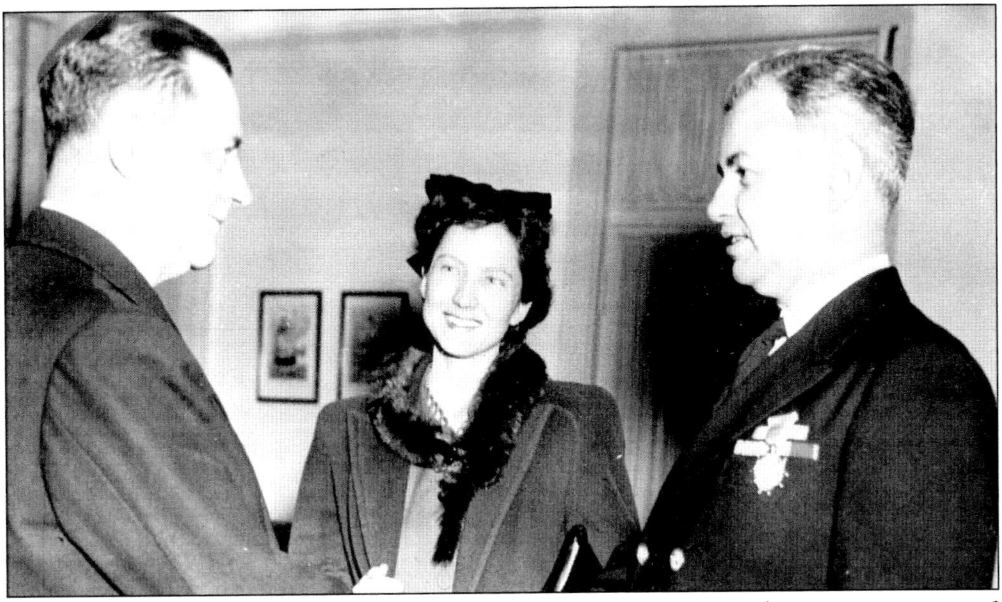

Dr. Francis J. Braceland graduated from LaSalle College in 1926. He was appointed chairman of the Committee on College Affairs and was instrumental in bringing alumni back into the LaSalle community. Braceland was one of the founders of the Mayo Clinic and became chief psychiatrist at the Institute for Living in Hartford, Connecticut, in 1951. He was president of the American Psychiatric Association and edited the *American Journal of Psychiatry* for 13 years. LaSalle awarded him an honorary degree in 1941. Braceland and his wife Hope were given a citation for his achievements in neuropsychiatry by Secretary of the Navy James Forrestal (right). (Photograph courtesy of Paul Braceland.)

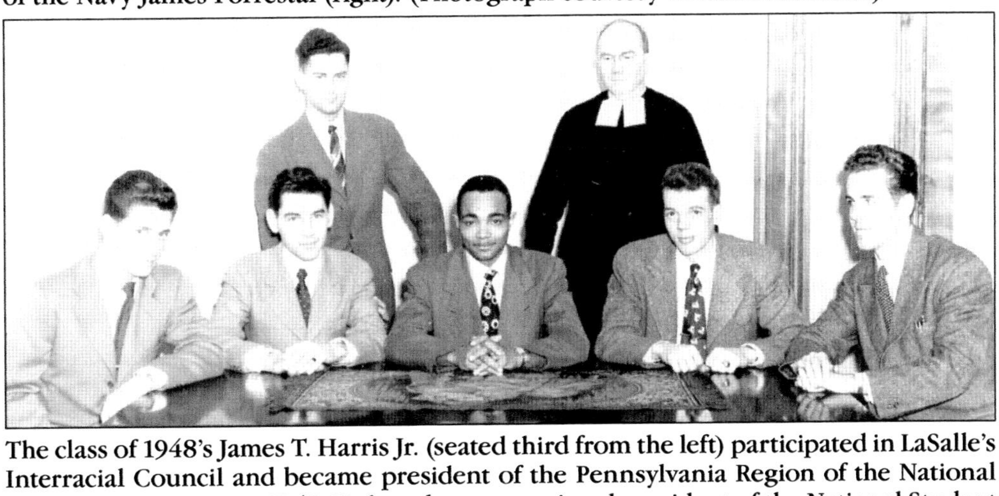

The class of 1948's James T. Harris Jr. (seated third from the left) participated in LaSalle's Interracial Council and became president of the Pennsylvania Region of the National Student Association in 1947. He later became national president of the National Student Association and assistant director of the Ford Foundation's Middle East and African Development Program. Harris was secretary general of the Institute of Law and Public Administration in the Republic of the Congo in the early 1960s, and he was executive director of the U.S. National Catholic Conference for Interracial Justice. LaSalle recognized him with an honorary degree in 1964. Other members of LaSalle College's Interracial Council were Jess Cain, Thomas Roger, Tom Harper, Frank Scully, Frank Rausch, and Brother Augustine.

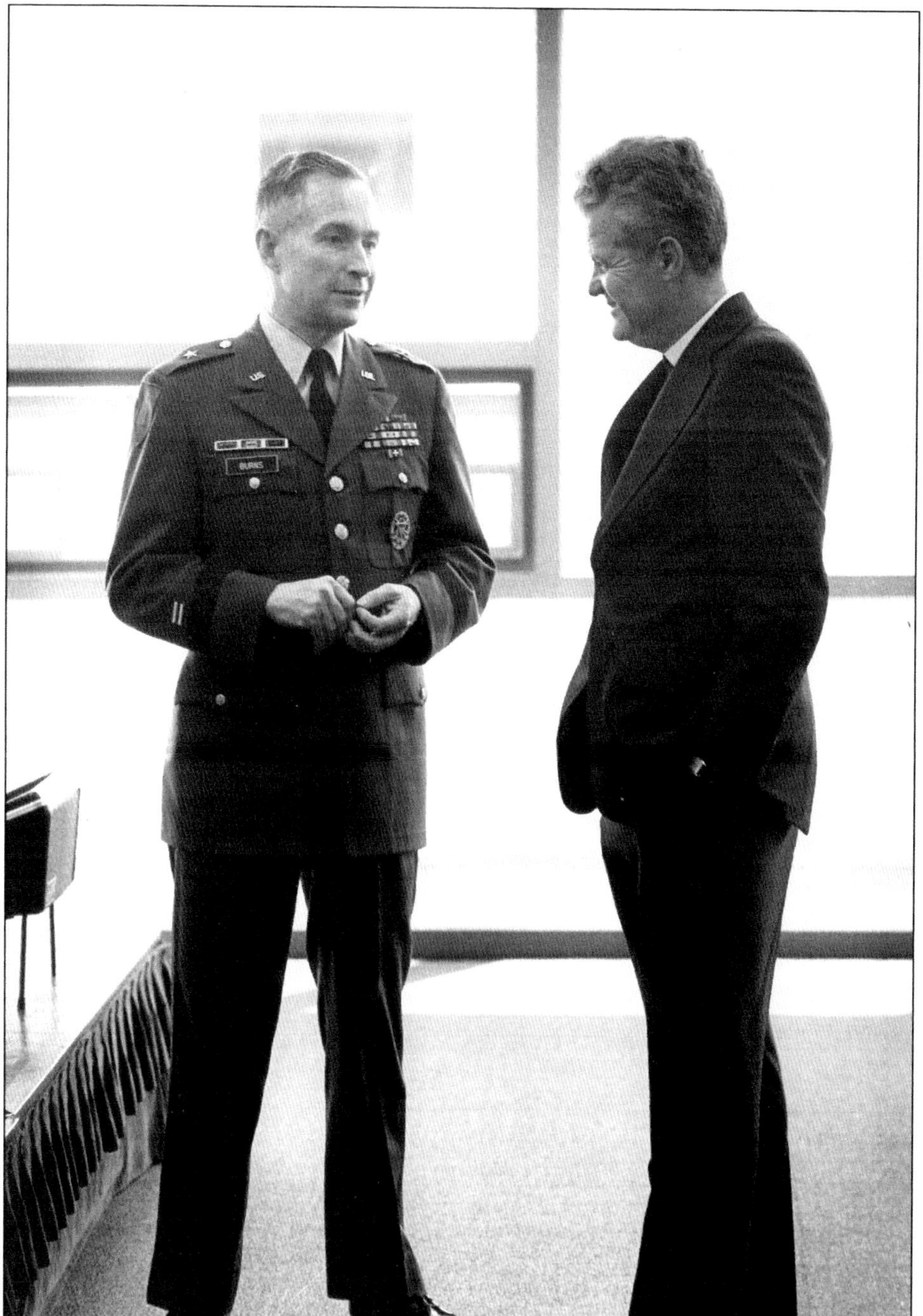

Maj. Gen. William F. Burns graduated from LaSalle in 1954 and served in the Vietnam War. He directed political/military affairs at the U.S. Army War College in Carlisle, Pennsylvania, in the 1970s. Burns was the representative of the joint chiefs of staff at the Intermediate Range Nuclear Forces Negotiations with the Soviet Union in 1981. He was Pres. Ronald Reagan's director of the U.S. Arms Control and Disarmament Agency, and was Pres. George H. W. Bush's special envoy to Russia on nuclear arms reduction. Burns was awarded an honorary degree from LaSalle University in 1988.

Dr. Warren E. Smith was a member of the class of 1954 and became a psychiatric consultant for LaSalle and public and parochial schools across Philadelphia. The university's Warren E. Smith Award is given to an African American alumnus who embodies Lasallian intellectual and spiritual ideals.

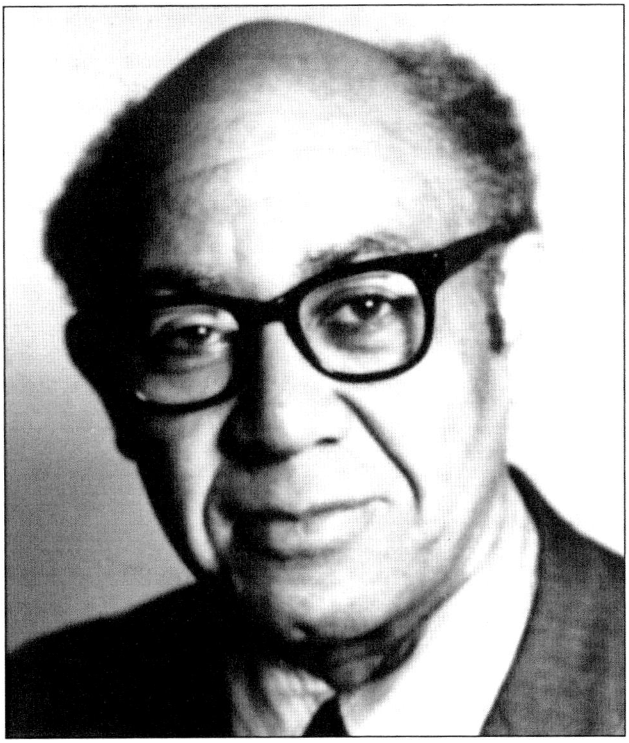

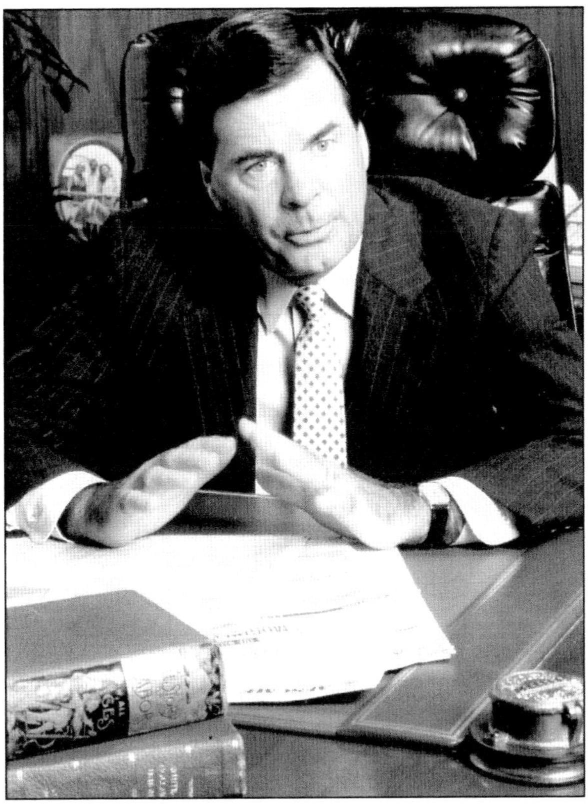

The class of 1956's Gerald W. McEntee was president of the American Foundation of State, County, and Municipal Employees.

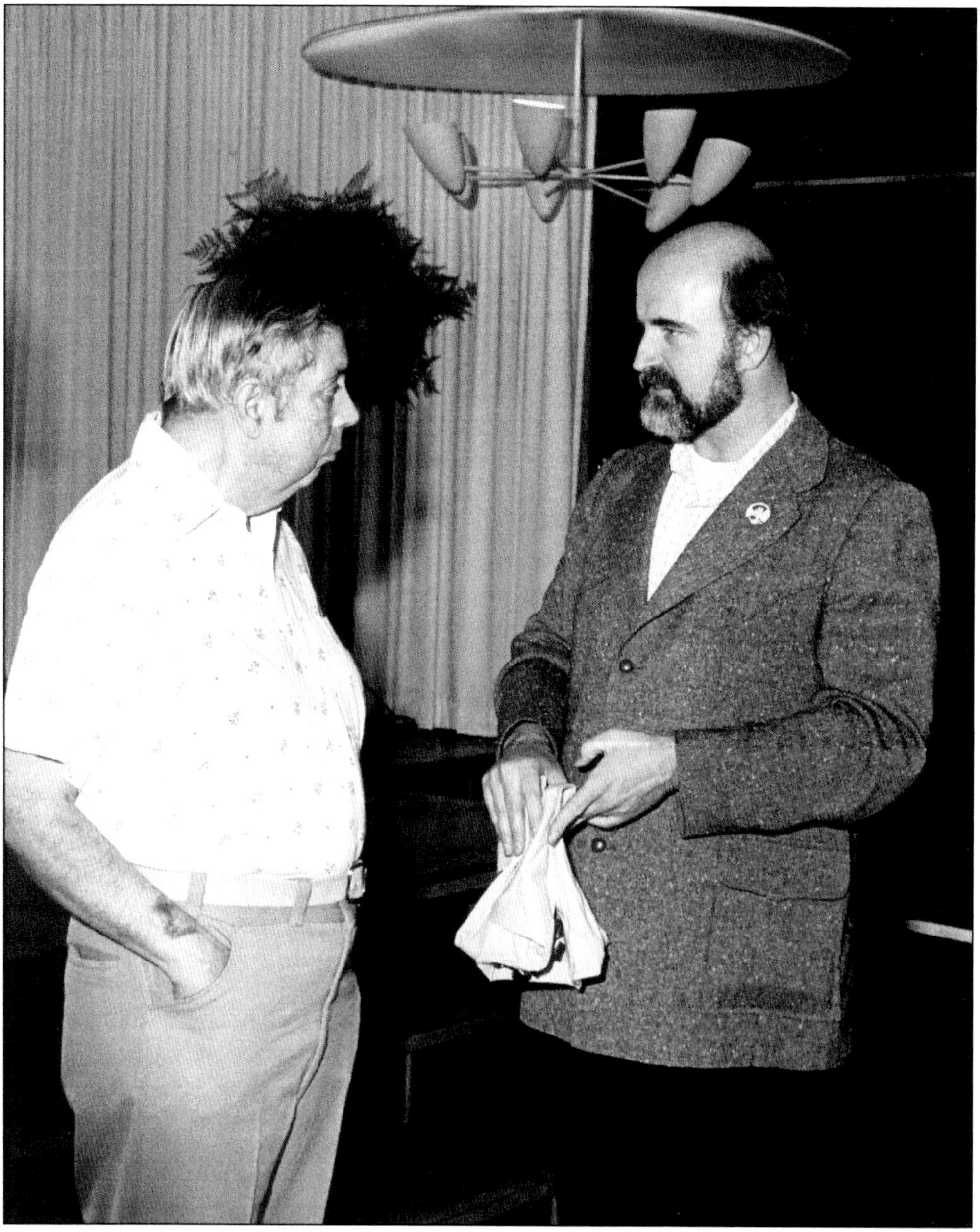

Peter Boyle (right) graduated from LaSalle College in 1957 and was a Christian Brother before becoming an actor. After several movie roles, including a lead in *Young Frankenstein*, he became a regular character on CBS's *Everybody Loves Raymond*. Boyle was awarded an honorary degree in 1993. He met with English professor Dan Rodden during a visit to LaSalle in 1977. Rodden was director of LaSalle's dramatic society the Masque and won the Lindback Foundation Award for Excellent Teaching in 1966. The theatre in the LaSalle Student Union was named in his honor.

J. Hugh Devlin became managing director of Morgan Stanley, was one of the founders of the Barr-Devlin Company, and cofounded the Navesink Foundation. He graduated from LaSalle in 1964.

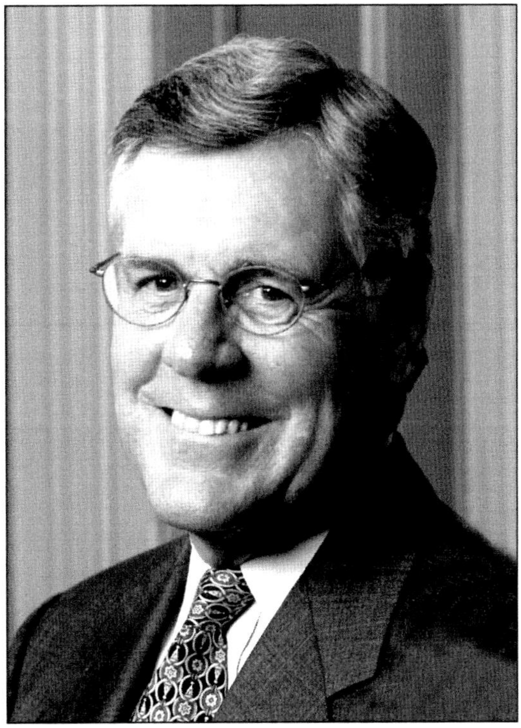

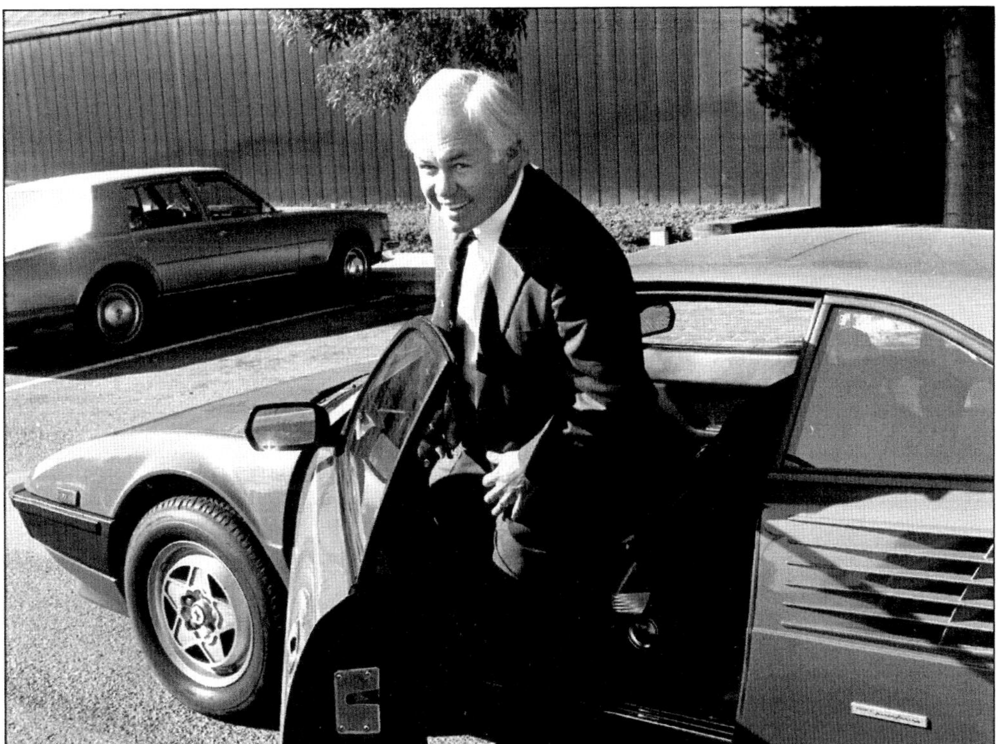

The class of 1964's Joseph F. Keenan became head of Chuck E. Cheese and was a founder of ATARI.

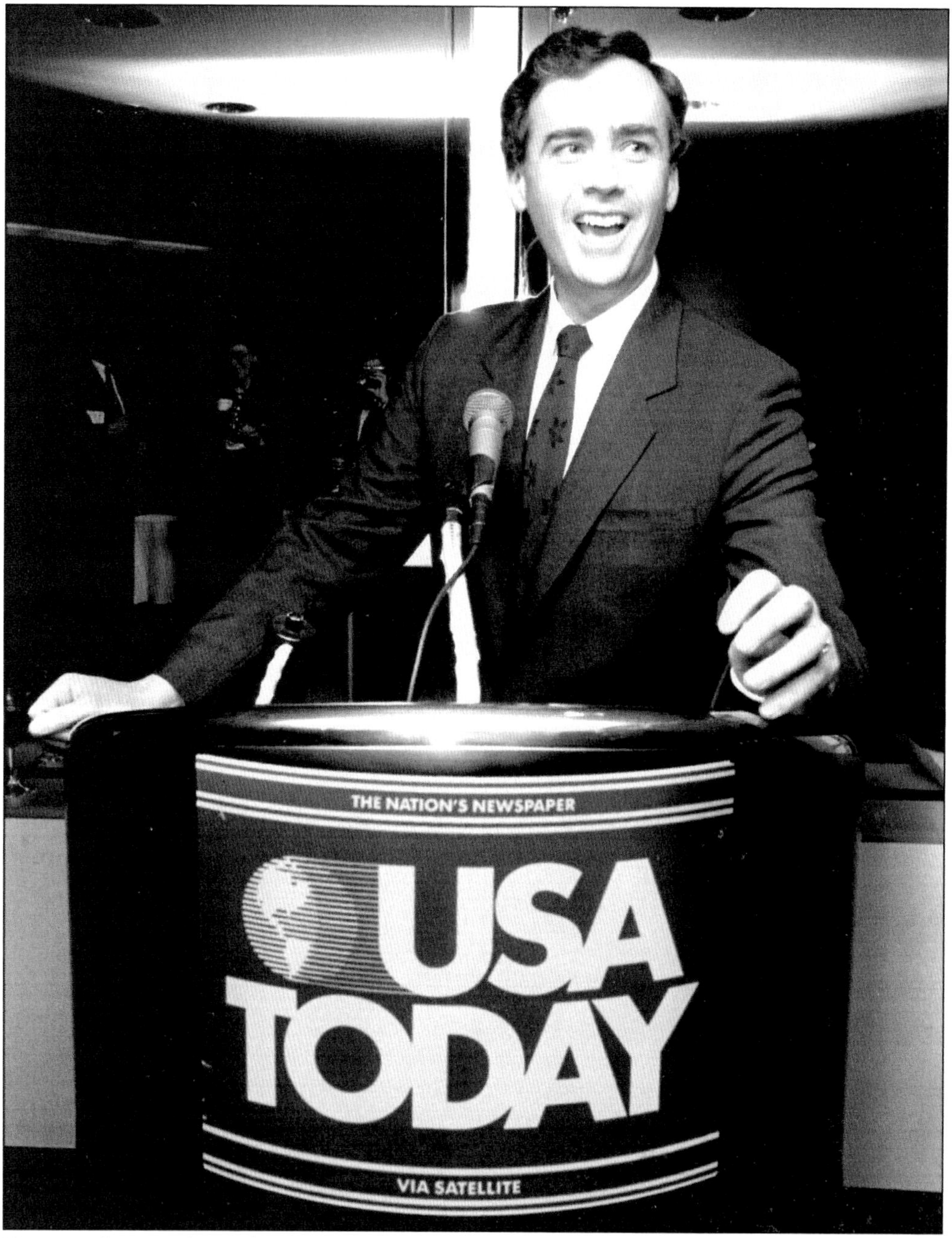

Tom Curley graduated in 1970, helped create *USA Today* in 1982, and became the newspaper's president in 1986. He became president and chief executive officer of the Associated Press in 2003. Curley received an honorary degree from LaSalle University in 1994. He was editor of the *Collegian* during his time at LaSalle.

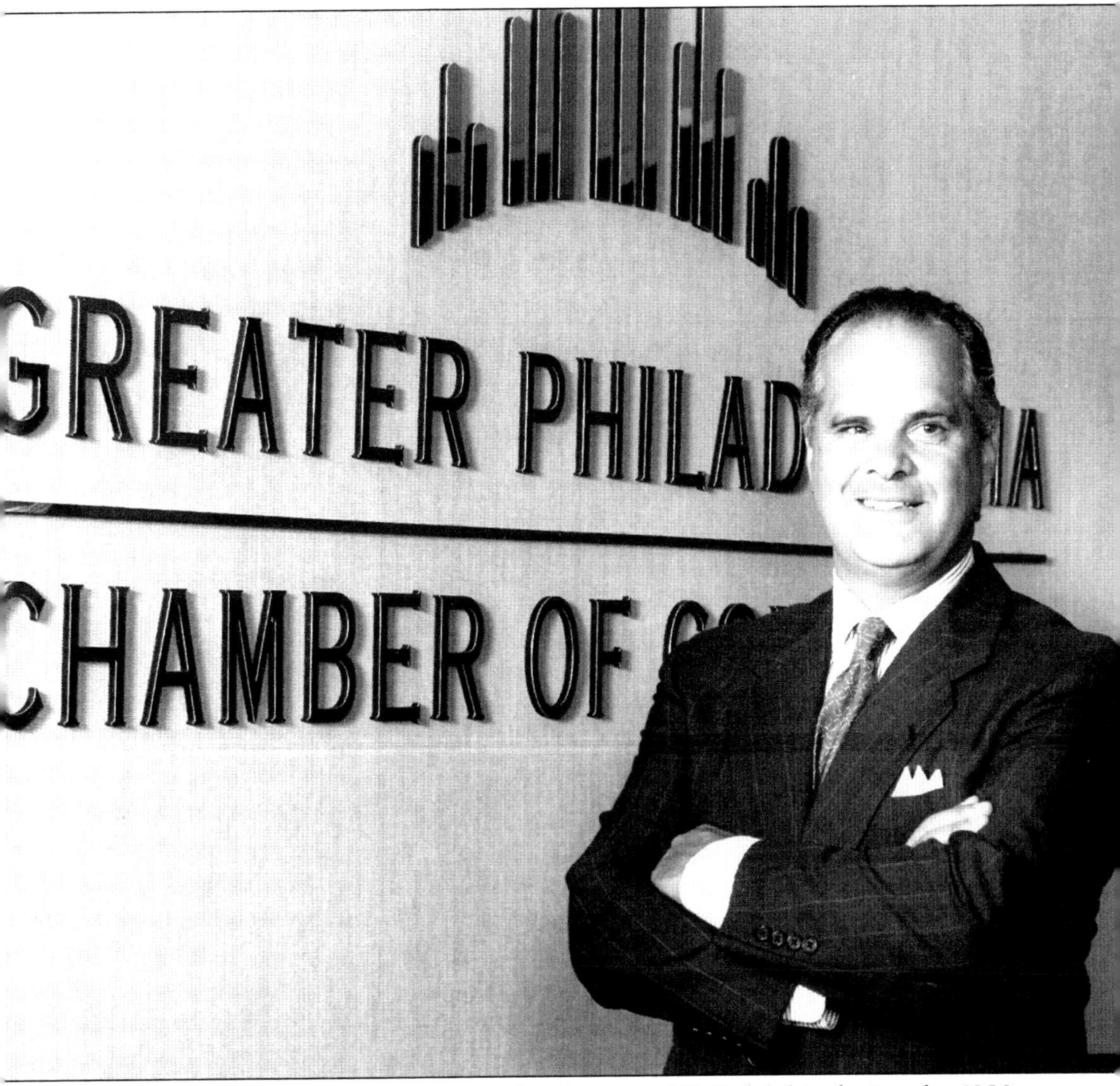

Charles P. Pizzi was commerce director for the City of Philadelphia during the 1980s and was president and chief executive officer of the Greater Philadelphia Chamber of Commerce from 1989 until 2002. He became the president and chief executive officer of the Tasty Baking Company in 2002. Pizzi was a 1972 graduate of LaSalle College.

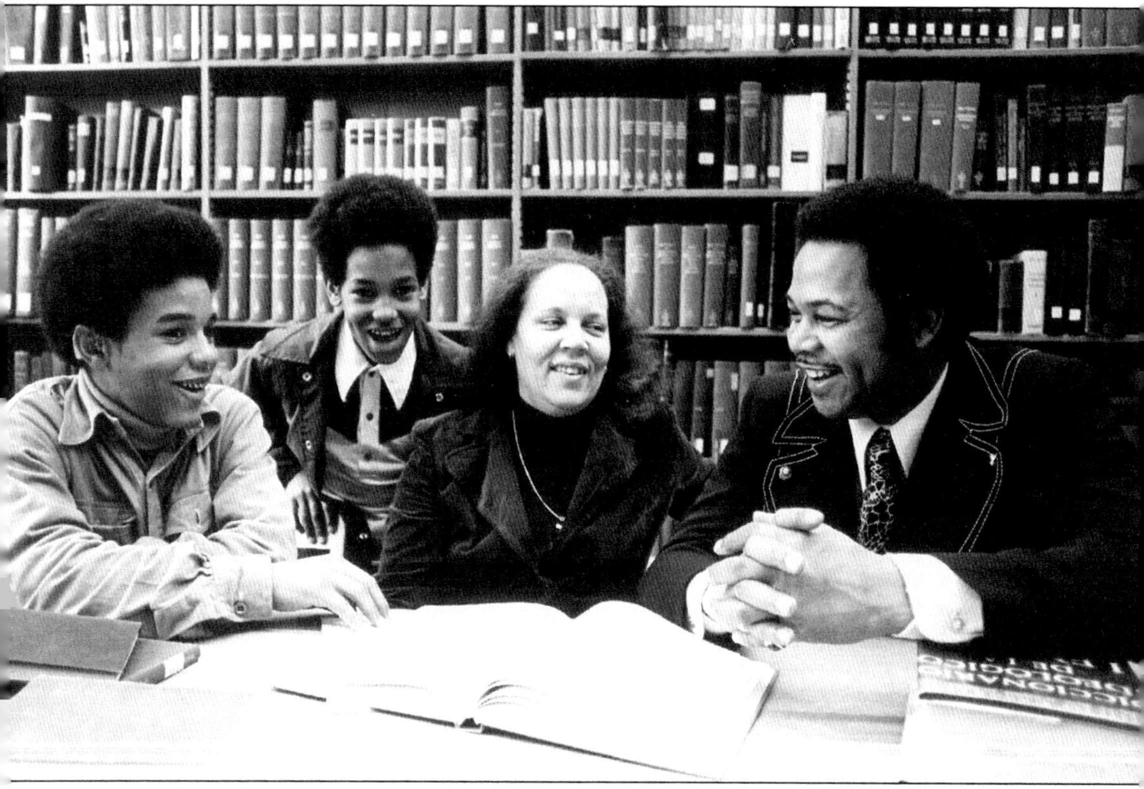

The class of 1975's Suzanne R. Brooks entered LaSalle after serving on the Philadelphia Police Force. She won a Danforth Graduate Fellowship for Women, went on to write prose and poetry, and own Creative Concepts Systems in California. Brooks was selected as the LaSalle University Alumni Association's Outstanding Graduate of the 1970s in 2000.

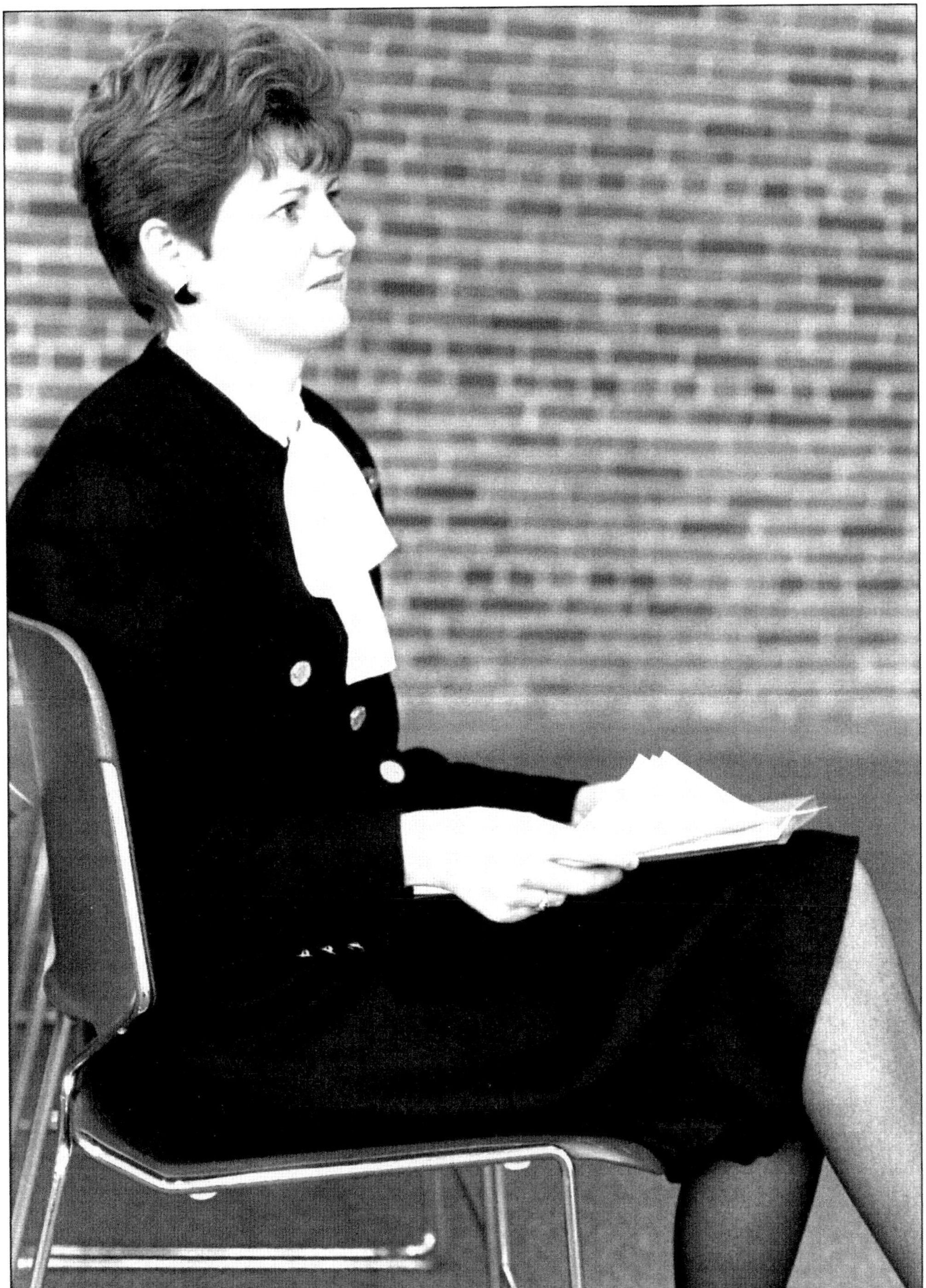

Sallyanne Harper graduated in 1976 and helped to found LaSalle's Women's Center and Building Blocks Day Care Center. She served in the U.S. Navy for 10 years, was chief financial officer of the Environmental Protection Agency, and worked in the United States Government Accounting Office. She was awarded an honorary degree in 1999.

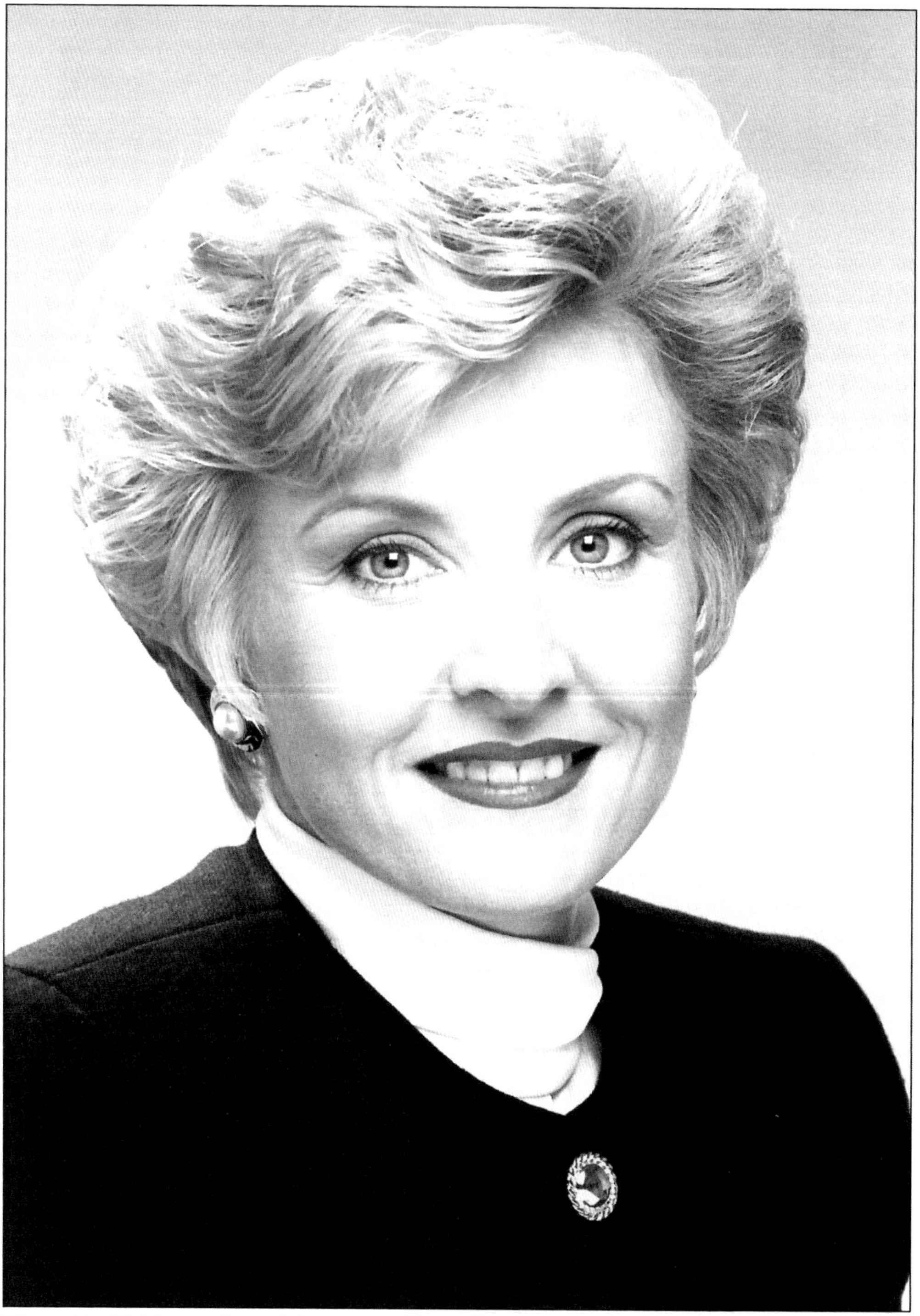

Diane M. Welsh graduated from LaSalle College in 1976. She severed as counsel to the Deputy District Attorney of Bucks County, Pennsylvania, founded the Child-Abuse Prosecution Unit, and wrote *The Bucks County Victim Witness Handbook*. Welsh became a United States magistrate judge for the Eastern District of Pennsylvania in 1994.

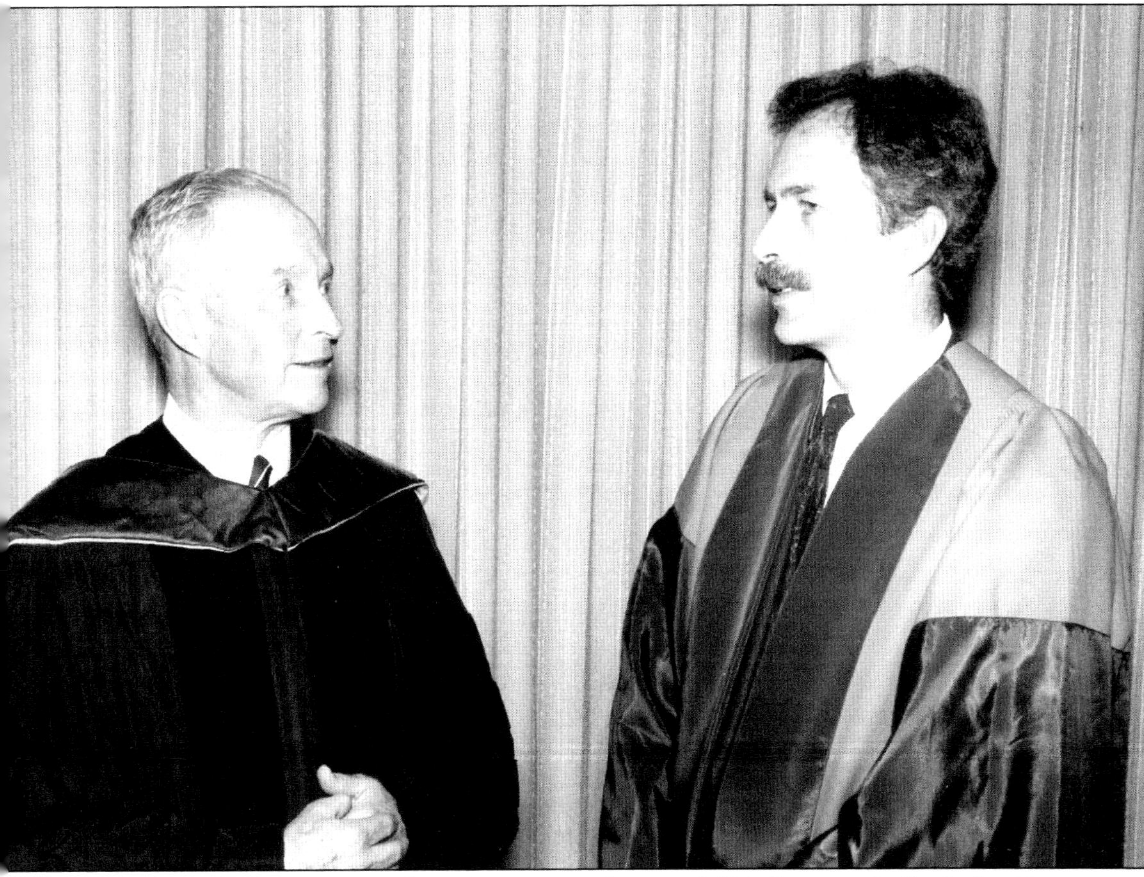

Dr. William J. Burns (right) graduated in 1978 and was LaSalle's first marshall scholar. He entered the U.S. Foreign Service in 1982 and was the U.S. ambassador to Jordan. Burns became assistant secretary of state for Near Eastern Affairs in 2001. He appeared in *Time* magazine as one of 1994's "Fifty for the Future" and received an honorary degree from LaSalle University in 1997. His father was LaSalle alumnus Maj. Gen. William F. Burns.

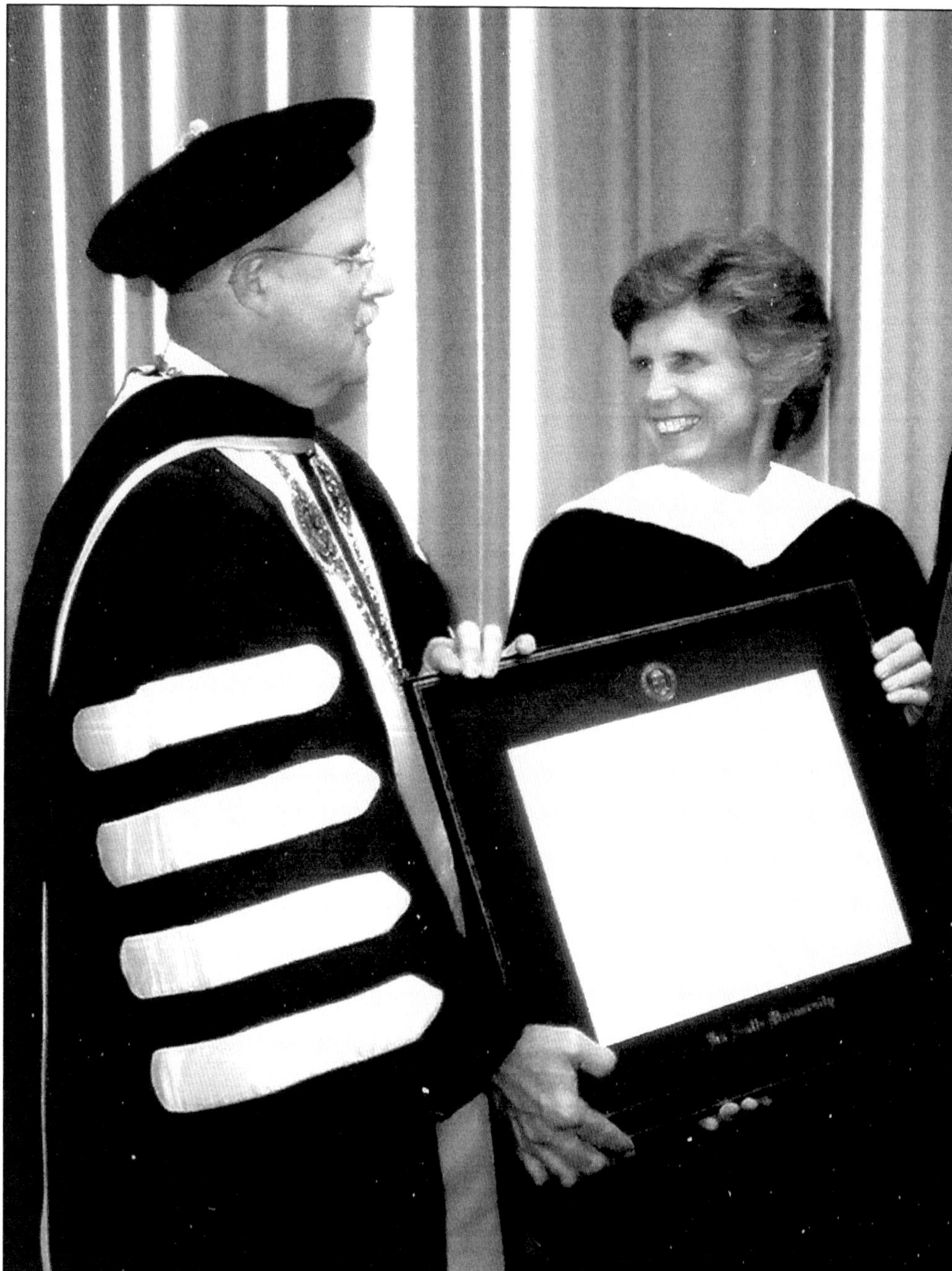

The class of 1977's Dr. Angelica M. Stacy's research in solid state organic chemistry has been applied to catalysis and energy conservation. She received awards from Cornell University and the University of California. Stacy was a founder of the Committee for the Advancement of Women Chemists and was awarded an honorary degree from LaSalle University in 2000.